RADIO R

"I was a BBC radio reporter ... in North Wales, a fabulous and beautiful land full of ... ng characters and incredible tales, like the lady who took her army to invade London on a bus, and the man who set out for Australia in a floating lorry, hugging the coast.

Having worked in both news and features I recall a vast range of stories involving everything from the sad to the comic, from fanfares to fun fairs, poodles to politics, mouse traps to mountain tops, puzzles muddles and downright mysteries. Stories like the spy school, the devil locked in a box, and the holy grail locked in a bank vault.

I can take you behind the scenes too, deep into the fading and secretive world of radio broadcasting, to reveal how to survive in the job and outline the tricks of the trade that I used to conjure up and maintain the magic of radio, when many in the BBC sought to devalue it.

I always managed to plough my own furrow, although sometimes only from one bog to another, and because I always wanted to be more of an entertainer than a journalist it was usually great fun, at least for me. So if you have a taste for the absurd, the curious, the bizarre, and even a few white knuckle rides, plus for good measure a shattering assortment of 'behind the scenes' disasters, read on and share a few of my favourite memories and nightmares."

First published in Gt Britain in 2008 by
Toby Books
enquiries@tobybooks.co.uk

www.tobybooks.co.uk

ISBN 978-0-9535716-1-1

Printed and bound by
C.P.I Antony Rowe,
Eastbourne.

2

CHAPTERS

A. Adaptability, Atmosphere, and Action.

B. Beasts, Blunders, Boats, and The Brave.

C. Crime, Cheating, Cuts, and Competitions.

D. Disasters, and Dramatics.

E. Entertainers.

F. Fools, Farmers, and Festivals.

G. Ghosts, and Games.

H. Heroes, Helicopters, and History.

I. Interruptions, Invasions, and The Inept.

J. Jungle Survival, Journeys, and Jurassic Park.

K. Keep Going.

L. Largest and Little-ist, Little People, and Lady Luck.

M. Money, Monsters, and Mavericks

..........continued

N. Newspapers.

O. Occupational Hazards, The Occult, Overtime, and Opportunism

P. Pets, Participants, and Politicians.

Q. Queer Ideas.

R. Races, RAC, RAF, Rescues, and Red Tape.

S. Snowdonia, Singers, Spies, and Scientists.

T. Terror, Tourism, Trains, and Treasure.

U. UFOs, and Other Unsolved Mysteries.

V. Very Queer Ideas, Including Vicars.

W. World Service, Writers, and The Weird.

X. X-rated.

Y. Yet More Blunders, and Disasters.

Z. Zoos, Zeniths, and Zeros.

CHAPTER A
Adaptability, Atmosphere and Action.

In the spring of 1968 the message was blunt. I'd been offered a month's trial with the hugely successful BBC radio programme 'Good Morning Wales' and on that first day I was given a letter to remember. The letter was 'A' and it stood for..... 'A'daptability. With the programme being an all embracing daily news magazine I was told that I would have to cover every type of story under the sun or be dropped.

The programme was the flag ship of BBC Wales and the invitation had come from the programme's editor Brian Evans, and I can say that accepting his challenge gave me a license to lead an amazing life in which I would learn to compile industrial and political reviews one day, and drive steam engines the next.

However, I also found the 'A' word meant more than adapting to different stories It also meant adapting to different and difficult situations. Daily programmes are ravenous beasts and you must never come back empty handed. When you're sent out to record an interview you not only have to do that interview, you also have to get it back to the studio in time or the programme's got a hole in it, and you're history.

In time I was with several other programmes as well, and going on the air at 4-30 in the afternoon the 'Home Run' type of programme was the most demanding, often requiring desperate measures. Once, with only an hour before going on the air, I even had to become a song writer. According to a newspaper report a young man at the Anglesey Sea Zoo had written a special love song to persuade the fish to mate. When I got there though he wasn't singing. "Sorry," he said, "The newspaper exaggerated a bit, I just strum."

In the first place, if you too become a reporter, you will learn that a love song written and sung to a tank full of gawping fish is a story. Strumming a guitar to them just aint. Secondly you will learn that as well as the 'A' word there is also the 'I' word. When stories are in short supply reporters feed off each other. Stories do the rounds and there's nothing wrong with that, but beware. You will sometimes find (with a considerable measure of irony) that you've become the victim of another reporter exercising his ability to be - 'I'nventive.

At times like this it's no good feeling sorry for yourself. Alarmingly, you know that very soon the programme's presenter is going on the air saying "This afternoon we bring you a song specially written for fish" - so you write one.

I quickly scribbled down a few sickly lines like - "You are the one I want to kiss, honest babe you're the one I miss. You're in my dreams every night, come on babe hold me tight." I then made up a tune and hummed it until he could sing it and I recorded it, and after hurriedly cutting out a few whispered asides it was in the bag.

(This, like all those that follow, is a transcripted excerpt from the actual recording.)

BCB31
(Singer sings his love song for the fish)

Barham	(As song ends) "Very nice, very nice. How long did it take you to write that ?"
Singer	(Whispering) "What shall I say ?"
Barham	"A few days."
Singer	(Loudly) "A few days."
Barham	"It's very good."
Singer	"Thankyou."
Barham	"Has your song got them mating yet ?"
Singer	"No."
Barham	"Look they're chasing each other, sing your song again quick."
Singer	"Right!" (Singer strums and sings loudly)

If my previous years working in the theatre taught me anything it was that most essential commandment ' The Show Must Go On'. No matter how good his excuses, the reporter who comes back without his story, whether it be to a newspaper office or a BBC studio, is a dead duck, out the door, and back on the dole.

It certainly made for a hectic life. Every day people had to be located and tracked down, and this was long before you could boast of having satellite navigation in your car, or even a mobile phone in those days.

During my 32 years with the BBC I reported on literally thousands of stories, hard news stories, soft news stories, general features, issues big and small, current affairs and not so current affairs. I was the real 'roving' reporter and my patch was a big one. It was the whole top half of Wales covering thousands of square miles.

It stretched from Chester west to Holyhead, down to Aberystwyth, then east to the English border, both sides, and up through Wrexham, and with a tape recorder hung from my shoulder I stretched the mileage allowance to its limit. I climbed to the tops of mountains and scurried around deep underground. I was sometimes up in the air, and yes sometimes all at sea. I was into factories, farmyards, fairgrounds and mansions, caves, castles, colleges and convents, even prisons, hospitals and asylums, anywhere where there were people with a tale to tell.

Wales is a wonderful place to work. It's beautiful and it's rugged, but the toughest terrain is within the walls of the BBC where no depth of plush carpet can hide the blood stains. In those early days, as I watched other reporters fall by the wayside, I realised just how vital those two letters were – 'A' for adaptability and 'I' for inventiveness. I could see that in time of famine successful reporters had to become as inventive as the sultan's wife, and for a lot longer than a thousand and one nights too, often cobbling items together by using old stories and simply bolting new angles onto them.

As a newcomer I was impressed. However, even when stories are plentiful, you still have to 'bring home the bacon', and if you're keen to try this way of life don't let anyone keep you from your story. Remember 'I' also stands for Initiative, and if you've got it - use it. If a man's too busy mending his shed to speak into your microphone, put it down and help him mend his shed. It works. I've done children's home work, I've done lots of washing up, and I once did a woman's shopping for her. She said she couldn't see me because she had to go for her husband's sausages, so I got some for her.

Although the roving reporter spends most days on a 'race track' with little time to deal with anything but the essential facts, I think there's another word that should go into the 'A' frame, and that word is 'Atmosphere'. Some people, even some of my colleagues, wouldn't agree, but atmosphere was always important to me. Infact I always felt that it was the essential ingredient that provided the listener with the 'picture'. Some referred to it rather blandly by using another 'A' word – 'Actuality', but providing the listener with the right atmosphere often means providing more than simple background noises.

For a long time there was certainly appreciation among producers and colleagues alike for a reporter's piece nicely done but it didn't last. As the emphasis swung further towards 'hard' news, even in magazine programmes like 'Good Morning Wales', attitudes changed and new producers wanted little more than straight colourless reports churned out with little attention to listeners needs.

I think many people among the policy makers for radio had given up. Television was visual and was soon in colour. Wrongly to my mind they saw radio as nothing more than a second best service, fit only to broadcast in black and white. I couldn't go along with that impoverished view, but it was an attitude readily accepted by many young producers who were only working in radio as a stepping stone across to more lucrative careers in television. Many of these birds of passage had no interest in radio, and would often miss the opportunity of covering a good story or event because in their opinion it would be too visual.

Nothing made me more angry. You the listeners will know that you can see anything on the radio. All you need is a reporter who can describe the scene and provide some atmosphere, and that can be found in anything, the sound of the wind rushing through the gaps in a stone wall, the ticking of a clock, a few footsteps on the stairs, anything, and of course a bit of music if it fits.

I remember the first half hour programme I put together. It was around 1970 at a big international scouts jamboree on the outskirts of Bangor. They were camping on the Penrhyn Castle estate and they spent the week indulging in all those wonderfully zany boy-scout practices in pursuit of self sufficiency, the sort of endeavours most of us left behind with the invention of brick built houses, proper cutlery and flush toilets. Every day they were making knives and forks out of twigs, carrying water in their hats, and building bridges with tree trunks over rivers that weren't there, and with their permission I set about illustrating all this lovely crack-pot activity with short bursts of crack-pot music. They'd come from all over the world and they'd assembled what must have been the world's worst boy-scouts band. It was marvelous, and they revelled in it. They spent their time marching around the camp enthusiastically belting out a selection of rousing marches that made you wince. Being made up of out of tune trumpets and a cracked drum they were appalling, wonderfully appalling.

When you're thinking of atmosphere however you also have to think of yet another 'A' word – 'Action', because often they come hand in hand, and you must always be prepared to get right into the action. You must let your listeners feel they really are at the heart of what ever is going on. If it's the action of people, you must let the listeners hear clearly what is being said, or indeed shouted. You must get in among those people and actually let your listeners 'rub shoulders' with them. Sometimes they will be celebrating, or arguing, protesting, fighting, rioting, even destroying something, but whatever they're doing you must get right in with them, and if it's an angry crowd it's even more important. Here I'm talking about your safety.

I first learnt this during the 1974 farmers riots in Holyhead. They were protesting about Irish beef imports arriving to swamp, as they saw it, an already depressed market, and for several nights a crowd of about two thousand big stick wielding farmers repeatedly smashed through the police cordons and barriers to literally stampede the terrified and bellowing cattle back into the docks. It was mayhem, and I warn you – an angry crowd is like a rugby scrum, it swings around. If you're on the edge you'll get smashed against a wall, hit by vehicles, or coshed by the police. If you're a reporter get into the heart of that mob and stay right in there.

Incidentally – 'tune' your recording level. Don't ever record on automatic. Learn to do it and appreciate the difference. The listeners will certainly appreciate it. There's nothing worse than hearing back-ground noises surge in like a tidal wave between every sentence.

It's possible of course to convey a radio picture simply by the tone of someones voice. A good example can be found later with a woman whose front garden had disappeared down a mine shaft, and there was definitely something in the voice of a football supporter whose parrot had been taught, by a so called friend, to loudly and enthusiastically support the wrong team.

There are lots of ways to paint a radio picture but if you get it wrong you can be in trouble. One weekend, when reporting on the annual miners gala in Cardiff's Sophia gardens, (a very political event) I allowed a gaggle of geese to take over from the guest speaker, government minister Michael Foot. He'd made his point and was now becoming repetitive, so when these geese came waddling along honking like old fashioned motor car horns I held the mic. out to them, gradually turned up the volume, and let them drown him out.

Even if you read no further you will have realised that I love radio programmes. I do have criticism of the BBC however but mainly this is a book of good stories, and if you too harbour a desire to become a radio reporter it may serve as a guide to your survival. I say survival because doing the job is easy enough, lasting more than six months is the hard bit, and with the BBC's ever growing determination to spend so much money on television at the expense of radio I fear the chance to follow quite so freely in my footsteps may already have gone. Unless you either have a fast pony or know the secret of Munson's mixture. (See chapter U)

CHAPTER B
Beasts, Boats, Blunders, and The Brave.

Having completed over three decades in this role I can tell you that much of the radio reporter's susceptibility to high blood pressure is accountable to beasts. These invariably turn out to be animals hoping to become rich and famous, laying claim to a whole spectrum of abilities ranging from juggling plates to doing the foxtrot, and in a manner of speaking, many are said to talk. However, these claims nearly always exceed their talent, and invariably their misplaced ambitions are over emphasised by owners who suffer from clinical delusion.

On the other hand, it has to be said that some animals are talented, and with the right agent could become stars of stage, screen and television, but regrettably not

11

radio. For some reason most are reluctant to perform on radio. I spent an entire afternoon once waiting for a couple of donkeys to say hello. As the sun went down and I slumped back into my car, the jubilant owner came skipping down the drive to tell me they'd said "Goodbye." This form of petulance was not uncommon. Countless award-winning parrots and Mynah birds clammed up as soon as I walked in the room, and if it hadn't been for the talking fish I might have become disillusioned.

I interviewed this fish in a Wrexham pet shop. The proprietor said he came from a jungle somewhere and he might well have done. I don't know what language he was speaking but it sounded pretty foul to me, especially when we took him out of the water. Every time in fact, and the stag that apparently came out of the water to gallop up and down Barmouth beach didn't appear too happy either, and when he ravenously devoured every flower and vegetable in sight, no-one was happy.

The experts identified him as a 'Red' stag, and as Red stags don't normally frequent Barmouth, it was thought he must have fallen off Scotland and floated down on the gulf stream. It seems they're very good at floating, but the poor thing was starving when he turned up in Barmouth. On the whole though he had very little to complain about when you compare him to the kipper I was sent to see in Rhyl's public library. Someone had used him as a bookmark.

The kipper might have been very good at being a bookmark, talented in fact, but he had absolutely nothing to say of course, and that in itself says a great deal about the working relationship that sometimes exists between radio reporters and their producers. Unfortunately the type of producer who wants a dead kipper on his programme can be found in almost every department. The problem, as far as the reporter is concerned, is that visiting a dead kipper doesn't give you much to go on. You look at the kipper, it stares back at you, you describe it, it still stares back at you, and then the librarian says "We found it in this 'ere book."......And that's about it really.

Much of the reporter's time will be spent looking for escaped animals like wallabies and black panthers, but the stag at Barmouth was a good animal story, it had plenty of life to it, (the people trying to get it out of their gardens were certainly animated) and it had a genuine air of mystery to it. After all, you don't expect to find anything more than donkeys on a beach, and they had some nice ones in Barmouth, and also in Llandudno where the local donkey man, Mr. Llew Hughes, was given an 'award' for his services to tourism. This resulted in one of my favourite tapes. I'll play you a snatch. He was reminiscing one day with his daughter.

BWB A3

Olwen "Tell the story about Stella when she used to get fed up. She used to go and lay down, didn't she ?"

Mr. Hughes "Oh, behind the deck chairs! We used to have a white donkey called Stella, and we used to send them up, you know, they used to go themselves, they knew where to go, and I said to my father one day, 'I wonder where the white ass is, she hasn't come back'. I used to go up and have a look for her and d'you know where she used to be – with a kid on her back, lying down behind the deck chairs, hiding. You see a lot of people taking them and thinking they can go further. But those donkeys have been on the beach a bit, and they knew where to turn. Aye. Aye."

There's really no doubt about it, some animals are very clever. Some of them devilishly so. I have a feeling that animals have a bar fixed into their brains which stops them short, and one day someone is going to genetically remove that bar and that will be the end of us. I think the young man who lived in Nantlle might go along with that. He was after foxes one day with terriers and a shovel. Having dug his way into a den he rescued a lamb. It was alive and far too big to get through the entrance. He was convinced that the fox had taken it in when it was small to fatten up. Christmas was coming.

Then of course you get the senior citizens. The oldest horse and the oldest cow, and the oldest duck too. The oldest I was introduced to was twenty-five years old, and I don't know how old the owl was at Penrhos near Holyhead, but it flew into this couple's bedroom one night and landed on the wardrobe where it stayed for twenty-three years. It might have stayed even longer after my visit, I don't know, but it had obviously found its grandstand view more interesting than hunting for mice.

I think the oldest horse I met was fifty-one, and I remember a cow near Melin-Y-Wig having twenty one calves in twenty one years, and I think the oldest cow was 34 at Llanaelhaearn, but then Mary's little lamb has been around for a long time too. Remember the nursery rhyme ?

Mary had a little lamb,
Its fleece was white as snow,
And everywhere that Mary went,
The lamb is sure to go.

That's one we all know, written in the 1840s about a girl who lived on the edge of Llangollen. Her house can still be seen close to the golf course, and yes the lamb really did follow her to school. The writer was a lady from America who saw them walking along the road and cashed in on it.

I don't know how long Mary's little 'Larry' lived in the flesh, not very long I suppose. And for obvious reasons turkeys aren't known for their longevity either, which explains why they get very worried if you start talking about dinner, and you've only got to mention words like 'pluck' and they become downright hysterical.

This transcript is taken from a recording I made in a shed full of turkeys near Penyffordd. It was

December and when I walked in with the proprietor they were making that gentle little 'gobble-gobble' noise that turkeys make as they stroll around contentedly pecking at the ground. It was all very peaceful to start with, until they heard me say the word 'seasonal'.

BWB 8

(Occasional gentle 'gobble-gobble' noises).

Barham	"Well, that's a nice noise, isn't it ? A very seasonal noise".
Turkeys	"Gobble! Gobble!" (turkeys suddenly alarmed).
Barham	"Well, they're chatting away like mad now aren't they, do they think I've come to feed them or something ?"
Proprietor	"Oh, they react to strangers".
Barham	"Perhaps they're worried I've come in to wring their necks".
Turkeys	"Gobble! Gobble! Gobble!" (Turkeys running around in panic).
Barham	"I didn't mean it! I didn't mean it!"
Turkeys	"Gobble1 Gobble1 gobble1"

The noise was deafening. There were three hundred in that shed, all big birds, and they were literally stampeding, threatening to knock us off our feet. It took some time for them to settle down, but no sooner had peace and quiet been regained when I put my foot in it again. I was told they were twenty-six weeks old and I asked "Are they all going for Christmas dinner ?"

Turkeys	"Gobble!! Gobble!! Gobble!! Gobble!! Gobble!! Gobble!! Gobble!! Gobble!! Gobble!! Gobble!!
Barham	"I didn't mean it!! I didn't mean it!!"(They gradually settle down) Can we come and see them being plucked ?"

15

Turkeys   "Gobble!!! Gobble!!! Gobble!!!Gobble!!!Gobble!!!"

Strange things – Turkeys. A man in Amlwch made galleons from their carcases every Christmas. They didn't float though, but enough of beasts and birds, now we're into boats and I've seen some pretty strange craft built around our shores. There were several concrete boats, and a huge steel yacht built at Borth near Aberystwyth to sail the high seas as a cargo boat of all things, and I often wonder what happened to the leather boat someone was building behind the pub at Nant Peris.

As a reporter, I got invited aboard a lot of boats – shooting down slipways on lifeboats, skimming the waves in speedboats, even scooping up mud on a dredger, and on several occasions a variety of naval craft, but I must say I always felt drawn to yachts. Nautical beasts thrust forward by powerful engines are okay but I always felt I had a deep-rooted connection with sail power. This I put down to the fact that one of my ancestors was a sail maker on the Thames, and with this background, and through the considerable experience I'd gained from various maritime assignments, I was eventually given my own 'command' and was sent to sail the Norfolk Broads with my wife and two very young children as crew. Here I acquired a great deal of sympathy for Captain Bligh.

BBWB101

Barham   (Becoming exasperated.) "Come on Gareth, get the tiller over, we're going into the bank."
Son   "It won't go over any more."
Barham   "Well you'll have to try a bit harder for goodness sake.
(Crashing, crunching noise. Inexplicably the boat has stopped.)
Daughter   "The mast is up in the trees."
Barham   (Now totally exasperated.) "Oh! For goodness sake!"

The BBC never did believe in free speech. No matter how infuriating the situation became you were never allowed to 'express' yourself. Instead you had to contain yourself to things like "Oh bother!" - "For goodness sake!" - "Crumbs!" Or just occasionally "Well I'm blessed!"

When we got the mast stuck in the trees we were taking part in a holiday feature, and you have to be careful with holiday features. As I might try to explain later - you can 'publicise' a holiday, but you mustn't 'advertise' it. You can't actually persuade people to come and part with their pennies by painting too rosy a picture, and on that occasion there was little danger of that.

BBWB
(Deciding with wife which rope to pull on. Gale blowing. Both shouting to be heard).

Christine	"I don't think that's right! That one ?"
Barham	"What ?"
Christine	"No!"
Barham	"Well I think it is."
Christine	"No, no!"

(Wind howling, waves crashing)

Barham	"Well, let's just pull on the blessed thing anyway. Now hang on!"
Christine	"Whoops."
Barham	"I've got my foot tangled round the bottom of it! Now then, okay ? Now then, right!"
Christine	"Over this one ?"
Barham	"Yes, I think so. Oh, crumbs, well hold it! Look, look (getting annoyed) can you hold this rope away from my ankle ?"
Christine	"I'm doing my best!"

(Loud crash as sail balloons and swings across wildly).

| Barham | "Oh crumbs!!" |

(General commotion).

Christine	"We're drifting!!"
Barham	"We can't be!!"
Christine	"We are! We're right over here!"
Barham	"We can't be drifting.I've got the mud-weight down!"
Christine	"We're right on the other side of the lake, now look. We were well over there before!"
Barham	(Giving up) ".....I think you're right.

I do actually love the Broads and that wasn't the only Broadland adventure, and there was another on the Llangollen canal as well, and I remember on one occasion a woman writing in to complain about the BBC paying for the Barhams to have a holiday, but the BBC paid for very little. For example a boat company would supply the boat free of charge, but we only did a few family holiday features, all the rest I produced entirely unaccompanied as was the norm, or just occasionally with a party of other journalists. Some were at British destinations and others were abroad and I will tell you more of those later, but food, flights, hotels, were all paid for by tour operators, hotels, or National tourist board.

They were all paying for publicity of course, but don't let anyone ever tell you there's no such thing as a 'free lunch'. There is, because there has to be. You 'say' what you think. Your only loyalty is to your listeners who may be tempted to buy the product, and if you think that something is disappointing you say so. That yacht broke down. The wind dropped and the engine wouldn't start. I had to say so. If you think the price of a cup of coffee is a rip-off then you have to say so. If you're treated to a nice dinner on a train then of course you say so, but if the train misses its connection you say that too. It's a responsibility you cannot shrink from.

Sticking with boats for a bit, I've always thought that boats should be leisurely things, but as we all know some people just love getting wet and cold and prefer to race them, and the strangest boat race I ever came across was the 'Three Peaks Yacht Race'.

It's an annual event, starting on a Saturday, and I was often sent to cover the start for the afternoon's sports programme. Not that I ever saw the start. In order to be back at the studio in time I always had to leave before the gun went off, but it's a strange race in which umpteen big yachts sail off from Barmouth with fell runners stowed aboard to run up and down mountains. They race to Caernarvon to run up and down Snowdon, then they race to Whitehaven to run up and down Sca Fell, and then they race to Fort William to run up and down Ben Nevis.

It has to be said that it involves a good deal of navigational skill, but what it's like to race up and down a mountain having spent several days tossing around in a boat goodness only knows. It provides plenty of atmosphere on starting day however, which is what you need on the radio. As I have already said, because of the distance involved in getting the tape back to the studio, I was never able to wait for the start. Time on those occasions was always desperately short, but it was especially desperate one year when I got marooned.

The event is run from the yacht cub at Barmouth, and on this occasion I'd recorded the start of the feature with an organiser explaining the logistics of the race, and my next step was to include an old acquaintance who was playing a major role that year. It was his turn to be commodore, and he was going to describe the colourful scene and explain where some of the competitors had come from while driving me around their boats in his launch. On reaching the Australian's boat I was going to record something with them to round it off, and then commodore X was going to return me to shore, and that would be it, job done and dusted, and off I would rush on the long journey back to the studio.

However, when putting together a radio feature there are often days when you have to be 'flexible' in your approach, and this was one of those days. Also you will notice that I refer to my old acquaintance as commodore X. This is because he may have been a perfectly sober individual normally, but on this particular day he became anything but.

Also, there were other problems. He needed to get changed into his commodore's suit because he was short of time. Therefore he decided that he should take me out to the Australians first, then go back, change, and then come back for me and do his bit then. Seeing as I still wanted the Australians on the end of the piece, doing it out of order was obviously going to give me some extra editing to do – cutting them out and sticking them on the end of the tape, but that's something you get used to. Assembling a radio feature is just like putting a film together, recording the bits as and when you can, and sticking them together in the right order later on.

As with a good many blue prints laid down by mere mortals, it didn't quite happen like that. With the interview with the Australians done, they decided they would go ashore and I remained aboard waiting for the return of the commodore.

I can't remember how long I waited, but the mooring was on the very outer edge of the harbour and after literally jumping up and down and shouting my head off for what seemed like eternity, I was eventually rescued by a passing canoeist !

At the yacht club I found the smart commodore in the bar and tapped him on the shoulder. I've rarely seen anyone look more horrified, and looking incredulously at his watch, and with time now desperately short, we flew down the stairs and leapt into his launch, off at long last to do his bit – reviewing the fleet. It was something he could have done very nicely, sober.

Over those many years I had several nightmares, and this one is particularly memorable. Following on from the interview with the race organiser explaining how the race is run, commodore X was supposed to be telling me about the competitors, how many were taking part and where they'd come from, but now, as he grappled with his memory and strove to say something - anything, we were doing nothing more than 'zoom' around in a tight circle. We were going round and round as if caught in a whirl pool, cheered on enthusiastically I might add by an extremely noisy crowd hanging over the railings.

Eventually he'd at last managed to say something that was just about usable and we staggered, heads spinning, up the harbour steps, and saying goodbye to him, I turned towards my car and fell into a pile of lobster pots.

Sadly I never saw him again, but the strangest boat I ever saw was called the 'Fire Dragon'. It was built by a motley crew from the Rhyl Fire Station and launched onto the River Elwy just below the old road bridge at Rhuddlan. It was just before Christmas. I don't remember what year and I cannot remember why they did it either. In fact, I can't imagine why they did it.

As any actor will tell you, the worst calamity that can overtake anyone engaged in speaking to the public is to become paralysed with a fit of uncontrollable 'giggles'. We all remember it happening to Brian Johnson once during a cricket commentary and I can tell you it's agony. Actors call it 'corpsing' though I don't know why, but you you feel so guilty. You feel such a fool. You know you've got to get yourself under control, but you just can't. You just can't.

These firemen had decided they could make a boat using only the things they carry every day on a fire engine. They used ladders of course, and plastic sheets, and sticky tape, and then having put it all together they climbed in. Half a dozen firemen, and Father Christmas.

Their boat was to be driven exactly the same way as some of the big cross channel ferries, that is to say - water was to be sucked in by a portable petrol driven pump and thrust out the back. It's a sort of 'water' jet propulsion. However, instead of shooting the water out beneath the surface, they thought for some inexplicable reason, that they had to shoot it up in the air !

I'm wondering if I can go on with this, my ribs are starting to ache already. I was talking to one of the fire officers while the crew got the thing ready.

BWB 2

Barham	"Shiver me timbers, this is a fine looking craft, Paul."
Fire Officer	"This is the Fire Dragon, Alan."
Barham	"So, how far are you going on this fine ship ?"
Fire Officer	"We intend to stay on the river for as long as possible."
Barham	(Laughing) "I thought you were going to say you intended to stay on the surface as long as possible.
Fire Officer Fire	"Yes, it's built from equipment that you find on a Engine. If you look closely, you'll see the hull is constructed of ladders. They're aluminium ladders, they're strung together with lines and ropes, even rolls of sticky tape and then it's covered with what we call salvage sheets which are waterproof. We've got airbags which we use at the back. We've got hose lines and a small pump to give us some propulsion on the water".
Barham	"So, it's jet-propelled".
Fire Officer	"That's right".
(Loud noise as motor on pump is started.)	
Barham	"Ah, there we are, dear me, the engine has started, smoke and steam everywhere and they're all clambering aboard now, that's it - Oh they're really going now. They've got four fire hoses I see sticking out of the back of the boat – they're squirting out water as hard as they can go, Oh, (starting to laugh)

they're going in circles now because only two of the hoses are working (laughing) and they both happen to be on the same side ! (laughing) Now they've got the other two working again – Oh (still laughing) they're going to collide with the bridge ! Are they going to get through ? No! (laughing). Oh dear, they've hit the bridge and they're having to push themselves off the bridge now, the water is coming through there quite rapidly this morning and, Oh (laughing now uncontrollably), as the boat swung round the fire hoses absolutely drenched some people on the bank (laughing still) and they've got stuck under the arch ! (Engine revving loudly, Barham hardly able to speak). They're really stuck now! (Barham now hysterical) Now Father Christmas has fallen over ! He's upside down in the boat !!"

I've been exhausted just listening to that tape, but sand yachting makes a nice change. It is a form of yachting on wheels that's been around for many years and this also makes for good racing. Black Rock Sands is a good venue but I had my first lesson on a very wet beach at Borth near Aberystwyth. A reporter gets lessons in all sorts of things.

CB3K

Barham	(At speed, shouting to be heard) "Oh! We've just gone for a paddle and I've got a face full of salt water! (laughs) Oh dear, Oh dear, this is tremendous isn't it Geoff ?"
Geoff	"It's fantastic".
Barham	"We're really going at a tremendous speed now". (Splash) "Oh my word! Another mouthful of salt water" (Laughs).
Geoff	"This is ….. this is the first leg".

Barham	"We're absolutely tearing along this beach".
Geoff	"It's fantastic".
Barham	"I wonder what speed we're doing ? Oh! There we go right round to the left, Oh, Ooer, we've just done a tremendous turn to the left, Jeff's controlling this thing of course, with a rope in his hand."
Geoff	"I'm just pulling the sail in now to pick up speed again after that turn".
Barham	"Oh, … Ooer".
Geoff	"We just hit a rather bumpy bit then".
Barham	(Laughs).
Geoff	"It's quite exciting at times, but there's a tremendous feeling of achievement you know, I've only been doing this for two days."
Barham	(Horrified) "Only two days ?!"
Geoff	"Yes, I've never done anything like this before."

It was then that we just missed another yacht going in the opposite direction, and it wasn't long before I was having a go at the helm, and I can personally recommend this past-time. This is sailing without having to lean over the rail or look hurriedly for a bucket.

It's amazing how attached people can get to boats – real ones that is. I was on the last voyage of the Hibernia, or perhaps I should say crossing because she was the last of the old passenger boats that plied the route between Holyhead and Dun Laoghaire near Dublin before the introduction of the car ferries. Like her partner the Cambria, she'd been on that run since the 1940s.

Of the two, I knew the Hibernia best. She was a grand old ship. I particularly remember the beautiful main staircase, which I think was mahogany, (can you imagine that elegance today on a car ferry?) but then everything about her was elegant and certainly the crew thought so.

The stories people told coming back that night from Ireland were wonderful. There were tears in their eyes when they spoke of the dreadful storms when only the old Hibernia and her sister would venture out, and how she'd get them across even though they had to lie on the floor because no-one dared stand. And then there were the tales of countless celebrities, drinking all night and buying drinks for everyone, like the Hollywood film stars going home to seek their Irish roots, and then there was the girl who'd served behind a counter on the ship and who was now a housewife, tied to her kitchen sink in Holyhead. She now looked out for the old ship every day from her window, longing to be on her again. She was aboard that night, crying her heart out. It must have been something very sad. Altogether it was a massively emotional experience, but that's 'boats' for you, and out on deck, a lone Irish piper was playing a lament.

The scene on leaving Dun Laoghaire had been incredible. Absolutely incredible. Thousands of people came to say goodbye to her. I have never seen anything like it. A band was playing and all the while the crowd was cheering and shouting "Goodbye old Hibernia." There were flags flying, ships were blasting their sirens, men were running down the jetties to hand crank more sirens, and there were fog horns booming. It was a wonderful send off.

I was on the bridge with my son Gareth who was only six, and I was glad he was with me to see this remarkable side to human nature. Those people must have had so many deep and very personal memories tied up with that little ship, and she sailed that evening on a flood of tears.

As I write this, I am beginning to think I might be painting too rosy a picture. There were plenty of less memorable stories to cover, stories concerning strikes and walk-outs, and tragic stories involving deaths and injuries, and of course sometimes these stories emerged with the discovery of a body, and one of these certainly qualifies as 'memorable'. I know we can all make a few blunders but this one is just unforgettable. One day when a couple of coppers on the Llyn peninsula reported that a burnt and mutilated body had been found on a beach, they then rushed it off to Bangor to present it to Dr. Donald Waite, the 'Home Office pathologist.'

I love this story. It conjures up the most wonderful scene. The pathologist in his white coat is studiously discussing the case with me in the dissecting room.

WL21
Dr. Waite   "Well, I knew immediately that it wasn't human, although it had a grey shape, and rotting flesh has a grey appearance from the sea, but it was too hard. It was too firm and not soft. There was no smell with it, and it was with what appeared to be a pair of jeans. It did seem to be some kind of dummy".

I've not got much against our Police Force but I did enjoy that story. To give them credit, the North Wales Police were quick to respond with one of their Press Officers scoring a brilliant last minute equaliser. My producer had been very keen for me to find the two policemen who'd brought in the 'body' of course, but they'd very quickly closed ranks and wouldn't let me get to them, and so at Police headquarters I asked if perhaps they'd suffered any embarrassment.

WL22S
Press officer   "No, but we're thinking that perhaps if we hold a reconstruction, that we might very well ask the reporter concerned if he'd like to play the part of the dummy".

Brilliant, and like I said – we all make mistakes. I've made a lot, and looking back it's is hard to categorise them. For a start, I once introduced the Welsh Director of the Royal Society for the Protection of Birds, as the Director for the Prevention of Birds. I didn't realise what I'd said, but he did. I saw a strange look come into his eyes, a very strange look – panic really.

It's so easy to make mistakes. There was another occasion when I was interviewing a young lady blacksmith who'd made a name for herself with her strange Gothic designs, especially in huge door fittings, handles and things. She'd been showing me her hinges when I most unfortunately said "Right, now show me your knockers."

A few years ago, in 1975 I think, the WI was celebrating its Diamond Jubilee. Celebrations were being held all over the UK, but as the movement had come first to our shores via the island of Anglesey, the first major celebration was held there. The institution had originated in Canada and came to an Anglesey village through someone's garden summer house. Naturally it was thought that the first celebration should be held in that very same village. It's a nice little place, as you can tell by its name-
Llanfairpwllgwyngyllgogerychwyrndrobwllllantysiliogogogoch.

The Summer house was still there but in order to seat so many people due to attend this prestigious event, it was held in the assembly hall of the naval college alongside Plas Newydd, and on the night it was packed with people from all over the country.

Out in the long corridor, amid an atmosphere of huge expectation, the ladies taking part were lining up before going on stage. They were presenting a pageant to illustrate the decades in which the WI had been so active, and of course they were all dressed to illustrate the passing of those years. It was a great big fancy dress party with a costume representing every walk of life, and it was my job to describe them, but then .... this woman striding up the corridor looked different. I could see immediately that she was in a hurry and that she wasn't dressed as a first world war nurse, or a 1920s flapper, neither was she a factory worker or a shop girl, but she certainly had a 'purpose' about her. As she drew near, I laughed and said into the mic. "I can't make this one out. What's your fancy dress then ?"

They say that looks can kill, and it was a very close shave. She glared at me and I could see that she was furious, infact she was livid! "Do you mind!" she hissed. "This is my best dress and I'm the compère!!"

As they gathered round and tried to console her, I slipped out of a side door for a bit, but when all is said and done, it has to be said (even admitted) that occasionally a broadcaster's blunders can be more firmly rooted than in a mere slip of the tongue or a fundamental lack of dress sense. There may indeed have been times when my efforts to be creative might have gone a little too far.

For instance, it has been suggested that one of my more notable blunders was to come up with a 'Radio Mime Competition'. This was always going to be a novel departure from what was, and no doubt still is, perceived as normal, but I saw it as an interesting blend of suspense and reflective calm. In the end I'm not sure if it was in any way reflective or calm, but it was certainly quiet.

Exactly why I did this I 've no idea. It was a very long time ago and it may have been a tongue in cheek response to 'alternative humour'. We did it in dead-pan seriousness, and I remember the competitors went under assumed names, and who can blame them ?

AB21A
Barham   "Now listeners at home, I must remind you that we
              want you to award marks for each piece on two
              counts. First we're asking you to award marks out of
              ten for technical merit, and then out of ten for artistic

interpretation. Now can we have the first contestant? Thank you very much. The first contestant is Miss Blodwen O'Reilly telling the milkman that she doesn't want four pints of milk tomorrow thank you, but could she have a carton of cream."

(Rapid footsteps heard as Miss O'Reilly comes down hall and opens door.)

Barham   (In hushed tones) "Yes.... she's talking to the milkman, erm,pretending to talk to the imaginary milkman I should say, and she really is being very firm with him. You can see in this interpretation of hers that she really is having to be very firm with him.... I think it comes over very clearly infact, that he's given her a lot of trouble in the past, but there we are it's going very nicely, very nicely, now here she comes again, here she comes."

(Door slams, rapid steps back up hall. Spectators applaud.)

The next mime was too ambitious. The artist chose to engage herself with the art of speed flower arranging, but when a poisonous thorn caused her to faint, the 'yell' that came from her as a result of hitting her head on the piano, meant immediate and irreversible disqualification, and unfortunately the very same fate awaited the third contestant too. He was losing love fourteen in a badminton match when he was foot faulted. He argued with the umpire and was disqualified for using abusive language. That caused trouble. I didn't realise what he'd said, but apparently some of our listeners could lip read.

Overall I don't think we got many letters of complaint, but upstairs 'management' didn't like it all. They couldn't understand how marks could be awarded for technique and artistic interpretation by listeners at home. I didn't try to explain, I thought it might be too difficult. After all, if you need to ask....?

Upstairs they later expressed similar criticism, not to say concern, when I broadcast an award-winning conjurer doing card tricks - on the radio. I couldn't quite understand their concern because I always saw radio as being very visual, but they were also critical of the fact that the recording had taken place in a disused railway tunnel.

I don't think they were being very fair really. On the one hand they were saying that radio wasn't visual enough for card tricks, and on the other hand they were saying it was too dark for the cards to be seen in a railway tunnel. That was largely true of course, it was difficult to see the cards, in fact you couldn't really see the conjurer, but it was the only place where it was quiet. He worked as a printer on the square in Caernarvon printing the local paper, and faced with the noise of the printing press and the noise of the traffic outside, we went down the steps that lead to the harbour and nipped into the old tunnel.

Although he wasn't actually a full-time professional, Ivor (stage name Rovi) had just been made president of the Magic Circle. It was a great honour and one richly deserved. His skill with the cards was incredible. You literally couldn't see how he did it, especially it has to be said, in a tunnel.

It never did me any good but I've always liked that saying - 'The man who makes no mistakes makes nothing.' And I certainly saw some pretty big mistakes in my time, but management apart, some of my interviewees made a few mistakes over the years. Two in particular were fatal. One man in Caernarvon set straight off from my interview to canoe across the Irish Sea and half way across capsized, and in Llanrwst another bought a pulverising machine to salvage waste paper and fell in it. Incidents like these are particularly tragic to the reporter because one day the person is enthusiastically telling you of his plans, and the next you're hearing what went wrong.

I don't know if the Snake Man in Rhyl's funfair lived to tell the tale, I think he was American, but anyway he built a bedroom in the funfair solely to sleep with umpteen very poisonous snakes. On that very first day I very carefully put my head round the door and saw him lying on the bed with them crawling all over him, and soon after, and for the very obvious reason, he was rushed off to hospital.

There have been plenty of snakes. Among the more unusual was the adder that smiled up at the mechanic in Connah's Quay when he opened the bonnet of a car. The car had only just pulled in so it had travelled at least ten miles there in the engine compartment, and it then took an RSPCA Inspector all the morning to get it out. The poor thing probably liked it in there because it was nice and warm, but at the University in Bangor a Professor Thorpe had a pen full of big cobras and they were incredibly noisy.

I didn't realise that cobras hissed so loudly and having been rudely woken they weren't in the best of humour. The pen was only about six foot square with the walls standing at about four foot high. There must have been at least half a dozen of them in that pen, and as some reared up hissing at us, others were rising higher on their backs! I was then persuaded to hold my microphone over the edge, and time and time again they hammered its spongy wind muff with great stabbing bites. It was an amazing sight, and the professor's aim was to try and unify a series of anti-venom drugs, and for that he had to 'milk' them of their venom, but I didn't ask if I could stay for that.

I've purposely reserved the last part of this chapter for some very special people and for some very special memories. I have met quite a few brave people and there's a particular group that I would like to mention. They call themselves the 'Milton Mountaineering Club'. They come together from all over the United Kingdom to climb, and they are all blind. Each one has a guide quietly giving them a constant trickle of advice, but they don't choose the easy routes and on the occasions that I've been with them they've had to use ropes, particularly on Cader Idris.

BWB 12

Lady Guide   "If you put your right hand on the rope …. it's there.... and if you follow your hand along the rope ….I'll just hold the other hand in front of you."

Close by, another guide, a man this time was helping a lady stretch a foot across to another rock. She was struggling and starting to perspire.

Male Guide   "Further …. further …. a bit to the left …. that's it, up a bit, up a bit more, to the right a bit, a bit more, that's it."

At that point, the blind lady suddenly remembered an old television programme, "Eee," she said with a big grin. "It's just like the Golden Shot".

I could never forget that, and on another occasion with them on Snowdon, I asked their leader David Blackall, himself blind, why they do it. This too is something I will never forget.

Mr. Blackall   "It's a kind of epitome of life when your feet are on a mountain. It's no good wishing you'd come from the other side, or you'd come on a different day, or tackled a different mountain altogether. The one you have to climb is the one that's under your feet, and the only way to live our lives is to live the life that's under our feet. We're sharing with each other in an enterprise, which is always a very pleasurable thing to do, and I think we are climbing the mountain not because we're blind, but because we're people and

32

because we think we're entitled to a share in the affairs of men."

CHAPTER C.
Crime, Cheating, Cuts, and Competitions.

Crime plays a part in every reporter's life. I saw all manner of things disappear. Farm gates often vanished and there was even a knocker 'nicker' in Nercwys. Before long there was barely a door knocker left in the village, and not far from Pwllheli somebody even stole a footbridge, and how well I remember being on the scene one night when officials of the Rhyl Urban District Council were bent on stealing a submarine.

Their workmen had been taking sand with a mechanical digger from the shore to dump in the harbour for some reason, when suddenly there was a loud 'clang.' They'd struck something big and hard. A little extra digging exposed a large metal thing with a pointed noise, and within the hour Council officials were dancing with joy. They thought they'd struck something that would bring gold rolling through the turnstiles.

They thought they'd found the Resurgam ! This was the world's first real submarine mechanically propelled. This 40-foot, 30-tonne vessel, which was built for a two-man crew, was lost off Rhyl in 1880, and its description in the history books inevitably compared it with the work of Heath Robinson because this submarine was steam powered. Underwater but steam powered, and designed by an arms dealing clergyman, a curate by the name of the Rev.George Garrett.

It had been on its maiden voyage from Birkenhead, but like the curate's egg the curate's submarine was only good in parts, and after major repairs in Rhyl he had it towed out to sea where it promptly sank. For years divers had searched for it, and now a Council digger was digging for it, and digging very quickly. Rhyl's border, as it was then with Colwyn, was very close to that spot and apparently this buried treasure was on the Colwyn side of the border.

I'd had a phone call in the middle of the night from one of the Rhyl Council officers. He was very excited, "We've found the Resurgam," he shouted and was soon telling me where they were going to display it on their promenade, and the pleasure they were getting out of pinching it from Colwyn Bay. However, by the time I arrived about three quarters of an hour later it was a different story. It was long faces all round. Long faces and red ones too. It wasn't the Resurgam. Once they'd dug down deeper they saw it had 'Mersey Docks and Harbour Board' painted on it. It was an old buoy.

The sad thing is that now, (and I'm writing this early in the 21st century) it's been found lying on the seabed, but it's still there. I interviewed the British Railways employee and part-time diver Keith Hurley who found it in the mid-nineties. At the time he told me it was in amazingly good condition, but now other divers are said to be ripping chunks off it.

I shouldn't give the impression, too pointedly at least, that Rhyl is what you might call a crime hot-spot, but the bird population is not too law-abiding. Over the thirty-two years that I was engaged in this business I was sent to Rhyl for a variety of reasons, usually reporting on everything to do with the holiday trade, day-trippers and fun fairs, but on one occasion it was a case of daylight robbery. Flocks of birds were following builders to building sites and pinching the putty.

While a couple of workmen shovelled sand and cement into a mixer - and the rest kept watch on the sky, Chief Works Officer Ray Edwards told me the birds had gone crazy.

BWB 6RT
Mr. Edwards "You can actually see the starlings hover around the

window frames clinging onto those parts of the frames while they eat the putty off, and the pigeons appear to stand on each other's shoulders on the sills eating it around the frame. We've tried various methods to deter them. We've put turpentine on the window frames, we've put masking tape over the putty, but all that seems to do is to add dessert to the putty. They carry on eating with more relish in fact."

Barham   "You say they even recognise your workmen's vans when they go out ?"

Mr. Edwards   "That's right. If we just put one window frame in a particular site they don't seem to bother, but when we go out in three or four vans on a big window replacement programme they seem to recognise the vans and follow us to the job."

Barham   "Like seagulls following fishing boats."

Mr. Edwards   "Exactly the same, and of course this has been going on for some time, and with them eating the putty, the flocks are growing bigger."

Barham   "They're thriving on it are they ?"

Mr. Edwards   "They're thriving on it yes. Another method we tried was to paint the putty as soon as it was applied, but the birds seemed to wobble about as if they were drunk, and they seemed to eat that with even more relish. We infact tried putting tins of putty in front of the windows so that the birds could help themselves and what they did was - they just ate that and went on the frames later."

Barham   "Have you tried a scarecrow ?"

Mr. Edwards   "No, perhaps we will."

Barham   "You might have the first scarecrow on a building site in Britain."

Mr Edwards   "Yeah!"

I'm told cockroaches like putty and crows certainly like golf balls. Gangs of them have been working the Machynlleth and Trearddur Bay courses for some time now, scooping the balls up in their beaks and flying off with them. This gets to be expensive, and although the birds at Machynlleth always seemed to fly off in the same direction, the location of their horde remained a secret.

They're very well organised and brazenly just stand waiting for the balls to arrive. When I was on the Trearddur Bay course with Club Captain Graham Kinder and some of his mates, he was faced with half a dozen waiting on the very first green. The ball flew through the air, fell onto the green and immediately the first one in line pounced on it, but on this occasion it was driven off. Almost before he'd finished his swing Graham was racing after the ball, shouting at the top of his voice. He then ran round the green trying to chase them away whilst his opponent quickly took his shot.

CAW 11

Barham	"This is happening all the time is it ?"
Golfer A	"Oh yes, they're a pest. They're costing us money."
Barham	"Well yes I suppose so."
Golfer B	"We're losing a lot of balls now. We've just had a four come in and they've lost six this morning."
Barham	"You've all lost balls have you ?"
All	"Oh yes, yes, yes."
Golfer C	"I was playing with Graham the other day and he lost five."
Barham	"Dear oh dear."

On the green I spoke again to Graham.

Barham	"You scared the crows off that one then Graham"
Graham	(Breathlessly) "Yes I managed to save that one."

36

Barham	It's not a quiet and relaxing game for you is it ?"
Graham	(Still breathless) "Not at the moment."

Thieving was just too easy for those crows, a lot easier than it was for the chapel minister who wanted to steal something one Sunday morning from a supermarket in Portmadoc. The motivation for this descent into the underworld was to protest about shops opening on a Sunday, and to bring a spotlight on his protest he invited the 'media' to come and watch.

I thought he was very brave because you could see that he was dreadfully torn by his action. The act of stealing I'm sure was very painful to him. Anyway, followed by a small crowd of us reporters, he tantalisingly picked up first one thing and then another, going around a number of shelves with, I might add, the manager looking on in dread. The last thing this young and possibly ambitious manager will have wanted was this sort of publicity, and with us there he had it in abundance. He tried to persuade the minister not to take anything but the man in black had made up his mind.

He really wanted to be arrested for shoplifting and no-one was going to stop him, so eventually he made up his mind and picked something up. I seem to remember it was a bottle of washing up liquid that he then took to the check-out. There he told the girl at the till that he was very, very sorry, but he wasn't going to pay for it, so would she please phone the police and have him arrested, but the manager had a cunning plan. He told the girl at the till not to charge him and let him go. The girl looked puzzled, the minister looked disappointed, and we must have looked devastated, so he politely said again that he wasn't going to pay for it, and she timidly whispered that he didn't have to. "It's a present" she said, very sweetly.

The brilliant young manager had averted a crisis, there was going to be no arrest and we left the store feeling cheated, until our minister suddenly came up with a brainwave. He decided he would walk round to the police station, declare that he was a shoplifter, show them the bottle and insist that they arrest him. So off we all went, happy now that we still had a story to report, but when we arrived at the police station it was closed. No-one was there. A note on the door said 'Back on Monday'. It was very disappointing but, as I said to him at the time, it was to be expected really, after all it was a sunday.

The letter 'C' also stands for cheating and there are times when you need to. Like when you have to write some-ones love song for him. It doesn't have to happen very often. Apart from dealing with emergencies it's usually done only to add some atmosphere, and it's called 'The Magic Of Radio. For instance if you're with sheep that have gone dumb, you have to pretend to be a sheep. Every now and then you have to say "Baaaa". I've often been sheep, even cows. It takes a little practice but you can get the hang of it - "The view from here is lovely. These lovely lush green meadows sweep all the way down to the river, but you have to watch where you put your feet. This is a dairy farm after all and I'm surrounded by cows - Moooooooooo, hallo Daisy."

You have to turn your head away from the microphone when you do animal noises to give them distance, it's not difficult, and actually it's surprising what you can achieve. On the World Service I once substituted the giant turbines of an atomic power station with our washing machine. Anglesey's Wylfa Power Station, which at the time was the largest nuclear power station in Europe, was having teething problems.

It was in the 1970s and it had just been completed at a cost of multi millions, but a ghost was on the warpath. Strange to say it was the ghost of an opera singer and she was being blamed for the breakdowns. Repeatedly problems would arrive and the great turbines would just start to run down. As you might expect, on the day I was there to report on this persistent problem the turbines were spinning beautifully, racing even.

So what do you do in a situation like

that ? After going all the way there you can't let the programme down so you complete the interview with someone in authority saying that supply to the National Grid is constantly being interrupted by a ghost, and then you go home. There you get out the washing machine. Then, when it's going full pelt, you switch it off and as the spinning tub gradually slows down, making a lovely 'whirring' noise, you say into the mic. - "Once again these turbines are running down. The ghost has struck again."

Naturally you only cheat when it's really necessary, when your piece needs a sound effect to produce the essential atmosphere which, at that particular moment or day, is not available by normal means. It has to be seen as a theatrical tool. It's purely theatrical, and without it, without the right background noises, the listener might just as well read a newspaper.

I feel sorry for to-day's broadcasters. For much of their time the prohibitive cost of motoring means they so often have to stay and 'cheat' in the studio, conjuring up the magic of radio by speaking over sound effects recordings, which must be very boring. Whereas I had the challenge of using my initiative and doing it on the spot with what ever came to hand.

On this subject – creating the right atmosphere and providing the listener with the sounds which obviously should be there, the most important thing to remember is never, never play around with a straight news report. No atmosphere is called for. Just record what is said and leave it at that. Atmospheric sound effects are only for features. Never for news. That rule is sacred, and for all sorts of reasons it's right.

Occasionally there are times when the sound effects for a feature are so important that the feature or programme cannot possibly proceed without them, and this is something that must never happen. Like the Mountie has to get his man, you have to get your story come what may.

It can get complicated though. I was sent once to Bala to go fishing with the town's best pike fisherman who was going to show me how he caught those big killers. The feature was going into a nature programme and of course in order to demonstrate his skill he needed to catch at least one pike. " He will catch one won't he ?" my producer asked with a very worried look."Don't worry," I said, and on the phone my fisherman said exactly the same thing, adding "It's not difficult really."

It was soon after 5 p.m. when he met me at the lakeside from where he worked at a nearby garage. He told me that he first needed to catch some small perch to use as bait. "This is easy," he said, handing me a bucket to keep them in, and soon we were clambering into a rowing boat with his little boy.

We rowed out onto the lake and two hours later it was getting dark. It was getting dark and he hadn't even caught the bait. He said there were normally thousands of perch there at the car park end, but not that day.

Eventually we were sitting under a big bright moon, wondering where the damn things had gone, until in exasperation I got hold of the bucket, filled it with water, and splashing my hand around in it I said "Listen. The sound of perch swimming around in your bucket." He raised an eyebrow "Good idea," he said, and we got down to work at last, sorting out the imaginary bait.

CBBW 101

Fisherman	"What we want is a good lively one to attract the pike."
Barham	"I see. How do you fix it onto your line ?"
Fisherman	"Well, (taking fish from bucket) you get hold of the perch ...."
Barham	"It's a lively thing."
Fisherman	"Well you get the hooks, you get the first hook, you hook it in the front of the dorsal fin .... and the second hook ..... you hook in front of the tail."
Barham	"Mm".

Every now and then we stopped and listened to what we'd recorded to see if it sounded realistic. It was good, and again I watched, microphone held outstretched, as he explained how he was setting two floats, one above the other, and then he threw the tackle over the side. This of course was time for another pause.

During this lull we had to decide on the size of the pike we were going to catch, and how we were going to illustrate those tense minutes when the floats would at first become agitated and then be pulled under the surface. We also had to decide how we would hook our pike and bring it to the boat. Having switched on and explained that process, we now needed something to 'strike' against. I suggested that we rowed across to the yacht club in order to tie the end of his line to the door handle of a car. This we did in total darkness, and once back on the water it was time for action again.

Fisherman	"There he goes!" (Strikes his rod against the fish).
Barham	"Now what do you do ?"
Fisherman	"You let the line go, let the pike travel along, you can watch the pilot floats go round the top of the water."
Barham	"Yes."
Fisherman	"And then you let the pilot float go right under...."
Barham	"There he goes!"
Fisherman	"You smack over the bale arm on the reel, and you reel in!"

It was very exciting, but then we had to bring the 'pike' to the side of the boat. Here was another problem to solve. Suddenly I thought of something. Taking off one of my Wellington boots I turned it upside down and swirled it round and round in the water. It sounded perfect. It made all the right sort of swirling and splashing noises a big fish makes.

41

Fisherman	"Here he comes" (reel noise).
Barham	"How long do you think it will take us to get him into the boat"? Fisherman "We'll get him in now."
Barham	"He's a beauty isn't he ?" (swirling noise) "What a cruel mouth he's got".
Fisherman	"They're vicious." (reel noise)
Barham	"How do we get him into the boat ? I'm not catching hold of him."
Fisherman	"No, I've got a gaff here. Just a minute! He's gone again. (swirling noise). You get the gaff and hook him under the chin. Here he comes."

I lifted my boot out of the water and commenced to flap it around the bottom of the boat. It sounded very realistic but it didn't go on for long. My companion grabbed a hammer and laid into my boot with a vengeance, continuing to bash it until he was sure that he'd killed my boot stone dead.

At that point I caught sight of his little boy. He'd not said a word and now he was watching us with a very worried look. His father eventually drew his breath, happy to have killed one more pike, the terror of all things in the lake. He then described how nice they are stuffed with sage and onion and baked in the oven, and I was able to go home. The only trouble of course was that next morning I had an awful lot of work to do, cutting out all the gaps in the tape.

Cutting chunks out of tapes is rather snootily referred to as editing. Today it no doubt corresponds to cutting bits from discs. These were just coming in when I packed up. Until then I'd seen no technical advances at all. Radio really was steam radio. For over three decades I cut magnetic tape with a razor blade and stuck the ends together with bits of sticky tape like everyone else. In time you could work very quickly, and from what I saw of the new computer technology, a razor blade and sticky tape were far quicker and more accurate.

Mind you, you sometimes got into a terrible mess with tape. I walked into a studio one day and found the religious affairs producer up to his knees in the stuff. His programme had shot off the spool at high speed. He was in a terrible tangle, and the language certainly wasn't in keeping with 'Prayer for the day.'

Cutting tape is quick and easy, but 'editing' is a pain. It's tedious. Imagine it. You've done the recording and now you've got to listen to it all over again. You've got to figure out where you can lose some precious seconds, because almost everybody who opens his mouth into a microphone says too much, and no programme is elastic. Pieces have to fit exactly. So most of the time editing only means throwing bits of what people have said in the bin. At other times it means deciding if your report or feature needs some explaining from you the reporter. These bits, that you record and stick in later, are called links, and you also have to decide where in the piece you're going to put them.

Apart from preparing some of the lengthier stuff at home, most of my editing was done in my car every day, parked in lay-byes with the tape recorder on my lap and the lid opened up behind the steering wheel. During all those years this amazed my colleagues but I can't understand why. I found the standard issue 'Uher' we used for recording was so much quicker to edit on than any editing machine. It was small enough to do away with all that fussing with a white pencil for a start, I just took the tape from the play-back head, kept my eye on the exact spot - and cut it. It was that quick and that easy, and with practice it was perfectly accurate.

Of course every studio had editing machines waiting for your return, but not only were they slow to use, there was nearly always a queue waiting to use them. Therefore editing on the way in avoided lost time, and sitting with a nice view and with a flask of coffee and a piece of cake, with your editing done for the day, was always very pleasant.

I always liked live broadcasts and I think everyone did because obviously a live broadcast didn't involve editing. As I've said, editing hour upon hour was extremely boring. You can sit for hours and hours with a razor blade clenched between your lips, searching and searching for bits that are either repetitive or not so important so they can be dumped. Reports and features have to be exactly the required duration whether they're recorded or done live, but with a live piece the content takes second place to finishing on time, and often suffers because of this.

With a recorded piece there's no excuse for not getting to the heart of the matter, but no matter how little someone's told you in a live broadcast, when your two or three minutes are up you just have to say "Thank you Mrs. Jones and now back to the studio." But if you're recording it there's no excuse for poor content. You go on asking questions until your interview tells you everything and then you spend the rest of the day or night cutting it down to size. That's why, with no criticism intended for the reporters, live interviews are often so inferior.

It's not something that happens in a short news report, but when putting together a 'feature' you often have to record things out of sequence, as I explained with the Three Peaks Yacht Race, and that's when you can get into a dreadful mess.

During my career I very often compiled features and indeed whole programmes up to an hour in length in my office come studio at home using clothes pegs, (I had the technology) and they fitted the purpose admirably. I numbered each peg and placed them in line to hold the 'ends' of all the inserts, and then I reassembled them all onto the spool in the order I wanted them, but out on the road it was a different game altogether.

Sitting in the car there was never anywhere to line up clothes pegs, so the various bits of tape used to get hung over headlight switches, heater controls, and even through the steering wheel. Then of course I'd forget which bit of tape was which. "Did I sling the Vicar round the gear stick ? Or is this piece

44

the church bell ?   No, I think that's the Verger.   Or is that the Verger's wife ?"

I got into a terrible tangle once, I got the bells of the Ruthin Parish Church under my feet. By the time I'd untangled them and got them back on the spool, they came out sounding dreadfully cracked.

Actually, if I can just say this for the benefit of broadcasters everywhere, cutting tape properly is an art. The joints must not be noticed, even when taking into account the fluctuations of passing traffic. Think of your editing in advance while you're doing the recording. For example if your interviewee dries up wait for the right background noise before you ask the question again. In other words if a car was passing when you asked the question in the first place, make sure a car is passing when you ask the question again. If this is not possible, cause an audible diversion. Slam a door or something.

There   are   times   when   editing   is extremely difficult, as it always was with someone speaking on a train. It's not such a problem now they've started to introduce continuous rails, but before modernisation every train made a 'clackety-clack' noise as the carriage wheels sped over the gaps between the rails. We always had a huge problem with that because the clackety clacks were always speeding up and slowing down. You may not realise it but trains do have a habit of speeding up and slowing down. They're doing it all the time, not just when leaving or approaching a station either, so when you come to cut a chunk out of someone talking on a train, if you're not careful you will get a train that jumps from thirty to sixty miles an hour in an instant.

Even on continuous rails the advice I would give any aspiring radio reporter is to keep interviews on a train to no more than thirty seconds at a time, and recording an interview with someone with bells ringing in the background is another hazard. A single bell tolling is particularly difficult, not to say impossible to cut into. Chopping a few words out of your speaker in that situation will almost certainly upset the regular timing of the bell and make it sound as if the bell ringer has gone berserk. Music too is another difficult background to cut into. You can only do it at the end of a particular phrase in the music, although I did manage to cut easily into stuff like heavy rock music because, by comparison, it's so disorderly.

Horses trotting was another field with a 'keep out' sign on the gate. I was producing a holiday feature in York once and I thought it would be nice to start by rolling into town in a horse and trap. They were running them from the station and the coachman was very good. He had a good strong voice that was easily heard above the 'trot trot trot' of the smart black pony, and as we approached the old town walls he was telling me what a wonderful place York is and what I was going to see that weekend.

He was great, but at the time I was a bit worried as I thought he might be a little long-winded, and when I got all my recordings together I knew I had to cut him shorter, but it was very hard. No matter how I tried I couldn't cut between his words and the rapid steps of the pony. Every time I cut out a few words I ruined the 'rhythm' of the pony, and in the end the poor animal sounded so lame I was worried people would report it to the RSPCA.

You may have noticed that 'C' is also for competitions and if you want to do this job beware of competitions and races. You will want to be at the finish but so will a race compère and at least a dozen loud speakers doing exactly what you're trying to do.

Goodness knows how many races there are each year and you get to cover them all in time, even take part. I once came third in a camel race, but some people here prefer to go sledge racing with huskies. Huskies, fur coats, hoods, gloves and boots, everything the Eskimos have - except snow. They would like to have snow and occasionally, if the weather's been kind to them, they do have snow. But, as often as not in North Wales, the sledges run on wheels making them look like chariots

On a very cold and windswept Talacre beach, a vivacious lady by the name of Miranda Taylor-Smith took me for a run on her sledge, and her dogs shot off with such acceleration that I nearly fell off the back.

ABWB 8

Miranda	"Okay off we go! …… Oh, are you still here ?"
Barham	"Well, oh yes, oh my word, we went off with such a jerk!"

She was great. I do love to see people enjoying themselves. I just cuddled up behind her and hung on!

Miranda	(Exhilarated) "Good boys! Good boys! Hyke, Hyke, Hyke on!"
Barham	(Shouting) "You don't shout 'Moosh' then ?"
Miranda	(Shouting) "No, no, it's Hyke. Hyke! Hyke! Hyke!"
Barham	(Shouting) "My word, we're going at a tremendous speed!"
Miranda	(Laughing) "Hyke! Hyke! Hyke! Hyke! Hyke!"
Barham	(Shouting) "Is this a good place to practice on the beach like this, on wheels ?"
Miranda	(Shouting all the time) "Come on boys, Hyke! Hyke! Hyke!"
Barham	(Hanging on) "What a bumpy part of the beach this is."
Miranda	"Go on boys! Hyke! Hyke! Hyke! Hyke on boys!"
Barham	"Crumbs!"
Miranda	"That's it boys, good boys. Whoa! Whoa!" (They stop.)
Barham	(Recovering) "Is it a good place to practice ?
Miranda	"Oh yes, I mean, the sand really works their muscles, and at the same time they don't damage their feet or jar their legs like they would on hard concrete."

Barham   "So if you can't get snow this is the place to come ?"
Miranda   "Yes that's right. Come on, let's do it again!"

There have been some very strange competitions. There have been people carving statues out of snow, and they looked very good too, but when I started in this business piano smashing competitions were all the rage.

It seems very odd but in the 1960s there must have been thousands of old pianos smashed to smithereens by teams of young men and women wielding sledgehammers. They just laid into them and the first team to have their piano lying at their feet in bits was declared the winner. They made wonderful noises of course. It sounded like musical thunder, but not all competitions are races and I mustn't forget I'm giving you races later, but the reporter will find competitive events everywhere and in the most unexpected places.

Agricultural shows harbour some of the more bizarre. Welly-throwing became obligatory at most of these events, and at the Flint and Denbigh Show they tried frozen haggis throwing. This, without a great deal of surprise, had to be abandoned when an orbiting haggis lost contact with mission control and gave a nasty headache to an off duty sheepdog.

Competitions come in a variety of guises. One marvellous example I came across completely by accident. It was all to do with the pride of two bulldozer drivers. One on the Llandudno municipal rubbish dump, and the other on the Colwyn Bay municipal rubbish dump.   I was sent to report on the fact that rubbish piled onto the dump at Llandudno was spilling onto the playground of a primary school. It wasn't very nice. The headmaster recorded a few words for me saying how dreadful it was, and it was clear that most of the problem was being caused by seagulls. They'd colonised the rubbish dump and were constantly picking it over and causing the rubbish to topple down into the playground.

This was another case of doing something out of order. I wanted my description of the scene to come first, and then I intended to follow this introduction with the headmaster complaining about the mess, but unfortunately he had to go to a meeting. I therefore recorded his bit first and then climbed up onto the dump to record the introduction.

In those days there were no fences and you could trample all over it, if you thought you could stand the smell. Anyway, I found I was looking at a very large area. In the distance a man on a bulldozer was spreading out a newly dumped load of rubbish, and in front of me there was a flock of seagulls. They stood watching me intently. The only problem was they'd gone very quiet and I wanted them making a noise of course. I wanted them 'squawking' while I said something like - "This is a very large rubbish dump here in Llandudno. Much of the rubbish is spreading down into the school's playground and much of it is being carried there by huge numbers of seagulls who have found this a more profitable place to rummage for food than on the beach."....But, the seagulls weren't playing ball.

I decided that perhaps I should get a little nearer, so I switched on the tape recorder and walked through the rubbish and mud towards them. They watched me coming but remained silent. I was getting very close now and still they watched in total silence, so to stir them up I started to wave my arms around, but it didn't work. They not only remained silent, they also flew off. They flew off and landed at the far end of the dump. I walked after them, picking my way through the muck, and when at last I reached them they rose into the air again, and without a single squawk, they flew back to where they'd been to start with.

Radio is all about sound. You have no pictures to back up what you're saying, just sounds, so there was nothing for it, I walked back again. On my arrival they once again flew up into the air, and flew silently back to the other side of the dump. It was at this point that the bulldozer driver switched off, and came to meet me.

"You after these seagulls mate ?" he asked, with the air of a man who'd already worked out the answer. "Yes," I said, "I want to record them making a noise, you know, squawking, that sort of thing." He shook his head. "Oh you 'aven't got enough of them 'ere mate," he said, "You want to go to Colwyn Bay. They've got thousands of 'em there, their rubbish dump's a disgrace, it's filthy. There are thousands of seagulls there, and you know why ?" I didn't know why so I shook my head. "It's because they don't bury their rubbish like I do. The place is a disgrace. You should see it. It's filthy, you'll get plenty of seagulls there I'm telling you. Chuck a brick in among 'em mate," he said laughing, "That'll stir 'em up."

Having been convinced, I settled for Colwyn Bay. I knew where the dump was, it was just outside Mochdre in those days and I knew it was much smaller so I reckoned I'd have a better chance of getting straight in among them. I parked on the road and by the gate I saw a bulldozer was at work. Beyond it, but still quite close, there was a gang of seagulls. They were standing around looking bored and numbered less than the gang in Llandudno. The bulldozer driver saw me coming, switched off and got out of his cab. I explained that I wanted seagull noises and he gave me a thumbs up. "Okay mate," he said, "Carry on."

He followed me round to the other side of the bulldozer and picked up a stone. This he lobbed into the middle of the seagulls and they immediately took off squawking like mad. At last it was just what I wanted and I got straight into my lines saying into my microphone - "This is a very large rubbish dump here in Llandudno, and much of the rubbish is spreading into this little primary school, and..." That's as far as I got. The bulldozer driver quickly clamped a big muddy hand over my microphone. "No. No !" he was shouting over the noise of the seagulls. "This isn't Llandudno, this is Colwyn Bay! Llandudno is five miles away! You go down the road here, and turn right at the

Black Cat garage."

In exasperation I was almost in tears. "I know this is Colwyn Bay," I cried "I'm pretending it's Llandudno." He now looked very puzzled. "Why ?" he asked, and watching his eyebrows knitting ever more closely together, I realised it would take a long time to explain and by then the seagulls were so far away they could hardly be seen let alone heard. "It doesn't matter where the seagulls are," I said, "I just want seagulls." He looked at me in silence for a few more moments, and then his eyes lit up and he said something I'll never forget. "Well in that case," he said, "You want to go to Llandudno. They've got millions of seagulls on their dump. It's disgusting. It's a filthy dump! They don't bury it properly like I do !" he said "It's disgusting. You go to Llandudno mate, it's an absolute disgrace !"

That is what you call 'Competition'.

CHAPTER D.
Disasters and Dramatics.

I've covered quite a few disasters and in spite of everything many had a funny side. There was a disastrous fire years ago at the huge Butlin's Holiday Camp near Pwllheli. It destroyed a large part of the camp including the theatre and several shops, but the managers were determined to talk people out of going home. 'Damage limitation' you call it, and what better way of doing it than by holding a gigantic party. This was seen as a great idea and it was planned to go on all day with everyone wearing party hats. This meant phoning the wholesalers and buying literally thousands of party hats, but never mind the whole idea was to forget the fire. However things rarely work out as planned. When the hats arrived every single one of them was a fireman's helmet.

The worst incident I was personally involved in came very close to being a major disaster. I'm told that if it had reached its conclusion I may have gone into the annals of broadcasting history as the first interviewer to kill his interviewee.

I'd heard that a charitable organisation had paid to have a seaside caravan equipped with a kidney dialysis machine so that kidney disease patients could have a holiday. The idea was excellent. I was told that a lot of people had to spend every other day of their lives lying in bed plugged into a dialysis machine in order to purify their blood, so going away on holiday was impossible.

The caravan was a big static caravan at Black Rock Sands. I was told a lady was using it that week and it was arranged for me to visit her. When I arrived her husband met me at the door and took me into the bedroom to meet her. She was lying in bed connected up to this quite large contraption which allowed no room for a chair, and so after a brief introduction I knelt by her side and started the interview. I asked her about having to be connected to it every other day, and what she thought of this idea, and was she having a nice holiday of course. At first she seemed quite happy, bright eyed and smiling. She told me about them having been walking along the beach and paddling in the sea, but gradually her eyes started to flicker, her voice went quieter and her words became slurred, and then suddenly a buzzer went off in the machine behind me. This brought her husband rushing back and I got up and went into the lounge so as to be out of the way.

He fiddled for a bit with the controls and then having told me it was okay, I came back and knelt again at her side. She was fine now and we re-started the interview . I asked her again about having to have this treatment every other day, and what she thought about having it in a holiday caravan, and all that sort of thing. But again she started to go quiet and her words started to slur, and again the buzzer went off and again her husband rushed in.

Once again I sat in the lounge until he'd finished fiddling with the machine, and now for the third time I knelt again at her bedside and once more we got down to the interview. I gave her a few more questions but unfortunately with the same result. Again she seemed to be fading away. It was then that her husband realised what was happening. The pipes connecting her blood to the machine went under the bedside mat. I was kneeling on them and cutting off her blood supply.

It's usually the reporter who comes close to an early demise. See 'T' for terror. But this chapter also has its scary moments. Gwilym Thomas, a director of the Llandudno artificial ski slope and toboggan run, was quite sure both he and I could ride on a toboggan together. He was wrong. When you hire a toboggan you find you're sitting on a sort of 'tea tray' that runs on castors down a steeply twisting stainless steel trough. I was told that if you don't use the brake you go at 40 miles an hour.

I was reporting on its opening but I was getting worried about the time, and as they finished bolting the last section of the trough into place, Gwilym cheerfully said, "Come on, let's jump onto this one."

CBWBC 12
(Toboggan flies down trough.)

Gwilym	(Shouting) "Right turn!! 90 degree turn!!"
Barham	"Oh my goodness me!!"
Gwilym	"Slide into this one ... we're coming up to the bridge now! Left turn, 180 degrees!! We're doing 30knots!!"
Barham	"Oh!!"
Gwilym	"Hang on, a right turn!!"
Barham	"Another bend!! ......"

(Crash, extended, with severe noise levels.)

The tape recorder miraculously went on recording as we slid down the track underneath the upturned toboggan. I got it on the air in time and it made quite a spectacular report, and in the Bala area another interesting little journey was down the River Tryweryn on a raft.

This river can be regulated as it comes from the dam built across Llyn Celyn, and half a mile down from the dam there's a canoeing centre. Previously I'd done some commentaries on the slaloms there, but on this occasion I was sent because they'd hit on the idea of taking holidaymakers down this twisting torrent on an inflatable raft.

It was a big inflatable raft and we did have a helmsman. He was at the back hanging onto a long oar, but I don't think it had much effect.

CBWB 15
(Rushing water.)

Barham   "Oh dear ... it's getting very rough now I'm afraid."

Passenger   (Alarmed) "Oh, ooh, oh! ...... Oh!"

Barham   "This is like sitting in a bath".

(Several screams.)

Barham   "We're up to our knees practically in cold water. I'm
                looking down the waterfalls as we go down them,
                and you feel a little bit dizzy shall I say."

(More screams.)

Barham   "Oh my word, that was quite exhilarating! We must
                have been dropping four or five feet at a time I would
                imagine there. This lady on my right, did you enjoy
                that ?"

Woman   (Shaken) "Yes very much so. (Laughs) Even though
                it went down my neck."

Barham   I think this one lasts something between twelve and
                fifteen minutes...."

Helmsman   (Shouting) "Hold tight!"

Barham   "..... between twelve and fifteen minutes according
                to the amount of water rushing down, oh, oh we've
                just gone over a rock underneath my feet there. I can
                see now why we were told to sit up on the side

	holding onto these ropes and not sit on the bottom, I wouldn't have liked to have got that rock underneath my back end, would you ?"
Woman	"I certainly wouldn't." (Laughs).
Barham	"Oh my goodness! Look at this down here. Is this the big one ?"
Someone	"Yes."
Barham	"Oh dear, oh dear, oh, we've hit some rocks! We seem to have gone sideways against …. this is a tremendous drop (alarmed) it must be about ten foot down and there are tremendous breakers at the bottom, here we go!"

(General panic, many screams.)

Woman	(Very alarmed) "Oh lord! Oh!!"
Barham	"Oh, I think this next one's the big one. I think we're going backwards!!"
Helmsman	(Shouting) "Hold tight!!"
Barham	"Oh my goodness me, this is impossible!!!"

(Much screaming. Water rushing. Gurgling noise. Tape recorder cuts out.)

I don't know if it might have been a miracle, but we all survived. The big dinghy went over the fall, we all tumbled on top of each other and the dingy then bent over the top of us, almost swallowing us up as if in a giant mouth.

Fortunately we all had a change of clothes and after we'd had several mugs of something hot I had to be away, but because the tape recorder had been under the water I couldn't spool off the tape. The thing was dead, and on the way back over the Ffestiniog moors I reeled the tape off by hand and sat with it strung out on the heather to dry in the sun.

That particular tape recorder dried out okay but I used to lose a few. Once coming down Tryfan, a marvellously rugged peak in Snowdonia, rather too quickly in a thick mist I slipped. My feet went shooting up in front of me and I fell smack on my back. The tape recorder in my rucksack was a write-off. A narrow pointed rock had pierced right through my rucksack and skewered the tape deck. I sometimes reflect now, rather ruefully, that during all those years I was never insured.

Naturally from time to time there were cases of 'misadventure' to report on in Snowdonia, and not all casualties were climbers dangling on ropes. Inspite of the advice tirelessly given by the wardens constantly roaming the hills in bad weather, most fatalities were among people simply walking, and quite often of course walking on snow and ice before going over a precipice. There were sometimes half a dozen deaths a year but the message seems to be getting through at last and the overall numbers appear to be falling. (Not that 'falling' is the best word for it.)

I was sometimes sent out into the hills to look for the search parties, very often overnight, and I came to view both the mountains and the search parties with enormous respect. People underestimate mountains that's the trouble. Mountains have a habit of leading you on, and in bad weather the inexperienced just don't realise until it's too late that they've reached the point of no return, exhaustion and the onset of hypothermia.

The glorious Snowdonia National Park measures 800 square miles and there are an awful lot of mountains here, but first time explorers all flock to 'Snowdon' of course. This is simply because Snowdon , or 'Yr Wyddfa' as its known in Welsh, is the highest of them all. Not by much, but nevertheless it is the highest at three-and-a-half thousand feet, and therefore it's the great magnet.

Snowdon is King of the Rockies, and many people come to Snowdon with the sole intention of doing something crazy on it. One group from a Lion's Club somewhere in the comfortable counties of the south of England came intending to walk up one of the paths in dinner jackets and bow ties etc.

They were coming for lunch and

intended to dine at a table on the summit complete with a starched white tablecloth and candelabra. To be fair, I think they were probably doing it for charity, I really can't remember for sure, but they certainly thought they had it all worked out. An advanced party took the table up on the early workmen's train (a rack and pinion mountain railway goes up on the easier side of the mountain) and the rest set out from Pen y Pass in good heart. So did I, but not in a dinner jacket.

The weather was fine to begin with, but as it so often does here, the weather quickly deteriorated. There were about two dozen of them and they'd chosen to go up the Miner's Track, which was a very rough and crumbling track having suffered enormously from erosion. It's one of the busiest of the Snowdon footpaths, and with so many people having strayed from it over the years the route is confusing even in clear visibility, but when the cloud descends it's deadly. A thick mist was just what they didn't need, and a thick mist is just what they got. It was so dense that before long they were strung out all over the place, with shouts coming from all directions, some getting further and further away. "Anybody there ?" .... "Where are you ?" .... "Over here".... "Where ?" .... "Where's here ?" .... "Where are you ?" .... "Where am I ?"

I knew those paths very well but even I wasn't sure how far we'd come, and not many weeks before I'd been out all night in that area because a party of Americans had disappeared. They'd got stuck a little further on having passed the 'zig zags' to where it drops steeply into Lake Glaslyn.

As for our lions, eventually the cloud lifted and we made it to the top, but it was a very sorry looking bunch of revellers that eventually reached its destination. They'd left the Pen y Pass car park looking immaculate in their dinner jackets and bow ties, but no longer. They now looked like a gang of soaking wet scarecrows. The advanced party had apparently done its job and laid the table, but by the time we arrived a gale was blowing and everything but the table had blown away. As we got there they were piling rocks on it to keep it down.

You can be lost in the mountains of Snowdonia for a long time. Early in 1973 four school boys hiking on the Duke of Edinburgh's award scheme were seriously lost in the Carneddi range when they became engulfed in low cloud. After a school teacher failed to rendezvous with them at the end of that first day the alarm was raised, and three hectic search and rescue days later they were still missing.

I then had a stroke of luck. A friend had discovered that a hill walker and his wife from the midlands had stumbled across the boys on the very first day they'd gone missing. They'd spoken to the boys, huddled together in their tent waiting for the teacher, and being worried about them they made a 999 call to the police as soon as they came down to a road and a public house. (This was in the days before mobile phones.)

The pub was the Newborough near Dolgarrog and the woman licensee confirmed this, adding she'd heard the couple giving the police the boy's exact location with a map reference. Having been told this I rang the telephone exchange and was told that all 999 calls from the area were put through to the police station in Llandudno. There they denied that they'd received it. But the couple had left their home number at the Newborough and when I spoke to them they confirmed the call and the details they'd given.

On contacting the telephone exchange again I was told the exact time the call had been made, that it had definitely been a 999 call, and it had definitely gone through to the police station in Llandudno, having been made from a number that was indeed the Newboro's number. It was clear that someone in Llandudno had failed to make a note of it.

When at last the search parties were given the right location the lads, wet cold and hungry, were found very quickly, and after the much needed reorganisation that followed all treble 9 calls in these parts were routed to the police head-quarters in Colwyn Bay.

I saw some pretty strange antics on Snowdon, but among the most commendable of these lunacies was the stilt-walking ascent by a young schoolgirl named Emma Disley. Like most others, she was raising money for a charity and I've singled her out because of her gritty determination. Her parents had been olympic athletes in the 1950's so she knew something about determination, but by the time we'd reached the top her hands were covered in blisters. I never forgot that girl, and in later years that determination slipped into overdrive again. She became one of the very first women to be ordained by the the Church of England.

Back on the subject of disasters though, few compare with one involving a fellow from Caernarfon who was emigrating to Australia, sailing off full of hope and brimming over with the spirit of adventure, but in a floating lorry.

His name was Bill Parry and he was marvelous. He'd bought an old Second World War Army lorry that could float. They were quite common during the war. They were fitted with a propeller and were used to cross rivers. He though was going to the other side of the world. I asked him if he was a navigator. "No," he said, so I asked him how he was going to find Australia, which I thought was a reasonable question, to which he replied, "I shall hug the coast."

Over the years I have often pondered over this radical approach to world travel, and particularly on its significance for global navigation. With the aid of fully up to date maritime charts, and at least one road map, I've come to the conclusion that his final destination could well have been Gloucester. Round South Wales, up the Bristol channel and follow the signs for the town centre.

An important element in the radio reporter's work is to describe things, and describing his lorry was easy. It was a lorry. A lorry with a cabin on top that he'd built himself. He'd spent months building it and it was obvious to anyone's eye, sea-going or not, that he'd made the whole thing top-heavy, but there wasn't much room in this cabin. Much of it was taken up by an enormous chest of drawers crammed with everything from socks to sweaters, and on top of the cabin he'd built a massive tripod mast made from steel scaffolding poles.

The mast was for the radio aerial, but he didn't have a radio. On the other hand, he did have navigation lights. He showed them to me. "I'm told I've got to have these," he said. "So I fixed these jam jars on either side. I've painted one red and the other green and there's a bulb in each one." He also explained that each bulb was powered by a separate torch battery, and in the end, trying to suppress what I can only describe as a 'sinking' feeling, I asked him if he had a life raft. He smiled reassuringly, "Inner-tube," he said, and pointed to a large lorry sized inner tube slung over the 'back'. (I can't bring myself to describe it as the stern.)

This bewildering little craft was sitting on the muddy beach opposite Caernarvon castle, and a few days later I was back there to witness its departure, and driving down that little road on the other side of the river I came up behind a lad carrying a suitcase. I suddenly remembered. Bill had advertised for someone to go with him. I stopped and wound down the window and asked if he was going to Australia. "Aye," he said in a broad Scots accent, so I told him to get in and took him to his ship. "There she is" I said, pointing to it sitting on the mud, and the amazing thing is that he actually got out, thanked me for the lift, and with not the slightest hesitation walked across the mud to meet his skipper.

I gave them a little while to get acquainted and then, after recording a few final words with them both, I waited in the car for the tide to come in. Within half an hour they were afloat, and with a small crowd of people I watched the two mariners pull up their anchor and set off for the other side of the world, in a cloud of smoke.

Next morning I heard the news. They'd moored a couple of miles down the coast so they could walk to a pub. They were having a last pint in Wales when the tide, still on the rise, picked the thing up and and turned it over. Although I don't suppose the Lutine bell was rung, it instantly became, in the language of the Lloyd's Shipping Register, a total loss.

I suppose if you're going to lose your ship you might as well do it on the first day, it's not too far to walk home, but I don't know what happened to the young Scotsman. I hope he was able to salvage his suitcase. His skipper was naturally traumatised. I went to see him the next morning and he was very disappointed, but after a few months the old spirit of optimism and adventure returned. He became a chapel minister, went to south Wales, and changed his sex.

Thinking of their departure though, among the little crowd watching had been an old boy leaning over the rail He was wearing an old navy sweater, and with a real old weather-worn face he looked a real old sea dog. He was watching them in silence, and when I held the microphone in front of him and asked, "What do you think of this ?" - his answer was probably the best answer I ever received. It came in such a gruff old voice, and without turning round he just said, "They'll be back for tea."

Picking up comments and off the cuff opinions from people, as I was doing there, is known as doing vox-pops. It means 'the voice of the people', (or something similar), but you're only looking for brief encounters so you don't ask for names, and this can bring forth some very outspoken comments on any subject under the sun. Nothing loosens the tongue like the cloak of anonymity, and it's very much like fishing. Even if you're running out of time, and even if you've collected sufficient comments, the temptation is always there to throw the line in once more. You never know, you might come up with a gem, but here's a tip worth remembering - generally approach little groups of people instead of individuals because they always spark each other off.

It's an uncomfortable, but nevertheless concrete fact of life, that other people's misfortunes can arouse twin reactions that are impossible to reconcile. Very often you arrive on the scene and feel so awfully sorry for someone, but in the end you can't get away quick enough because there's a black comedy element that's threatening to choke you. No writer could have written the lines that follow. It's the transcript from an interview I did with a lady whose front garden had suddenly, very suddenly, shot down a mineshaft. The entire garden had gone through an old mine cap, leaving one big black hole from the gate to the front doorstep. Her garden had completely and absolutely vanished without trace.

I won't say where it was because apparently there are lots of old mine shafts in that area and I don't want to give anybody nightmares, but I think this couple had probably moved there for their retirement. She had a broad Lancashire accent, and 'eeee' poor woman, she sounded so fed up.

CBWB 8

Woman   "Well, my husband was gardening for me and felt the earth collapse, he jumped off onto the step here, it's just at the side of the hole, and I was inside writing a letter and he came in to tell me. He said 'Just come out love and see what there is out here' and I said you'll have to wait until I've finished my letter. I never, - well you don't expect things like this do you ? Anyway, I came out, - I mean, he was upset, and so I came out and saw the hole. It was awful. It is really, there's no peace really is there ? You can see where it is for yourself. You've got to pass it every time you come out, every time you look out the window you see it, you can't get away from it can you? Oh it's awful, it is really. There's no, - nobody has any idea, you know, until they have it."

Barham	"Have you tried throwing anything down it, to fill it up.?"
Woman	"Oh yes, there's a boiler, there's a couple of chairs, kitchen chairs, there's all the garden rubbish that was accumulated, and it's all gone down the hole, and when it happened at first, my husband just went back and forth, round the back just in the first half hour. Probably it was just some sort of reaction, I mean, we couldn't stop him, he was going round to the back and coming back with some more rubbish to throw down, and everybody said, 'Do give up, calm down' but he was probably in shock."
Barham	"When the earth gave way under your husband, he was very lucky wasn't he ?"
Woman	"He was lucky. I think it's only with him being a miner that he did realise and jump."

The fascinating thing about radio is that if you can trigger the 'magic' you can show your listeners the scene just as well as showing it on a screen. All you need is the right atmosphere, but with this lady you didn't have to throw stones down the hole, it was all there in her voice. There was no anger, just a weary acceptance that things like this happen.

On the other hand some people can display a good deal of anger, like the poor man with the parrot I mentioned – taught to sing the battle hymns of a rival club, and at one time the air could become a trifle blue when dealing with the Forestry Commission. They loosened up eventually and it became a pleasure to work with them, but in my earlier days they were dreadful.

We had a story emerge in Llandudno once where roadside trees were dying because of the new North Sea gas that was being piped through the town. At least that was the expert's theory at the time. The tiny gas leaks that were occurring around joints in the pipe were causing a population explosion among certain bugs that were thriving on it, and these bugs were devouring the roots of trees. It sounded very strange but that was the story and I had to cover it

To be on the safe side council workmen were felling the effected trees before they toppled and caused an accident, but by the time I had a council official on tape, work for the day had finished . This was disappointing, but the piece wasn't needed till next morning's Good Morning Wales so I wasn't to be put off and I rang the Forestry Commission. I imagined they must be felling trees somewhere and all I needed was the ordinary sound of an ordinary chain saw, and a tree falling.

I rang their office near Llanrwst. "You'll have to get permission to ask us," the voice said. "Where from ?" I asked. "Aberystwyth." I was told. I was getting annoyed but phoned Aberystwyth. The voice there was just as helpful. "You'll have to write." I explained there wasn't time to write, but it made no difference. "You'll have to write," the voice said again, "And we'll need it in triplicate." Although I didn't often slam the phone down, I certainly did that day.

As usual there was no time to go looking through sound effects records in the hope of finding a tree falling. In those days those sort of facilities weren't readily at hand in our Bangor studio anyway, but fortunately I had a friend with a timber business, and Kieth told me where he had someone felling trees near Betws y Coed.

I found him in the woods (which wasn't surprising) and told him what I wanted. "Just saw one tree down for me," I said, "And as it comes down switch off the saw so I can clearly hear it falling, and I will say – There goes another roadside tree." He nodded. "Okay," he said, and went to start his chainsaw. After several attempts he gave up and tried another. At last this one started.

He put the saw through a tree that was

about a foot thick. Ideal. I recorded it whipping through the soft wood and the tree began to fall. Just as required he switched off the saw and as it leaned over and made all those wonderful loud 'crack-crack, - cracking' noises a tree makes as it falls, I dramatically spoke my words - "There goes another roadside tree, and .... and....oh dear." Unfortunately we didn't get anything like a 'crash' as it hit the ground because, to be precise, it didn't actually hit the ground. It just sort of leant over, and leaned up against another tree.

"Damn," the man said, and I could see he was now embarrassed. Lumberjacks pride themselves on dropping a tree through even the narrowest of gaps. With beads of perspiration appearing now on his brow, he turned to another tree. There were plenty to choose from, we were hemmed in by them, and soon his saw was noisily biting into another one. I switched on the mic. again, and within seconds the saw fell silent .... 'Crack! – Crack! Crack'! "There goes another tree." I said "Another roadside tree ...." Silence. This tree now was also leaning up against another one.

This extremely tiresome process went on for half an hour. When you get into this sort of situation it's like gambling. You can't go because the next one could be a winner, but suddenly and without warning we heard the sound of a tremendous gust of wind tearing through the forest and coming towards us. We looked around. We had six very heavy trees leaning up against each other. They were leaning very precariously, and any one of them was capable of crushing us both to pulp. I looked back to the man with the saw, and all he said was "Run" And we did.

In the end I got my tree, but not a real one. I don't know how the thought entered my head, desperation I suppose, but I went home and used an old laundry basket that I had in the cellar. It was the old wicker type used by laundries delivering to hotels, and simply opening the lid provided all the creaking noises you could wish for - all those terrible creaking noises of a doomed tree coming down. Then, noisily screwing up a piece of grease proof paper gave me a few million leaves, twigs and branches, all smashing into the ground. The sound was perfect and no one back at the studios ever realised that it wasn't a real tree.

A colleague reckoned that I should have worked for the sounds effects department, (not that we had one) but sadly I never got around to the coconut shells. However I did discover one day, when I was short of snow, that grinding a table spoon into a dish of icing sugar sounds exactly like walking in snow, and I did once manage to create the 'static crackle' you often got on a two-way radio set.

This was when I was working on an extraordinary story. A lady by the name of Ruth had arrived from a big town somewhere to live out in the hills, (but not for long) and one night she discovered a couple of hill walkers on her doorstep who'd got lost in the mist. Very kindly she took them in, dried them off, fed them, and put them to bed. Next morning she sent them happily on their way, but the incident worried her so much that she got hold of a couple of two-way radios and set up a rescue service called 'Station Ruth'.

You have to remember this was in 1969, so there were no mobile phones, but the most remarkable thing about it was that she gave the radios to her dogs. She had two very large ones. One was a great dane and each of them had a radio set strapped to their collars, then whenever it came over a bit misty they were told to roam the mountains looking for anyone who might be lost.

We could hardly believe it when we heard, but sure enough when I went up to find her cottage overlooking the Nant Ffrancon Pass I was met at the gate by one of her dogs, the big Great Dane, and having introduced myself to its owner it wasn't long before the lady was showing me how she attached a radio set to its collar. It was of course quite a big collar and it also carried instructions on how to operate the set.

So, I first recorded a few words of

introduction with the lady and then, to show the listeners how she ran her rescue service, I walked up the hill to act the part of someone who was lost. And not wanting to sit there all day waiting for the dog to stumble across me by chance, I took it with me.

About a hundred yards from the house I switched on my tape recorder, started the recording, told the listeners what I was doing, and read aloud the instructions on the dog's collar.

CBWB9

Barham	"It says here - When you meet this dog she is here as a friend. Trust her. Pull up aerial and call up Station Ruth. Wait for your answer. Well dog, we'd better do as we're told hadn't we. (Pulls up aerial and speaks into radio set).... Hello Station Ruth .... Hello Station Ruth....Can you hear me ? Can you hear me? .... Can you hear me ?"
Ruth	(Static interference.) "Hello. This is Station Ruth answering. Are you hurt ?"
Barham	"No I'm fine."
Ruth	(Static interference.) "Will you look to the left hand of the dog's collar please and tell me the number you will find there."
Barham	"Number 2."
Ruth	(Static interference.) "Underneath the dog's neck you'll find a small opening in the collar. Will you pull out the lead please ?"

Having been told what to do, I pulled on the loop sticking out of the dog's collar and out came a lead. I guessed what was coming next. She asked to speak to the dog.

Ruth	(Static interference.) "Thank you ..... Matilda! Matilda! Come home Matilda, good dog, good dog."

The dog recognised her voice instantly, and with me hanging onto its lead and my tape recorder still recording hanging from my shoulder, it bounded off down the hill to meet the lady at the gate.

Barham   "Well I must say this is a very novel idea. What made you think of it ?

Ruth   "Well one dark night there was a knock on my door and when I opened it there were a couple of hikers who had got lost. I brought them into the house and made them a nice hot drink, and I started thinking."

It was a most crazy idea of course. Goodness knows what would have happened if those dogs had come across a flock of sheep, but she meant well, and I wanted to make a good job of her feature but I had a problem. On my arrival I'd found that one of her sets was away being repaired and the other one wasn't working very well. When she spoke on it very little of what she was saying came through to the dog's collar. But did it matter ? Well I thought so, so I decided to record what she said separately. I put some twigs in her stove to catch fire and sound like 'static crackle' and got her to say what she had to say – kneeling down by it. It worked perfectly. All I had to do was splice her bits of our conversation into the tape later and it was in the bag.
I always wanted to bring things to life. On another occasion when news was coming in about ginseng tea being good for Olympic runners, I ended an interview in a health shop by drinking some of it and then running off to the studio, accelerating to 100 miles per hour. This I did by altering the tape recorder's recording speed with a screw driver as I ran, crying out things like "Oh dear, what's happening ? I'm running so fast !! Oh dear !! Oh dear !!" Until my voice became a high-pitched supersonic squeal.

I used any reason I could think of to 'dramatise' things. There was never a script, and a lot of people joined in for the fun of it, making it up on the spot, and I remember dramatising an interview I did once with a lady wrestler. Her name was Nikki Monroe, she was a British champion and later that very evening she was going to be defending her title. She was very nice, and later I'll give you a chapter on people who became 'participants' – people who participated in the fun, and Nikki could well have fitted into that chapter, but here she is under 'D' for dramatics. I told the listeners that I'd been sent to test her abilities and that I felt a bit awkward about it because I didn't want to hurt her. (As if !)

CBWBC 3

Barham	"Are you sure you'll be alright ?"
Monroe	(Calmly) "I'll be perfectly alright."
Barham	"Okay. Here we go then. Are you ready ?"
Monroe	"Ready."
Barham	"Right." (Barham grunts, groans and gasps for some time.) "Phew. There we are, that's got my jacket off. Have you got somewhere I can hang it ?"
Monroe	"Yeah, just put it on the chair there."
Barham	"Right, there we are. Now have you got a favourite hold or a favourite throw, I mean, how would you describe your wrestling ?"
Monroe	"My wrestling is very skillful. I use various holds, moves, and submission moves."
Barham	"I see. Have you seen this variation of a half-Nelson I've perfected over the years ? You might find it quite useful actually .... now, if I get you round the neck .... there you see .... you see, you can't actually move from that can you ?"
Monroe	"Well, if I twist you here ..... and grab your neck .... and throw you from here !" .... (Long silence) .... (loud and prolonged crash into dustbin).

Monroe	(Worried)........ "Are you alright ?"
Barham	(Painfully in distance) "Yes .... I think so."

       The long silence before hitting the bin sounded as if she'd thrown me twenty yards or more but those precious seconds gave the wonderful effect of her victim flying through the air, and actually the crash was several waste paper bins piled on top of each other that I toppled with a flying cushion.

       Some people in the BBC didn't like me messing around like that, but fortunately I had a few supporters and I couldn't have done without my little flights of fancy. The magic of radio is wonderful and it's unique to radio, it's something television can never share. After all how could you be a television reporter and become Alice in Wonderland's dormouse and jump into a teapot for a nap ? When I jumped into that teapot Alice and her friends were enjoying their tea party in the garden of a hotel in Llandudno, and I landed in the gents toilet. A brief search of the premises had shown me that the inside of the gents toilets sounded just like the inside of a teapot.

       It was a nice afternoon in Llandudno, the seaside resort well known for white rabbits and things like that because Alice, the real Alice who inspired the story of Alice in Wonderland, used to stay there with her parents and every now and then the people of that town hold a Mad Hatter's Tea Party. It's lovely. It's like a picture book come to life with lots of children dressed up as the characters feasting at trestle tables sagging beneath the weight of wonderful goodies, like jam tarts of course.

CBWB 4

Barham	"So you're the Mad Hatter. What's your name when you're not being a Mad Hatter ?"
First Boy	(Shyly) "James".
Barham	"James eh ? Let's see what it says on your hat James .... it says '10/6d in this style'. You haven't taken the

	label off your hat, do you know that ?"
First Boy	(No reply).
Barham	"Are you the King of Hearts ?"
Second Boy	(Laughing) "Yes."
Barham	"Hello Your Majesty. Are you enjoying your jam tarts ?"
Second Boy	(Enthusiastically) "Yes."
Barham	"That's good, and who's this over here, the White Rabbit ? …. Are you the White Rabbit ?"
Little Girl	"Yes."
Barham	"Wow! How old is this White Rabbit ?"
Little Girl	"Four."
Barham	"Just four. What a nice bunny. I can't see any flamingos here. Dear me, and there's no dormouse either."
Doris Tasker	"Oh no, well now, you haven't a costume. Have you thought of being a dormouse ?"
Barham	"Golly, do you think I could be ?"
Doris Tasker	"And why not? Can you get in the teapot ?"
Barham	"Oh, into the teapot ? Oh yes of course, he got into the teapot didn't he, and he had forty winks in the teapot."
Doris Tasker	"Yes he did."
Barham	"Well I am feeling a bit tired, but just let me ask Alice herself. Alice, would you mind, I mean, could I be your dormouse ?
Alice	"If you want to."
Barham	"Could I really ?"
Alice	"Yes."
Barham	"Oh thank you very much because I am feeling a bit tired. Let me just climb up here. That's it, I must get on the table (standing on table) can I take one of the tarts with me ?"
Alice	"Yes

| Barham | "Right thank you very much. That's lovely. There, woops a daisy! Mind the jug of milk. Right here we go into the teapot. Bye bye Alice, okay, just got hold of the lid. Toodle-oo." (Lid closes with a clang as Barham drops into echoey teapot)."Oh it's much quieter in here. That's nice (yawns) oh dear ... oh dear." (yawns, fade out.) |

As I said, the inside of the tea-pot was actually the gents toilet because it provided the echoey emptiness. I jumped into the air so as to get the sound of landing in the pot and it was all done there on spot with a few words and a yawn and completed in seconds with a razor blade and a piece of sticky tape.

Surprisingly, because it was a much more complicated piece, this next little drama also went very smoothly. Well, fairly smoothly thanks to some very willing helpers. We'd heard that someone on the border with horses and a stage-coach in the village of Alberbury was planning to make some money by presenting himself at the summer fairs and agricultural shows as Dick Turpin. He had all the gear, the stage coach, a big black horse, a pair of antique pistols and a mask of course, in fact he was all set to play the part except for one drawback. He was French.

We had to admire him. There he was ready to pass himself off as the English highwayman but he had a French accent thick enough to cut on a cheese board. His "Stan an' deliv-air!" could have come straight out of 'Allo Allo' except it was several years too soon and again I'm afraid, I couldn't resist 'hamming' it up.

CBWB15

| Barham | (Stagecoach rumbling along) "Well, I never thought I'd have a ride in a real stagecoach. We've been rattling along through the most beautiful villages, absolutely beautiful. You know there's something |

rather special about this border country, it really is lovely. It really is beautiful. There are castles here and ruins of all sorts, scattered villages, lots of woodland, lovely trees, lovely villages, and …. lots of lovely …. erm ….erm."

I was running out of words! It was becoming very embarrassing. The problem was that I was waiting to hear the sound of a shot.

Barham   "It's really beautiful. Everywhere you look there's a little bit of English or Welsh history along this border country between Powys and Shropshire, and...."
(Pistol shot.)
Coachman   "Whoa ! Whoa !"
(Coach slows down.)

The real coachman couldn't come that day so into the breach had stepped a colleague, newspaper photographer Ron Broster who very kindly put aside his camera, picked up the reins and drove the coach for us. He was excellent. He sounded like the perfect sturdy Yeoman.

Coachman   "Whoa ! Whoa !"
Barham   "Oh I'm sure that was a shot. I can hear the coachman shouting whoa to the horses. He's having a bit of a job to pull them up. Something's up. I'll look out of the window and see what's going on. What's up coachman ?"
(Coach stopping.)
Coachman   "I'm sorry sir we'll have to stop. It's a highwayman."
Barham   "Good gracious me!"
Highwayman   "Stan an deliv-air! All your money, all your jewellery, everybody out."

73

Barham   "Oh well there's only me here so that obviously means me."

(Barham gets out of stage-coach.)

        The highwayman, sitting on a great big Black Bess type of horse, was Frenchman Gerard Naprass, and when I asked him why he'd thought of this particular stunt to perform around Great Britain, he said, "To revive Eeenglish 'istory."

        (Cheek !) He was an extremely nice chap to interview and he thoroughly enjoyed playing his part for me. After a few more questions we entered Act III. For this I'd had an idea. I thought if he could pervert the past by turning Dick Turpin into a Frenchman, I could convert the present, so Gerard again let me have his coach and I enlisted another participant.

Barham   "Thank you very much indeed Gerard."

(Coach door slams.)

Gerard   "Bye bye Allan."

Barham   "Toodle-oo and off we go. Well what a nice chap. I must say once you get used to it this old stage coach is quite comfortable really, when you settle back in the corner like this. It's a very relaxing way to see the countryside drifting past the window. I wonder how long it will take to get home. We seem to be going a different way. Perhaps it's a short cut. It's very beautiful. We're just going through some trees here and …."

(Pistol shot.)

Barham   "Oh dear."

Coachman   "Whoa ! Whoa ! Whoa !"

Barham   "What's up driver ?"

(Coach stops.)

Coachman   "It's another highwayman, sir."

Barham   "Good gracious me."

Highwayman	(With Welsh accent) "Stand and Deliver! All your money, all your valuables."
Barham	"Good gracious it's catching on with the locals! Look as I told the other chap, I haven't got any money."
Highwayman	"You must have."
Barham	"I work for the BBC."
Highwayman	"Don't be daft."
Barham	"I don't have any money or valuables!"

CHAPTER E.
Entertainers

Having enjoyed a few years as an actor long ago in a now extinct form of theatre known as 'weekly rep' performing 50 different plays a year (my Equity card dates from 1954) entertainers are right up my street. Having a few holiday resorts dotted around my patch meant that I met a huge number of them too. They ranged all the way from film stars to buskers, and having been determined throughout my career to be more of an entertainer than a reporter, I enjoyed meeting them immensely. There's no point in mentioning all their names just for the sake of it though, instead I will try and recall those who stand out most in my memory.

Actually, some I remember for all the wrong reasons. There was the 72-year old belly dancer, and her friend on the glittering North Wales entertainment scene - the 100 year old woman whistler, and then there were the tap dancers who fell over, and the magicians who forgot how to do their tricks. The one who lost his rabbit was quite memorable, and one can't really miss out the one-eyed classical pianist who broke bricks with his bare hands, or indeed the 80-year old gymnast. As a spectacle he ranked right up there alongside the 72-year old belly dancer, there's no doubt about that.

Ann Ziegler and Webster Booth must have been in their seventies when they turned up in Penrhyn Bay. Older readers will know this classical duet was world class and world famous, but through the onset of hard times they'd left their sunny retreat on the other side of the world and completely unannounced they moved into a little retirement bungalow in Penrhyn Bay. It was sensational at the time. Most of their neighbours will have been pretty elderly and what a surprise they must have had. Just imagine singing in your bath the morning after they'd moved in next door, not knowing their identities, and they hang over the garden fence and join in. I don't know if that happened, it's just a fantasy that appeals to me.

Doris Hare was a good old age when I met her. Long before being 'On The Buses' She was a fabulous golden girl radio personality during the Second World War. She had a theatre full of rowdy sailors every week in her programme 'Ship Ahoy'. What a show, and what a girl ! She'd long since retired and was living with her family on a farm near Denbigh.

I was only a boy during the war but I loved that programme, it was a riot, and meeting her when I think I must have been in my forties was a schoolboy's dream come true. Sitting round the fire with her that evening, having such a good laugh, was something I could hardly believe was happening. It was a privilege to be with her, and it was also a privilege to meet Sandy Powell, another of my favourites from years gone by. I know I'm boring young people now but he was the first comedian to have a radio catchphrase. It came about in the 1920's and it was simply – "Can you hear me mother ?" Strange isn't it, not funny in itself but everyone loved it.

He was appearing in Llandudno and he told me how it came about, and it gives a fascinating glimpse into the old world of variety theatre, known then as 'music hall', and also a very clear insight into how broadcasting has changed over the years.

L198A

Sandy Powell   "It wasn't meant to be a catchphrase at all, I was doing a sketch, I was broadcasting a sketch from Broadcasting House. By the way in those days you know, we all had to dress, no audience, but dinner jackets you know. Funny, nobody to work to. Well I was doing this sketch called Sandy at the North Pole. I was supposed to be broadcasting home you see, and I said I'd like to speak to me mother. Well half way through the sketch I dropped my script on the floor, and filling in to pick up the pages, I repeated this two or three times you see, and I didn't think any more about it. Then on the Monday we were opening at the Hippodrome Coventry, and the manager called and he said 'Sandy you'll do that tonight won't you ?' I said, 'What ?' He said, 'Can you 'ear me mother ?' I said 'Why ?' He said 'Well everyone's saying it. Try it.' And when I went on, I said it and the whole audience joined in with me you see, and that's how it was born."

I always had a great affection for the great comedians of his era, and as an actor one of my favourite memories was performing with the legendary Max Miller when I was in a television series in the 1950's with Alfred Marks. He was a good comic too and I enjoyed those days immensely. There were others who were good to work with as well, like the light comedy actor Jack Hulbert when I was in Portsmouth in what we called the 'legitimate' theatre. They were good times, so is it any wonder that I found it difficult to take anything seriously for too long with my background ?

I met a lot of old timers, mostly in Llandudno where they take a pride in offering holidaymakers a traditional holiday, but these encounters can be sad. I felt so sorry for one. She was such a nice lady but she'll turn up later in the chapter dealing with singers who, I believe, are very special people, but on the other hand meeting with these high flying performers can sometimes be a disappointment. I remember in Colwyn Bay being disappointed when I met Harry Corbett. There was nothing wrong with Harry, but when I asked to meet Sooty he showed me a suitcase full of Sooties.

Carrying a BBC microphone provides you with a ticket into anyone's dressing room and meeting these people can be revealing in a variety of ways. Irene Handel asked me to stay at her side for a rehearsal once, but this very funny lady (catchphrase – "He knows you know") got into a row with the Stage Manager that went on for the whole afternoon. He was a very brave man because she was a very hard lady.

That made a great feature, very revealing, and Julie Felix deserves a mention. I know you can't rely on first impressions, but I thought this American singer was nice. She was appearing in Bangor and I found that she had an unusual habit. Just before going on stage I discovered that she always stood on her head for a while. The manager thought I'd wait a bit before interviewing her, but no I wanted her upside-down. Always go for the action. It's so much better to get people talking when they're doing something, even if it's standing on their heads

CBWB 14

Barham	(On all fours) "Do you know, this is the most incredible thing interviewing somebody standing on their head like this."
Julie Felix	(Laughing) "You can hear my voice change."
Barham	"Kneeling down like this I can look right down your nose, do you know that ?"
Julie Felix	(Laughs) "Yes. Can you take the hair out of my right eye please ?"

Barham	"Certainly, yes ….. this one here ?"
Julie Felix	"Yes, thank you."
Barham	"Well at least I've done something useful today."
Julie Felix	"That's lovely, thank you."
Barham	"How do you get around to writing your songs ?"
Julie Felix	(Laughing) "You look as funny as I do."

She was nice, and I find people at the top of their chosen tree often are, but they can usually afford to be, and one entertainer appears to have been able to afford a double. His name was Roy Rolland and in 1971 or perhaps 72 he was appearing in Rhyl as 'Old Mother Riley'. We all know Old Mother Riley was played by Arthur Lucan, and her so-called daughter Kitty was actually his wife, but the man playing the part of the old washerwoman in Rhyl claimed to have been Arthur Lucan's double. He was very convincing in the part and claimed that Arthur employed him as his double in the last few years of his life, both on stage and in films.

BBWB 76B

Mr. Rolland	"Oh yes, yes on numerous occasions, in fact towards the end of Arthur's life I was playing the part more than he was."
Barham	"But why was that ?"
Mr. Rolland	"Well I think first and foremost it was his age, he was a much older person than I was. His life wasn't too pleasant shall we say, tragic circumstances, and I think that was the cause that I was on more than he was."
Barham	"And did people realise this, did they realise that it was you and not him ?"
Mr. Rolland	"Not at all, not even management knew, I think the only time I got recognition if you like was when he died."

Barham	"But what about outside the theatre ? Arthur Lucan was very busy at private engagements wasn't he ?"
Mr. Rolland	"So the public thought, yes more or less I did all his private engagements. I even signed his autographs for him, and I even witnessed weddings for him."

If that's true then those people aren't legally married, but never mind it was a long time ago. Naturally his dressing room was full of Old Mother Riley's old fashioned clothes, in particular that scraggy old shawl, and then there was the grey wig and her famous bonnet. I picked up the old bonnet to have a closer look.

Mr. Rolland	"It's a little tatty now but of course it makes the character, and of course I shouldn't feel the same in new ones. They were Arthur's and now they're mine, and I feel very honoured to possess them."
Barham	"Well I never thought I'd be holding Old Mother Riley's bonnet."
Mr. Rolland	(In character now) "Well as long as it's the bonnet you're holding and nothing else, that's all that matters."

It's a great temptation to spiral down to name-dropping here and I'll allow myself a handful.. Remember the Beverley Sisters ? Their dressing room hospitality was great, second to none. A joy to be with.. Danny La Rue was very funny, and Gregory Peck making a film with two working titles – 'The Chairman' and 'The Most Dangerous Man in the World' hardly opened his eyes during the whole interview. He sat perched on a rock alongside Snowdon's Miners Track practically nodding off. I knew that he had a reputation for being relaxed, even laid back, but he went through most of the interview with his eyes closed, and I'm tempted to name many more famous names from all walks of life like Edmund Hillary and Sherpa Tensing, the first men to conquer Everest. I had a nice stroll up Nant Gwynant one afternoon with Sir Edmund, but getting back to show business I must swing the spotlight back onto a couple of locals who could steal any show.

Margaret Lacey was - in her own words, a 'failed actress'. A single lady of advanced years but with the most devilish sense of outrageous fun I've ever known. She ran a dancing school and she lived in the village of Rowen, not exactly in the limelight, but every time John Slezenger was in the UK to make a picture, he wrote a part into it for her. That really is being a star. Apparently it had been a long friendship and he'd never forgotten her, and I'm not surprised. In the James Bond film 'Diamonds are Forever' she was the crooked missionary smuggling diamonds in a hollowed-out bible, but I featured her on the set of 'Yanks' with John Slezenger and Vanessa Redgrave. They thought she was wonderful and like so many of my 'special' people, this old girl is sadly missed. She used to hang presents on a tree for my children.

Also gone from this world is the greatest entertainer I've ever seen, let alone met. Here in Wales he was the 'Scottish' local I knew as Mr. Llandudno. Alex Munro was his name, the Glaswegian whose quick-fire jokes and supersonic vitality, even well into his seventies (at least), kept the town's open-air theatre going until it became the last in Britain, and before he died the curators of the Victoria and Albert Museum wanted to preserve his jokes, they were so old. To many comics this would have been an insult, but not to Alex. To him it was an accolade and he made as much publicity out of it as he could.

No-one in this world could beat this man for showmanship. He'd make use of anything and everything for a laugh or a headline. If I went to ask him about his shows, he'd have me on stage introducing me as anything in broadcasting. He would instantly make you part of the show, and for a practical joke one afternoon I walked on instead of the girl singer he was introducing. His jaw had barely hit the boards when he bounced back and told the audience I was the BBC's Head of Programmes who'd come to sign him up for a series of shows, and he took the applause too. Lot's of it. People must have spent months searching for that series.

You could not throw this man. He'd keep going come what may. Every year he'd produce a big pantomime in either the Pier Pavilion or the Astra. They were big theatres (both gone now) and every year they were sell-outs, and I was sometimes sent to feature them.

On one occasion it was at the big Pier Pavilion. It was the night of New Year's Eve and the show was going superbly. It was packed. It was great. I was backstage recording bits here and there with the cast. We were having a ball, and during a scene change I changed places with the man hiding behind the grandfather clock, moving the hands. It was of course 'Cinderella'. Alex, who was playing a rather aged Buttons,didn't know it was me behind the clock, but I was now in control of the 'time.'

As you will guess, this was the big ball scene and I don't think I've ever enjoyed myself more than I did that night. Every time Buttons tried to tell Cinderella it was nearly midnight, I dropped the minute hand by half an hour. That huge audience loved it, they were rolling in the aisles, the cast was in hysterics, and Alex was milking it to the full ! Nothing now was coming from the script. That went out the window. He frantically ad-libbed and joked through it every time the clock went berserk like the great old trooper that he was and it just got better and better ! Alex you were fabulous, absolutely fabulous.

The only interview I can find of him now was when he was selling off some costumes, and he even made capital out of this. I don't know if he made any money, but he certainly made publicity, claiming that everything there had a direct connection with somebody famous. It's a shame you can't hear that broad Glaswegian accent, with sentences shouted at full volume and tumbling out at top speed with barely a moment for breath.

CBWB 3

Alex Munro	"Allan! There are two thousand! Two thousand different costumes here! It's taken me all my life to gather these but now I'm getting so old I thought I must get rid of them 'cos these costumes started years ago when I was in the first circus in the Waverley Market Edinburgh, and I was booked as a clown with my brother and this 'ere, this old policeman's helmet, that was given to me by Jack Warner – Dixon of Dock Green. I'll put it on for you, there you are, Dixon of Dock Green" (he sings the Dixon of Dock Green signature tune)
Barham	(Mimicking policeman) "Evening all."
Alex Munro	"I'm a lovely singer."
Barham	"Yes you're marvellous but what about this top hat here ?"
Alex Munro	"This top hat here belonged to Raffles. He was a burglar, he was a gentleman burglar, you know like a gentleman farmer. He milked the cows with his gloves on. This other hat Allan, I'd love you to see this one, it's like a flowerpot; it belonged to Rasputin. This was worn by Rasputin, he was called the 'Mad Monk'.
Barham	"The Russian."
Alex Munro	"Yes a Russian man. I'll put in on for you and see I become a different person entirely."
Barham	"Good heavens. Tommy Cooper."
Alex Munro	"Tommy Cooper ? No! I'm Rasputin."
Barham	"Oh I see, I beg your pardon."
Alex Munro	"The Mad Monk, and I also have a beautiful stick here. Now this stick belongs to one of the greatest

Scottish comedians, a man called Sir Harry Lauder and he said (sings) 'I love a lassie, bonnie highland lassie.' This belonged to Harry Lauder and every costume you see here has a history."

I didn't believe a word of it of course but who cares, he was just a fabulous showman, totally immersed in his trade.

Janet Munro the film star, who died very young, was his daughter (remember her in 'The Day the Earth Caught Fire' ?) The day one of the cable cars on the Great Orme fell into Alex's auditorium, I was trying to find out what had happened. Fortunately the cable car was empty and it didn't land on anyone, but I was at his house late that night and Janet was with us sitting in the kitchen. She was nice but looked awful and she died soon after.

CHAPTER F.
Fools, Farmers, and Festivals

Of course the first thing you have to realise is that when you join the BBC as a reporter they will have no hesitation in making a fool of you. You get sent to feature any amount of silly things and you always have to join in.

These occasions crop up with painful regularity. Many of them annually. There are special anniversary days, even weeks, and many of them appear to have no foundation. Why we had to endure a National 'Hug' Day I can't imagine, or the National 'Smile' Day for instance. That may have had something to do with teeth, but the National 'Hallo' Day was another nightmare when you were sent out into the street simply to say hallo to people.

Always wanting to be original, I went into a police station on one of these occasions and said to the extremely bored looking sergeant at the desk, "Excuse me, do you realise today is National 'Allo 'Allo 'Allo Day ?" It seemed a good idea at the time, and then there was the National 'Politeness' Day. I said to this harassed looking bloke working up a lamp post, "What do you think of this National Politeness Day ?" He shook his head, "I 'aven't got time for that," he said. So I said, "It won't take long," and he said "Sod off." And of course we mustn't forget the 'Children in Need' appeal. I used to get sent to a supermarket in order to sing. I was given a song book and staff carried buckets around for people to throw money into.

On the first occasion I was quite flattered when I was sent on this mission, but then I found people were being asked to throw money into the buckets to stop me singing. This they did, and people can be very hurtful sometimes. Some were soon throwing coins into the bucket before I could even open my mouth. These people were obviously tone deaf but it's all in a day's work, and on one stunt I had to submit to a bunch of old ladies dressing me up as a woman. This was so that I could meet their friend Billy. It sounds ridiculous now, but at the time ..... well yes it was pretty silly at the time, however you just have to get on with it.

Billy was a ram and he'd escaped from a farm to scrounge a living around an Old People's Home. This was in Penmaenmawr and the old girls were feeding him cakes and stuff, and whenever the farmer came to collect him he bolted, only to come back later and eat all the flowers. In the end this wily old ram ran off at the sight of anyone in trousers, so I had to be dressed up in a blouse and skirt, supplied of course by the old ladies who were having a lovely time.

CBWB 5

Barham	"What do you call him ?"
Old Ladies	"Billy."
Barham	"Billy ? Sounds like a goat."
Old Ladies	"No, no."
Old Lady	"No he's a very dear ram."

Barham	"I must say I haven't worn a skirt for a long time."
Old Lady	"Hold on, pull it round the front."
Barham	"Right."
Lady	"Have you got a safety-pin ?"
Barham	"No I've just tucked it in the top of my trousers."
Old Ladies	(Laughing).
Barham	"Well it's very nice, it's a pretty shade of blue."
Old Ladies	(Enthusiastically) "Yes, yes, nice, lovely."

This, I thought, was getting rather out of hand, so I quickly led them out to where Billy had last been seen curled up on a step in the sun.

Old Ladies	"Oh you've caught him."
Old Lady	"Look he's sleeping." (To ram waking up) "Come on Babe."
Barham	"How is it then that he's developed this fear of trousers, why doesn't he like men ?
Old Lady	"Well you see the men have been trying to catch him to take him back to the smallholding where he should really be, among his own clan."
Old Ladies	"Come on Billy."
Barham	"He obviously knows he's better off down here."
Old Lady	"He knows his name you know."
Barham	"Does he ? Let's see if I can catch hold of him."
Old Lady	"We'll give him a shampoo."

That did it. He heard the awful word shampoo and he was off quick, and I asked if perhaps they ought to stop feeding him.

Old Ladies	"Oh no, no we don't think so."
Barham	"You don't want him to go away do you ?"
Old Lady	"We don't. It's a shame really that he does so much

damage. He's such a lovable fellow. I think he is anyway."

I felt pretty silly dressed up like that and I must have looked pretty silly standing in goal trying to save penalties taken by the premiership's leading goal scorer. At the time it was Ian Rush of Liverpool. Another stunt, another nightmare. Ian Rush had just become top scorer and as he lived in Flint, someone thought it would be a good idea for me to see just how hard he kicked the ball. I limped off to the studio black and blue.

You can be made to look a fool anywhere at all, even in your own home. For several months the Australian Broadcasting Service had me broadcast live into their breakfast show every week on nothing more sophisticated than the telephone. The new fangled satellite clarity was so good I didn't have to go to a studio, I just sat in my kitchen and talked to them on the phone. On one occasion I was telling them about the re-opening of a railway station. It was the station in that Anglesey village with the longest name. I'll spell it for you, Llanfairpwllgwyngyll – (Oh dear, do I really have to go through this again ?) - gogerychwyrndrobwllllantysisiliogogogoch. After years of neglect it was now open, all spruced up and ready to serve the village, and I'd chosen that for my talk that morning (morning for them in Australia, but evening for me).

They loved this long name. I said it several times, but never having been able to remember it, I was reading it from a book, syllable by syllable. I then gave them the English translation. This they loved even more. I said "So now if you want to travel there you say to the ticket clerk – Hello, can I have a ticket please to St. Mary's church in the hollow of the white hazel near to the fierce whirlpool and the church of Tysilio by the red cave ?"

Long before I'd got to the end of it I could hear them in the studio laughing their heads off. Splitting his sides, the presenter said, "Give it to us in Welsh again Al," so I obliged, still reading from the book. The guy at the other end was trying to get his tongue round it so I said it again, nice and slowly – Llanfair ... pwll .... gwyn .... etc. "Great," he said, "Join us next week Al, see ya." That was it. "Toodle-oo," I said and thought no more of it.

The following week I was telling them about the 'Hound of the Baskervilles' because evidence had come to light that Sir Arthur Conan Doyle had found his inspiration in tales of a big fearsome dog that had once terrorised an area of mid-Wales, somewhere around Knighton I think. Anyway, as most people are familiar with the stories of Sherlock Holmes, I thought this was a good story to tell. It certainly seemed to go down okay, but when I'd finished the presenter said, "Thanks Al great story, but 'ere mate, that long place name you told us about last week, how's it go again ? Lan-fair what ?"

To put it mildly this was very, very, embarrassing. The book was no longer on my kitchen table. I was struck dumb. I couldn't do it without the book "How's it go mate ?" the presenter down under asked again. "That long place name, give it us again Al." I was stumped, I didn't dare try and do it from memory, I just had to admit that last week I'd been reading it from a guide book.

Bill Curran learnt something about embarrassment on a trip to Scotland. He was a favourite colleague who covered a part of South Wales, and on his way back from Scotland he came a long way off his route to tell me about his trip. He was working for an amateur talent programme and he'd been sent to Scotland to audition a boy bagpipe player. Old Bill was a fine pianist but he didn't know much about bagpipes. He told me that when the boy finished playing he was so impressed that he stood up and gave him a round of applause. At that point the boy's father came storming in from the kitchen and said, "You bloody fool, the boy's just warming them up !"

As Brian Evans had demanded I had

to report on every subject under the sun, which sometimes meant attending concerts, even those of a classical nature where it was always necessary for the quality of the music to be matched at least, if not surpassed, by the well mannered responses of those attending. It was therefore quite refreshing to receive a very noisy phone call one afternoon from Ken Howells who ran the harmonica festival in Colwyn Bay. He was a very experienced professional player and people came from all over Britain and beyond for the event. He was laughing his head off. "Come over quick mate," he said, "They're all accusing the judges of fixing the results. There's a hell of a fight going on here."

Of course when you're sent to festivals you have to do your best, even at those where you don't know a note of what's being played, or a word of what's being said. I covered the National Eisteddfod a couple of times but being a non Welsh speaker that was a bit tricky, and so was the Urdd Youth Festival, but the International Eisteddfod held every year in Llangollen was altogether different because it's bi-lingual. It's a gorgeously colourful event, it lasts a week, it's crammed full of song and dance, spilling out sometimes into the streets, and because there's so much going on it was always hard work getting your pieces into the programme on time, even though we always had an outside broadcast unit there.

Every day it was a tremendous thrill to be with great choirs and dance troupes from around the world in their spectacular national costumes, and for me it was like being at the races. With a combination of insider tips and my own guess work I used to try and predict who was going to win each event so as to be among them when the announcement was made, and when I got it right it was mind blowing ! The electrified screams of delight, and the spontaneous singing that erupted, made fabulous, fabulous radio, but all day long there were the sad stories too.

It was a gigantic roller coaster of emotion. There were winners and there were losers, there were people who were going places and there were people who were lost.

There were foreign exiles now living in Britain (when exiles were refugees and not simply immigrants) clinging to the remnants of their culture and their dreams of happier days gone by. And there were those who, every day, were searching for news of their loved ones, because in those days much of the world was locked behind the Iron Curtain. At first the BBC used to book a room for me in a beautiful hotel, but I never wanted to stay. Each evening I just had to drive home to be with my own family.

I mentioned the Welsh National Eisteddfod just now, the one that's all in the Welsh Language, and a few years back I had a fascinating insight into its history. For ten years I had the pleasant responsibility of being the chairman of the Trefriw and Llanrhychwyn community council, and early one spring the youngest and most fit amongst us took on the task of rebuilding the monument to the bard Taliesin at lake Geirionydd. There were five of us, and although not builders by a long chalk we enjoyed ourselves over the course of several freezing cold evenings, and when we finished we had a party up there.

We took the village marquee up, along with a buffet lunch and crates of beer of course, and invited 'everyone', and among them was Dennis Davies representing the organizers of the National Eisteddfod. We had invited him because this is where, in the late 1800's, a local poet known as Gwilym Cowlyd staged his hugely popular alternative gatherings as a protest against the anglicized festival of the day. Mr. Davies told us that in the 1800's the Welsh National Eisteddfod was open to the world, even the Pope and the Emperors of Russia and China had been co-opted into the Eisteddfod circle.

CBWB 644

Mr. Davies   "There were many high people from all over the
              world, I mean all the way from Russia, Turkey,
              Persia, China, and the King and the Pope even. He
              was even a member of the Gorsedd, and then King

90

	Edward VII, I think it was to come, and he didn't agree with that and he put on this Gorsedd, the Arwest, and it was exactly the same week as the National Eisteddfod was held you know, which of course made quite a fuss at the time."
Barham	"So he really did have an effect didn't he because these dignitaries from around the world, these high ranking people, are no longer part and parcel of it."
Mr. Davies	"No, no they're not, no, no."
Barham	"Apart from the Queen."
Mr. Davies	"Apart from the Queen, she is still, yes, yes."

Now for farms and farmers, and what can I say ? It's been a slow and lingering process, but the decline is here for us all to see, and as the decline has accelerated I 've reported on an ever-widening selection of diversification. That's the name given to the desperate search our farmers have been forced to make for other ways to make ends meet. Diversification has materialised in so many shapes to disfigure our landscape. Fields now support ostriches and water buffalo. Hills support ski- runs and wind farms, and farm houses have become hotels, with grazing land reverting to jungle.

John Wynne knows something about this subject. He farms the hills above Harlech and has shown to us all what happens if you destroy the farming industry.

In 1982 having seen what was coming, he fenced off an area of land about the size of two tennis courts so that neither sheep or cattle could get in to graze it. This was about 300 feet above sea level, typical open hillside, and at the same level he did the same to another plot nearly ten years later. When I saw that one in the mid-nineties it was already becoming impenetrable. It was thick with gorse and saplings. He told me that before long the saplings would throw a canopy over the gorse forcing it to give way to trees, and that's what had happened to the plot he'd fenced off earlier. He showed me this plot too. It was a forest. He agreed we need trees but his message was plain and simple. Once you've lost the grazing land that we've relied on for centuries, you won't get it back again. Reclaiming it would cost too much.

Most of the time however, it's a peaceful existence here in North Wales, and especially out in the countryside, but there are banana skins to slip on, and once again another blunder comes to mind. If anyone has the ability to see my ramblings as a sincere attempt at confession, will he or she please exorcise my nightmares ? Especially this one. I once managed to arrange a meeting between a farmer and the President of the Ramblers Association, two parties that are often at each other's throats. The lady farmer, Claudia Bryan, was being pestered by ramblers who insisted on walking past her kitchen window to show they had a 'right' to be there, even though the path hadn't been a public path and went no further than the stream at the back of her house, and of course the head of the Ramblers was very keen to support them.

The two arrived and parked at either end of the car park. It was hight noon. They got out and walked warily towards each other. They met face to face. I introduced them.......switched on the mic...... and recorded the 'shoot out'.

It went very well with neither of them giving an inch to the other. When at last they'd exhausted themselves they turned to me as if to say, "That's it" and for some reason I looked down at the tape recorder......and found that I'd left the pause button down. I'd failed to record it!

To put it mildly it was enormously embarrassing. At first I just didn't know what to say, but gradually I realised there was only one thing I could say. Very sheepishly I asked, "Do you think you could do that again ?" For a moment I thought they were going to say no, but after they'd heaved a few very heavy sighs, they looked at each other like a couple of rams weighing each other up and nodded, and to their eternal credit they had that argument, word for word, all over again.

CHAPTER G.
Ghosts and Games.

Of all the ghosts I've reported on, ninety-nine per cent of them existed only in the scheming minds of hard-up publicans, and furthermore – only at pubs that do not offer accommodation. In places where customers are sold a good night's sleep, ghosts usually find there is no room at the inn.

The BBC reporter is sent to investigate ghosts in all manner of places, but a substantial dose of cold water inevitably lowers the temperature when you realise how predictable it all is. The ghost in the castle is of course someone who's been locked up there. The ghost in the theatre is of course an actor never a cleaning lady, and in the old farmhouse it's the murdered farmer not the VAT man, although that could just be a matter of time. However, it has to be said that here in North Wales the mould has been completely shattered at a nuclear power station.

I think I've mentioned this ghost already, but in more detail the power station is 'Wylfa' on the North coast of Anglesey and it's said to be haunted by an opera singer. You see what I mean about the mould having been broken. Rosina Buckman's house on the cliff was demolished for the power station to be built, and although long since gone she's still a bit miffed.

Ann Farrell, who used to work there, has made quite a study of her and she told me the lady can sometimes even be heard singing.

CBWB 7
Ann Farrell   "The power station was built on the site of a house

on the cliff owned by the opera singer Rosina Buckman. People, including security staff and cleaners, sometimes refuse to work in the reception area at night. Whether she's here just because she was happy here, or whether it might be because her mother-in-law's ashes were taken to Llanbadrig churchyard because they had to be dug up from Wylfa when the power station was built, whether that has disturbed some spirits, but it is definitely Rosina Buckman because I have a description of her as a beautiful lady with long golden hair and a long white dress, and every time she's seen this is the description I have given to me.

Barham	"Have you seen her ?"
Ann Farrell	"No."
Barham	"Are you wanting to see her ?"
Ann Farrell	"No, and I certainly wouldn't go there after dark."

In the dark, very late one night, I drove up a stony track to a bleak and lonely house close to those cliffs, and there, with the eerie unworldly sound of the power station humming across the fields, an old man living there alone showed me a photograph of Rosina Buckman's house. It was taken just before it was demolished. Standing outside was a woman, you couldn't see her clearly enough to describe her, but he swore there was no-one there when the photograph was taken.

You get used to going into 'spooky' situations, and seeing some pretty weird things too, like the human chess game played each year at Portmeirion. The people are members of a world wide club, an appreciation society formed to perpetuate interest in a 1960's television series called 'The Prisoner'. It was a weird series in which a British secret agent was trying each week to escape from a colourful seaside village where he'd been incarcerated with a crowd of other retired agents. Filming had finished by the time I came on the scene towards the end of the sixties, but I often visited the place.

Portmeirion is the Italianate creation of Sir Clough Williams Ellis. As an architect his work was both fun and sensible. He didn't like anything cold or harsh, and once, when he was knighted I think, he told me that buildings should be designed to accommodate the soft and cuddly animals that we humans are.

He was a noble sight, noble yet genial. He was tall, white haired, and he was always wearing knee length breeches and long lemon socks. I always remember him wearing a casual jacket too, I think in corduroy, with a handkerchief flowing from his breast pocket. He was always a joy to talk to and on one occasion I have a favourite memory of having tea with him and his wife at their old home Plas Brondanw. They'd invited my wife and I and our two very young children for afternoon tea, and the children were fascinated by the revolving centrepiece in the table which held the condiments, and when we walked around the grounds he told me how ships in the old days used to tie up at the gate at the bottom of the garden. That was before Mr. Maddocks built his cob and kept the sea back from what must have been as fine a sea loch as anything in Scotland, with its islands and sandy shores reaching almost up to the Aberglaslyn bridge.

They were a remarkable couple, and his wife gave us a book she'd written before I was born, explaining to children how they'd come into the world. It was called 'How you Began' and I'm sure that in those days writing a book like that must have been a very daring thing to do. Even in the thirties like everyone else, I was told that I was found under a gooseberry bush.

The human chess game was supposed to lead me straight into other games, but better late than never, and with no connection whatsoever between a fairy tale village on a wooded coastal hillside and a game of golf played in the dark, please allow me to introduce Peter Stebbings.

CBWB 6

Mr.Stebbings "Allan, if you look down there you'll see an
illuminated marker left and right of the green.
They're the magic light-sticks that guide us round the
course, and you'll also see one on the pin as well.."

This was recorded on a course at
Kinmel Bay where Peter, an expert on the subject of night-time golf,
was the resident professional and my guide to the game. In such
total darkness you need a guide, and what's more of course, you
need a ball that you can see in the dark.

Mr.Stebbings "This is the night-light golf ball. It's a transparent
golf ball with a magic light-stick inserted in it, and as
you can see it's glowing very brightly, giving the
effect of something like Dr.Who."
Barham "Yes, a pale greenish light."
Mr.Stebbings "Well that's right, and the thing is this, if this goes
through the air as it should do, it will give you the
effect of a tracer bullet."

It did too. We watched his shot soar
through the air and land almost on the green. It was a good shot,
and at this stage I should declare that I'm not a golfer.

Barham (From the tee) "Oh dear."
Mr.Stebbings "Well it's alright."
Barham "It's scurrying over the top of the grass like a
demented glow-worm."
Mr.Stebbing "But you can still see it."

That was hardly surprising, it hadn't
gone far. But by then I thought it was time to start the questions and

96

there was one particular question I wanted to ask. A pretty obvious one really.

Barham   "Peter the question is, why make it possible for people to play golf at night ?"

Mr.Stebbings   "Well the thing is there's a problem in this country where we have so many golfers and too few golf courses to play on, and the thing is the winter months when members can only play at weekends, we're saying to people who can't get onto private courses at the weekends, come here and play night-time golf."

It was at this point that we bumped into somebody, quite literally. This was someone who said he'd finished work at 8 o'clock, had a bite to eat and was still able to have a round of golf. He was obviously a satisfied customer and after we'd said goodbye to him I eventually got to the green. This was lit, as he'd said, with a light on top of the pin and another little light at the bottom of the hole. It was a strange experience but after a while I got used to it. My game started to pick up, until I found myself in a particularly dark area somewhere in the rough, and it all started to fall apart again. My opponent was full of encouragement though, telling me that it was all right as no-one could see. "Remember," he said, "Swings look better at night."

There's something irritating about golf. And I remember a friend giving it up and saying "It's got nothing to do with the game, it's the way it's played" and I when my producer saw that a hotel in the Vale of Clwyd was running a weekend course on the etiquette of golf, I was told to put on my hobnail boots and go and sabotage it.

There have been times when I've felt a bit like Norman Wisdom. Several times in fact, and this was just one of those occasions.

CBWB 2

(On the Bryn Morfydd Hotel golf course.)

Barham	(Jubilant) "At last I'm on the green !"
Manager	"Well, actually you've made two mistakes."
Barham	(Shocked) "Mistakes ?
Manager	"Standing behind me when I was taking my shot is not acceptable at all. It's all very well saying ' I'll look to see where the ball's going'. I'm quite capable of doing that, but as I'm taking my back swing I can see you in my eye."
Barham	"Oh crumbs."
Manager	"And also, just when I was on my back swing, you were also jingling coins in your pocket. I could hear it and I could see it. Those were two distractions there."
Barham	"And I thought I was doing so well too. Mind you, I did see you frown a bit when I was shouting at those other players, you know when I went across their fairway place."
Manager	"Yes, well they were in the process of playing."
Barham	"Should I have shouted something like – fore ?"
Manager	"That would have been acceptable. It's the recognised word."
Barham	"Oh I see, not - Oi! get out the way !"
Manager	"No, not at all."
Barham	"Oh alright. It's your shot then."

(Manager takes his shot.)

Barham	"Oh good shot! (To the pro. Jubilantly.) He's on the green as well ! Right, I'll just drop my bag down here."

(Barham throws golf bag and clubs down onto the green.)

Club pro.	(Dismayed) "Do you mind if I move your bag ? It's on the green old chap."
Barham	"Oh mustn't I do that ?"

Club pro.	"Not really, no. Put it to one side."
Barham	"Oh I see, right. (Rummages in golf bag) I'll get the stick out I need to putt with. This is a putter isn't it ? Okay my turn. Let's see if I can get the ball down now.... with careful aim."
Manager	"May I interject ? It is my honour to take this shot first on the green. I am furthest from the pin."
Barham	"But it's my turn."
Manager	"Yes it may be your turn but I am however further from the pin, so I have the honour."
Barham	"Right, okay."
Manager	(Preparing to putt) "Allan would you mind removing the pin for me please ?"
Barham	"Oh this pole thing with a flag on ? Right, I'll chuck it over here." (Pin lands with thud on the green.)
Club pro.	"Oh! You've committed a sin. Throwing the pin down on the green !"
Barham	"Oh ?"
Club pro.	"Place it carefully or hold it."
Manager	"Allan be very careful not to walk across the line of my putt." You've left your footprints now on the ground !"
Barham	"Oh have I ?"

They were wonderful, and like the lady wrestler I could have saved them for Chapter P and the 'Participants' but never mind this is not a reference book. Also it comes to the mind of this particular vandal that I once had to go to a factory on Dee-side to see if I could smash up the 'vandal-proof' toilets that were going into the old Wembley Stadium, and on another day wreck a new vandal-proof BT telephone box. The telephone box was pretty tough and the toilets weren't bad.

There are so many games people play. The radio reporter gets to see them all but you wouldn't think anyone could invent a game involving cows, but someone did. This too was a charity stunt and it was a very good one. The field was marked into squares and it was called 'Cow Pat' Bingo. Forgive me if I don't explain how it worked, but nothing happened until they let the cows out.

Changing the subject, I saw the village of Trefriw find a niche for itself as the venue for the Welsh boomerang championships. This event was started by a the wonderfully innovative Jay Butters and it's proved to be very successful. Every year people just keep coming back. Apparently boomerang people always do.

I'll end this chapter with pancake tossing. Here in Wales we actually had a world champion. He was either the chef or the manager at a hotel in Nefyn. I can't even remember which one now (the one on the left as you go west through the village) and he even tossed his pancakes around the world in order to defend his title. His name was Philip Artingstall who explained that pancake tossing is something of a sprint. He was doing it 307 times in two minutes.

CBWB10

Barham	(Watching pancake tosser practising) "What do you need to become a world champion ?"
Philip	"Strong in the arm and weak in the head."

There was more, but not much.

CHAPTER H
Heroes, Helicopters and History

There are several ingredients that go into the making of heroes. With a lifeboat crew one of those ingredients must be sheer dogged tenacity, and it was occasionally my pleasure to talk to one of Britain's most decorated lifeboatmen – Dic Evans, holder of two gold medals. He was the coxswain of the Moelfre lifeboat on the east coast of Anglesey, and on one occasion he and his men rescued the crew of a ship in a hurricane when most thought it totally impossible. The ship was the Hindley, and at one stage the lifeboat was swept right across the ship's deck, but still they got the crew off.

There's always anxiety in a little seaside community when a lifeboat has to be launched, but on this occasion such was their anxiety people crawled in the teeth of that hurricane to the edge of the cliff to watch Dic and his crew pull off that rescue. They were a wonderful crew, and in 1966 they were in the news again for another great job they did with a ship called the Nassiporos.

On one occasion after his retirement I was sitting with him in his house at Moelfre when he stopped speaking suddenly. A sudden gust of wind had rattled a window frame and I saw him close his eyes. After a few moments he looked at me, and very slowly he said, "Even now when I hear the wind like that, I feel a shiver creep up my spine." It was a memorable moment.

It's a 'need' to do something that produces heroes, and I'd give medals to whole groups of people, and right now I'm thinking of the people who came to the rescue of the Ugandan Asians. You can say whatever you like about immigrants, legal or otherwise, but these people hadn't chosen to leave Uganda, instead they'd been booted out by their dictator Idi Amin. I think it was in 1972 that a thousand of them were brought to the remains of the old Army camp at Tonfanau near Towyn on the coast of Meirionydd, and what a pitiful sight they were with little more than the clothes they stood up in. The poor children looked so scared, and what a place to bring them to. They'd come from a hot African country to a barren freezing site where the wind whistled in straight off the Irish Sea, but fortunately help was at hand.

I was sent there several times and it was always a thrill to see local people coming to the aid of these poor families, bringing them so much that was essential – clothes, food, toys, comfort and encouragement. And I will always remember the look of bewilderment on their faces, especially the children when it came to Christmas. After all, what do you do with a pine tree ?   Perhaps some of those people now run 'open all hours' corner shops around the UK, but one thing is for sure, I know they can never forget the people of Wales.

Back now to individuals. I can't name them all, there are too many. However, two come to mind because of the unusual circumstances that launched them into my list of merit. I said I can't name them all, and the first one I can't name, but I certainly remember where she lived. It was in Machynlleth and I've never forgotten her because she was disgusted with the council for poisoning the pigeons.

They had some notion that pigeons were spreading disease and were repeatedly spreading poison pellets on the pavement outside her house. Each time they did it she dashed out quick and brushed them down the drain. She told me, rightly or wrongly, that they didn't need culling and other birds were being poisoned too. From what I remember she wasn't a demonstrative person, but she was determined that no other birds were going to be poisoned outside her house, and every time they put down the pellets, she whizzed out with a broom and brushed them down the drain. Then, each time they knocked indignantly on her door, she'd refuse to open it, and as soon as they'd spread more pellets and moved on up the road, she'd fly out with her broom again before they could run back and stop her. This went on for a long time and she's definitely on my list of heroes for her tenacity.

The next individual is Peter Aldous. He became the manager of the Llanrwst swimming pool and swimming is certainly his subject. His particular event is the butterfly stroke and his story starts in South Wales where he suffered a cruel disappointment.

He'd travelled all the way down there as a teenager to compete in a youth club event. It was a big occasion for the boy. He won through to the final, but then he wasn't allowed to take part. Someone down there said, "He's not keeping his legs together." Apparently you have to do that in the butterfly stroke, but this lad simply couldn't because he only had one leg. (Try keeping your legs together if you've only got one leg.) So he was sent packing, but before long he came back. Before long he was doing the butterfly again, and how ! And how ! At the Olympic Paraplegic Games in Holland he won the Gold Medal. At the Olympic Paraplegic Games in America he won another Gold Medal, and at the Olympic Paraplegic Games in South Korea he won the Silver Medal. Oh yes, and I mustn't forget the World Record. He held that for eight years. What a reject!

A policeman called Constable Ken Williams would have enjoyed that story. By the time I met him first he was well into middle age, a big red-faced jovial ex-Welsh Guardsman, who eventually acquired his own wildlife reserve. It was here that he did such a lot of good work with local kids, especially those in trouble with the law. That's why I've got him down as a hero, but old Ken knew how to be a sinner too. Without a doubt he was an individual my friends in the written press would have called a 'loveable rogue'. For instance, on one occasion, having eaten by mistake the evidence of a poaching case (a pheasant) he presented another one to the Court that he'd pinched himself.

The pheasant case occurred when he was stationed in Bala, but I interviewed him first when he'd become the village bobby at Trearddur Bay, a village close to Holyhead where incidentally, he'd turned his police house into a smallholding. Anyone coming to report a crime had to negotiate a quagmire on which ducks and geese waddled around in a gruesome mixture of green and brown mud. I managed it thanks only to an abnormally long dry spell, but access to the office was impossible due to a large number of nest boxes stored there, and when I reached the sitting room I almost sat on an owl. The room was crammed with birds, most of which he was nursing back to health, but after a while though it was the old policeman who needed to stretch his wings. This he did by persuading the directors of the new aluminium smelter being built near-by to let him have part of the old Stanley estate they'd acquired. This area was on the wooded shore of the beautiful Beddmanach Bay, and in next to no time he'd moved into the cottage on the shore and was turning the whole area into a wonderful nature reserve.

His opportunity had come one evening when he spotted the managing director's car parked without lights. This man was an American and therefore a little uncertain of his position when Ken rang his bell and issued a warning with regard to this minor, if not dubious, offence before taking off his helmet and inviting himself in for a chat. Ken told me this himself and I would love to have been there. Just imagine it. "Are you aware sir that people here are saying that your new factory, with its poisonous fumes, is going to decimate the local flora and fauna?"

The poor man must have been horrified. The last thing a big company wants as soon as it arrives is to be accused of harming the local environment, and Ken soon found himself with everything he needed. In no time at all he had the place 'teeming' with wildlife. It was amazing. Badgers and rabbits could be seen crossing the road to be there, birds and all manner of wild ducks and geese just fell out the sky to be with him. That was the magic of Ken Williams, and people flocked there too. Thousands of visitors went to Penrhos. You just had to pull off the road and you'd be surrounded by practically everything that ever hopped, waddled, crawled or flapped its wings.

I loved going there. He so often had a rare bird drop in, or some creature to be nursed back to health, and I will always remember how he used to come rushing home from a shift and race upstairs to change out of his uniform and into his working clothes, topped with an old fishing hat festooned with hooks and flies, but the only tape I have of him now is a rather sad one. I recorded it long after he'd retired from the Police Force and had left his beloved Penrhos, and it was the last conversation I had with him before he died. By then he'd married a lady who'd brought him considerable wealth and together they'd embarked on a lot of travelling. This had led him to become involved with the overseas arm of the 'Duke of Edinburgh's Young Peoples Award Scheme'. It was just an honorary job but it gave him the opportunity to fish in some very exotic rivers.

This interview was recorded at their smart new home, complete with indoor swimming pool, and I couldn't help feeling it revealed a man who'd lost his way a little. Ken of the jet-set was never quite the same old Ken Williams I used to know, and on this tape he is indeed talking about the way his life had changed.

BWB 7

Barham	"My word Ken, you've got a good suntan."
Mr. Williams	"I just came back from Kenya yesterday and am still jet-lagged a bit. I've been there for the last two months."
Barham	"These days you're involved with the Duke of Edinburgh's Scheme aren't you ?"
Mr. Williams	"That's right, It's an honorary job. When I go to these various countries, especially African countries, I can look up the people in charge of the scheme there and chat to them, see if they want something or whatever, and also visit the young people in action and take an interest in what they're doing."
Barham	"I was passing Penrhos only the other day. It was looking beautiful, the tide was in on the inland sea there. But nothing seemed to be going on there very

much."

Mr. Williams "Well no, unfortunately when I finished they didn't carry on the same as I did, they don't have the young wardens there any more. They don't encourage that sort of thing, which is a shame really, because it was a brilliant opportunity to bring in young people from the streets and from the courts to teach them conservation. To teach them to be kind to animals and so on. But you see the aluminium company, they change their managers so often, and some of them encourage conservation, others couldn't care less, they're more interested in making aluminium but the place is firmly established. It's on the map of Anglesey as a nature reserve. That's one thing that's been established, which is important in my view."

Barham "Yes, and its nice to see where you live now, you still do something along those lines ? With all your nice ducks and things in the stream you've made here ?"

Mr. Williams "Well yes, I've got a mini nature reserve here. You know, I've got 150 mallard around me and geese and I've got owls nesting, I've also got nesting boxes everywhere and people flock here in the summer and spring time to see what I've got here. They stand on that little bridge going over the river Criggych and take pictures and I still see schools. Schools still come in to me and I chat to them and talk to them about various things."

While he was still at Penrhos he'd become such a well-known policeman that I was even sent to see him when he retired. As the interviewer, it's up to you to ask the questions you consider relevant, but sometimes your producer will want a specific question thrown in and on this occasion I had to ask him why he'd never made it to the rank of Sergeant. "Well" he said with a wry grin, "It was because of those damned talking brooches."

He was referring to the small radio sets they carried on their lapels. Soon after they'd been issued his crackled into life when he was on his beat one night. He was having his usual 'unofficial' rest period at the time, enjoying a cup of tea with the butcher at the back of his shop. "Where are you Williams?" the voice asked. "Hello Inspector, I'm outside the post office," Ken said. "That's funny" The Inspector replied, "I'm outside the post office and I can't see you."

Forgive me please if at this moment I become a little public spirited. I was always being told by those in the newsroom who had 'idiot' stamped on their foreheads that good news isn't real news, but I can't help thinking that a few 'do-gooders' qualify for the hero tag. In thinking of Ken's nature reserve, I can't help remembering the work some people do to find homes for unwanted animals like horses and donkeys, and then there are those who fight tirelessly to keep the remnants of our democracy intact, like the people of Anglesey who overwhelmingly objected to being used as guinea pigs in the fluoride debate. The stuff might be good for most people's teeth, but the islanders were given no choice. Most people in this once free country can choose for themselves if they wish to use this poison mixed into their toothpaste, but here the whole population had it forced upon them through their water pipes. They were forced to drink it for years, bath and shower in it, boil their potatoes in it, wash their faces in it, and bath their babies in it - like it or not.

Dogs too can be heroes, but the one I'm thinking of right now is one that I didn't meet. His grave is on the cliffs to the north of Rhoscolyn on the Anglesey coast. He died in 1819 after rescuing the four crew members of a small sailing ship. It was a foreign ship and having struck rocks the crew found they were sinking with little chance of surviving the raging storm. The dog on the other hand knew what to do, and supporting each one of them in turn he swam to the shore. This Herculean task though took its toll, and having reached the shore with the last of his precious cargo he collapsed and died.

I was told this tale by an old coastguard Mr. Evan Evans, who took me to the little grave close to the black and white arches, arches cut by the tide through the great cliff buttresses there. The dog's name was Tyger and according to legend he was like an Irish Wolfhound, and I remember this visit very well. A mist had come rolling in off the sea and the effect was quite weird. As we arrived at Tyger's grave we could see a dog. He was looking down at us from a distant rock and he looked big, and none too friendly either. Then, as soon as we finished the interview, this large hound started to come towards us, and what a surprise, through a trick of the mist and half-light, he'd looked huge and quite a long way off, whereas he was actually quite near and tiny, and was soon scampering around out feet.

If you find that hard to believe a very similar experience came to a man who tried to canoe around the Lleyn Peninsula and then go on to circumnavigate Anglesey. He gave up the attempt to canoe around the island through exhaustion and the disorientation of paddling in a thick mist. We'd heard he was missing and I was given the task of finding him.

This was a pretty hopeless task really, seeing it was foggy and I didn't have a boat. But always the optimist I set out with my son and after several hours we found him staggering around in a small cove called Porth Colmon. We'd searched all the coves we could get down to along the north coast of the Lleyn, and when we found him I was able to record a remarkable interview. His face was red and caked with brine and his lips were parched, but he managed to tell us how he'd lost track of the days. He also told us that at one stage he'd quickly paddled after a fishing boat, desperate for a lift. He was delighted to see it, but it turned out to be much closer than he thought. After just four or five strokes of the paddle he reached it only to find it was a dead seagull.

His trip had been something of a

disaster right from the start. I felt sorry for him really. On the first day, when making his way down the River Dwyryd to the great ocean highway beyond, he was capsized by a cow ! He was a determined paddler though. Don Ashworth was his name and he went on to canoe in America where he came across a Mississippi paddle boat. I think it was the Mississippi, and apparently the paddle boat was real enough because for a while he became its helmsman.

Thinking again about Tyger the dog leads me to the subject of history, which is a very valuable commodity in a tourist area - witness the medieval costumes worn to sell things. The shop keepers in Ruthin used to dress up every wednesday, and reporters are always stepping into the past. There were always things like burial mounds to visit. I remember too several ancient houses being put right back to their original 'ancient' condition in places like Castle Caereinion and Bangor on Dee, and of course Bishop Morgan's house near Penmachno. Some of them going on the housing market, with bare stone walls heated by middle of the room smoky log fires with no chimneys, to really test the persuasive skills of estate agents. And I remember some being moved too.

I remember Wolverly Hall being taken brick by brick to Chirk and an old cottage near Holt being taken 2 hundred yards for a better view, but what I didn't like was to see people come up from South Wales to cart buildings off to the St Fagans heritage museum. I hated that, but there were always archaeological digs to peer into, and I even met a girl who was digging into history from the air.

Mary Aries and her husband Capel had an aeroplane. They belonged to the flying club at Anglesey's Mona airfield and Mary, who worked at the County Archives Office, obviously liked a bit of unpaid overtime. This next piece was recorded on a flight around Anglesey. I was being shown how remains can show up through the turf.

CBWB 7

Barham	(Above noise of plane.) "I'm flying once again with Mary and Capel. They've told me that we're flying at 1,500 feet at the moment over Cemlyn Bay, north coast of Anglesey. What are we looking at, at the moment Mary ?"
Mrs. Aries	"Well down there below us just to the south of Cemlyn Bay itself, you can see a little hilltop if you look carefully. In this dry weather during the summer it's been possible to discover that it's the site of a hill fort."
Barham	"So the lines of the walls become visible in very dry weather ?
Mrs. Aries	"That's right. It's quite amazing sometimes. It's magical the way the buried landscape can sometimes become visible."
Barham	"What are some of the most interesting things you've seen in recent years ?"
Mrs. Aries	"Well the most interesting contribution that our photography has made really is the contribution to our understanding of early agriculture, because from the air we're able to make up field systems, and we can make up very, very faint traces sometimes of cultivations and of settlements, and of other human activities."

I remember they were producing a very interesting book called 'The Historic Landscape of the Great Orme' and on another occasion I remember them flying me over a field close to Mona where you could see the outline of all the streets of a village, abandoned because a plague had devastated it. At some later date all the houses had been dismantled and the stones taken away for use elsewhere, but at least from the air you could see exactly where they'd stood.

An old pilot, who'd 'crashed' out of the RAF, and who'd started giving trips to the public from an airfield near Caernarvon, was fun to fly with. He wanted the publicity and I enjoyed obliging. Any excuse was found to dive bomb Fort Belan, and then there was the lady who was giving flying lessons. She was fun to fly with too. She once let me steer down the Menai Strait and bank steeply round Puffin Island like she'd done careering round and around Caernarvon Castle, but as a reporter you get a lot of rides in helicopters as well.

Helicopters come in a variety of sizes. Someone once opened a passenger service between Holyhead and Dublin using a huge twin rotor thing and I was aboard its inaugural flight. It was very good too, it was the only helicopter I'd ever been in where you could just manage to shout your way through a conversation. It was very comfortable as well, carrying about a dozen people I seem to remember, but the service didn't last, within a few days it packed up.

The first helicopter I flew in belonged to a General. I needed to get to the studio in a hurry from the top of a mountain where I'd been covering an Army exercise, and the General cheerfully said, "Take my chopper old man." which wasn't how I was accustomed to being spoken to when I was in the army, but it's remarkable how nicely people speak to you if you work for the BBC.

Most of my helicopter trips were either on RAF exercises (something I will return to in a chapter on 'terror') or on mountain rescue events, but it was on another army exercise that I had a very strange experience in a helicopter. I'd gone with the pilot to refuel from a road tanker down in the Nant Ffrancon pass and on the way back up the mountain a mist swept in so quickly that we were surrounded by it in no time. It might have been the end of the exercise as far as we were concerned, but because I knew the tracks around there we were able to reach our destination. It was like taking somebody hill walking. We crept along about ten or twelve feet above the ground and on a couple of occasions we even climbed over stiles.

I don't know how I got onto the subject of helicopters, I thought I was dealing here with history, and two of the most memorable encounters with this subject involved a suffragette and the Holy Grail. The suffragette was a very old lady, as you might expect, by the name of Leonora Cohen. She lived in an old people's home in Colwyn Bay and amazingly had once been a prisoner in the Tower of London, and if I'm talking now to very young people I had better explain that suffragettes were women who campaigned in the early 1900's for women to be allowed to vote. Up until then, even here in Britain, only men held that privilege and the women's campaign was sometimes quite violent. They were mainly drawn from the ranks of the well educated, but they were certainly the 'lad-ettes' of their age.

I don't know why I had to go and talk to her, but I think it would have been in 1968 or 69, and it was obviously one of the last opportunities to talk to a suffragette. She sat very still and very upright. She was very old, I think in fact she was 101 if I remember rightly. She spoke with a frail but very clear voice, and with a slight but unmistakable Yorkshire accent.

CBWB 13

Mrs. Cohen	"I never slept a wink that night. I didn't fancy smashing a window or anything, I didn't bargain for doing anything like that, so what I did, I bought a guide to London and I went and sat in the park one morning to reflect on what I could find, a place I could go, and I looked at the art galleries and I looked at all the different places, museums and what not, and I couldn't make up my mind. I came down the T's and ...."
Barham	"To the Tower of London ?"
Mrs. Cohen	"I'd gone all through, and that was the Tower of

London. I was electrified. Oh the Tower, that's the place. I won't hurt anybody. This of course reasoned in my brain until I reeled, that was just the thing. I'd go back to Mrs. Morrison and she said she'd never heard such a crazy thing in all her life."

Barham   "So what did you decide to do ?"

Mrs. Cohen   "I had to go."

This lady, who in later life became a Justice of the Peace (time does heal) was determined to smash something and she and Mrs. Morrison (the lady she was lodging with) spent the whole night cutting a hefty iron bar from the grate with a file. Then they made what she described as an apron to conceal it. After that it was time to go. Her target was the Jewel House! On arrival however she found the main glass cases were surrounded by so many people that she feared hurting someone, and selected a less well attended display.

Mrs. Cohen   "I found a suitable place over the heads of everybody where I wouldn't hurt anybody, and I threw this missile right into the case which held the Order of Merits. There was the most ghastly crash, it was like an air raid. I was terrified and nearly fainted myself."

Within moments she was grabbed and locked up there and then in the Tower, and as I've probably said already the reporter often stumbles into the past, and of all the first hand accounts I've listened to there's one I remember with particular interest. The old blacksmith from Aberdaron was retiring and he showed me his treasured diaries, and wonderful they were too. Aberdaron is a tiny sandy-beach village at the far end of the long and wild Lleyn peninsula, and his observations provided a fascinating glimpse into rural life covering many years, and what I remember best was his account of that day when the last of the old Bardsey Island families came ashore.

113

Many of the younger people had already gone from the island and time had moved on. The old way of life, the old way of family farming, had passed them by, and the old blacksmith had described how their little boats had swept up onto the beach that morning, and how they'd stood forlornly on the wet sand clutching their few belongings, and how the people of the village went down to the shore and took them into their care. It was so very moving.

We're all watching history being made, but it's not always apparent until something is dislodged and time's big hand lurches forward with a 'clang' - revealing that someone, somewhere, has caught up at last.

One such revelation came in the 1970's when the Betws-y-Coed Urban District Council put up the rates to buy a lorry. Until then its Lilliputian existence had survived without motorised transport thanks mainly to the Swallow Falls turnstile, but the council did have property to maintain. This included an estate of council houses, and in spite of the workload such responsibilities bring their only means of transport until then had been a wheel-barrow. For the really big jobs a lorry was borrowed from another town, and somebody else emptied the dustbins, but for the day to day care of civic property and amenities – it was the wheel-barrow.

By the time this came to the attention of the modern world, it was time to take stock. The last wooden barrow had gone to that big council depot in the sky and in its place was a gleaming metal one which was being looked after very well indeed. It was being serviced regularly by 2 men, Bob Williams (ex 'handyman' at the old Waterloo hotel) and his mate, who's name I cannot recall, and they made sure they kept it under cover every night too, in the building where they used to keep the horse-drawn hearse.

Sometimes little snippets of history pop up in the most unexpected ways, and in the most unexpected places as well. Inconsequential things perhaps but nice to find. Take the 'Ovaltine' lady for instance, the beautiful girl on all those tins of Ovaltine. She wasn't a professional model, she was just a girl in the office at the time, and when I met her she was a cheerful old lady living in an old peoples home in Prestatyn - still drinking Ovaltine.

The last story in this chapter comes from another elderly lady and is one of the most intriguing stories I ever came across. It took me some time to decide whether it should be under 'H' for history or 'T' for treasure, after all many have searched high and low for the Holy Grail, but this lady in Aberdovey thought it might be in an Aberystwyth Bank. With the years quickly passing she thought it was time to tell her story, and this centred around the much supported belief that the Holy Grail was brought to Britain and held by monks at Glastonbury for a while before bringing it to Wales.

In the 1930s this Mrs. Smeeton of Aberdovey had been friends with the owner of a large house near Aberystwyth called Nant yr Oes. This mansion still stands and apparently it was on this spot where the monks had eventually settled, and the lady was convinced that an old wooden bowl kept in a cupboard there was the Holy Grail.

It sounds disappointing, I know. You feel the Holy Grail should have been something enormously mysterious, shining and 'untouchable', glowing with divine light and almighty power, ready to 'frizzle' unbelievers the moment they touched it, but no, according to Mrs. Smeeton, it was a very dull old wooden bowl, the sort of bowl that dirty beggars might hold forth in a Hollywood epic.

CABWB 8

Barham   "Who did this bowl belong to ?"

Mrs.Smeeton   "Well the custodian and the person who owned the house was Mrs. Powell, a sister of Sir Lewis Price, and she lived there all her life and kind of inherited

	this trust when the last monk had died."
Barham	"And what did it look like ?"
Mrs.Smeeton	"It was a plain wooden bowl, not very large, looking very worn, but I would say olive wood."
Barham	"Is that what you were told at the time ?"
Mrs.Smeeton	"Well I thought it was olive wood, and I asked what it was and she said yes, it must have been."
Barham	"Why did the owner think it was in fact the long lost Holy Grail ?"
Mrs.Smeeton	"Well I suppose she inherited it down the ages. I don't know, when was Joseph of Arimathea at Glastonbury ? Because, of course the monks had charge of the bowl. They moved to Margam, then during the dissolution of the monasteries they fled again to North Wales and were given sanctuary at Nant yr Oes, but I suppose some of the Prices or Powells were in residence and took charge of it when the last monk died, and he handed it to the family who therefore looked after it until the last member of the family died."
Barham	"Was she convinced that it was the Holy Grail ?"
Mrs.Smeeton	"I'm sure she was. She was as a matter of fact a bit irreverent in her manner and she just said – would you like to see the Holy Grail ? And then of course I did."
Barham	"Was she really convinced ?"
Mrs.Smeeton	"Oh I'm certain of it. She treated it with great respect, although it was only put in a cupboard in her study, but as I told you, there were hundreds of letters and documents and testimonials to the power this had given to people who had consulted it about their ailments."
Barham	"It had been used in treating people ?"
Mrs.Smeeton	"Oh yes for years."

Barham	"In what way ?"
Mrs.Smeeton	"Well they used to go to the place and ask to see it, kneel down and touch it, kiss it, pray to it, and I understand that it had even been loaned out to bedridden people who couldn't get to see it, but they might not have told the world in general, so I suppose nobody else really knew, it is rather an isolated part of the world."
Barham	"Do you know what happened to it ?"
Mrs.Smeeton	"Well I was always told it had been put into the care of a Bank in Aberystwyth while they were deciding what to do with the property, which was eventually sold."

Once in the Aberystwyth studio I had the task of phoning the Banks. I was on the air very soon now and time was short, and so too were the conversations.

"Hello, it's the BBC here. Do you have the Holy Grail ?"

"The Holy what sir ?"

"The Holy Grail, you know it's a wooden bowl thing. Have you got it in your vault ?"

"No I don't think so sir."

"It belonged to a Mrs. Powell of Nant yr Oes. She's not there now but some monks had it first. Can you nip down to your vault and have a look ? …..Hello ? …. Are you still there ? … Hello ? … Hello ?"

CHAPTER I.
Interruptions, Invasions, and the Inept.

Depending on what you're doing, interruptions are either ideal or catastrophic. If you want a busy atmosphere to your feature with people buzzing in and out and exchanging comments with you and your interviewee, that's fine, but on the other hand, an unwelcome interruption can kill your piece stone dead.

It can either happen suddenly or it can build up slowly. It can happen in a thousand different ways, but anything that forces you to stop an interview usually causes a hefty problem. It's very difficult to re-start an interview. The farmer and the ramblers leader I mentioned earlier were unusual, brilliant infact. They got straight back into battle as if there had never been a cease-fire, but if you disrupt people's pattern of thought, most dry up on you. Then of course, even if you go back only a short way in the recording, you're almost bound to have problems matching up the background noises. Remember what I said ? You either wait for the right background noise to come along before you re-start, or take the recording back to a spot on the tape where there were no particular background noises cropping up at all.

When it comes to live broadcasts they're particularly vulnerable of course to interruptions, and I'll give you some hair-raising examples in a later chapter, but even with a recording the wrong sort of interruption can be absolutely fatal. To be a good broadcaster you need good luck and good blood pressure, and if you work for the BBC you mustn't hit anybody.

How well I remember this incident. The date was sometime in the sixties and it was one of my very first broadcasts. I was standing on rough open land where a fairground had stood. This had been Rhyl's original fairground and all that was left was the Big Dipper, a huge old structure built of heavy timber beams and dating back to the early nineteen hundreds. Four steel hawsers had been attached to the top of it about sixty feet off the ground, and they'd been shackled to the backs of four enormously powerful towing vehicles. Workmen had partially sawn through the base of the thing and at any moment the lorries were going to edge forward. It was all going to come crashing down in a wonderful

118

orchestration of splitting-smashing timber.

My producer had wanted a feature registering the fact that a bit of Rhyl's history was being swept aside for a more up-to-date fairground. So I had all the interviews I needed with the people involved safely in the bag, and all I needed now was the great 'crash'.

"Make sure you get that Big Dipper coming down." I'd been told. "It should make a tremendous noise."

The lorries were reving up now and as they inched forward the hawsers began to tighten. As the enormous structure started to crack and creak, the crowd held its breath, and I said ..... "This is it, this is the moment we've all been waiting for .... yes here it comes !"

It was spectacular, they'd tipped it over and now it was hurtling to the ground. At the precise moment of impact a spotty-faced imbecile appeared out of nowhere to shout into my mic "Is this your hobby then ?" His words coincided exactly with the crash. I can't remember what I said, but he left quickly, and I was left in a state of utter confusion. I found myself walking through the dust towards the lorries and the jubilant workmen, and I found myself wanting to ask them if they could do it again. I remember feeling so – so utterly at a loss. It was my first disaster and I was feeling dreadful.

I know I've written a chapter headed 'disasters' but there were too many for one just chapter. Others follow in different guises and right now I'm thinking of those that come under the heading 'interruptions' and being interruptions they usually arrive unannounced. This is invariably the case with live broadcasting.

When the counties were reorganised in 1974 we reporters were sent to cover the new county elections. On the night of the poll a room was set aside by the local authority at each of the county headquarters for us to phone the results live into an election programme. I was given the brand new county of

Clwyd and duly turned up for the count in Ruthin. I was shown my room with the all important telephone on a desk, complete with notepaper and pretty well everything I might need. As the evening progressed I kept an eye on the results as they came in, and in general chatted to people about the swings to one party or another, and every now and then I went to my room and phoned through a morsel of news to the programme in Cardiff.

Always, the plea from late night election programme producers was, "Try and send us something to keep us going before the result," which is why 'election specials' are so full of waffle, but eventually the full count was declared at long last, and with people filing out of the building I now had the final result in my hand. At last I could sit down in my little room and go on the air giving the result and the whole political make up of this brand new county council – so many Conservatives, Labour, Liberals, etc.

On these occasions, when you ring through to the programme the producer comes on the phone and says, "Okay I'm putting you through to the studio," and then you hear the presenter say something like, "Now we have the result from Ruthin, Allan Barham is on the line, hallo Allan, what's the picture up there now ?" To this you respond by saying something you think is fitting, and then you start to read the details from your notes.

As I got under way I remember thinking it was going ok, I wasn't fluffing my words, and I thought I was reading it at the right pace – not too hurried and not too slowly, and then the door opened. It was the caretaker. "Come on, come on !" he shouted, flinging a mop and bucket into a corner with an almighty clatter. "I haven't got all night. Come on I'm locking up now, come on."

Of all the rooms they could have given me, they'd given me the caretaker's room. In situations like this you just have to carry on. You just have to. It's ridiculous really, pretending that nothing is happening, but there we are, it's tradition. You just have to carry on even though someone is standing in front of you pointing to the clock and telling you that it's time to go.

Incidentally, having touched on the subject of background noises and atmosphere earlier, I'll tell you this - I was recording a talk with a zoo keeper once about the new chimpanzee enclosure. This was at Colwyn Bay, at the Welsh Mountain Zoo, and as work for the day had finished I was pleased to hear during the interview someone behind us starting to saw a piece of wood. It was just what I needed. It didn't go on incessantly, it was just intermittent, it was infact perfect, except that it wasn't a man sawing wood at all. Neither was it a chimpanzee. It turned out to be a leopard. Apparently they sometimes make a noise exactly like a man sawing wood, and the next morning he went on the air - as a man sawing wood.

On the subject of invasions, which seem to fit into this chapter, I was lucky to have only been involved with one and a half invasions. The first was only half an invasion because it petered out only a stone's thrown from where they came ashore, and also I have to admit that I was 185 years late getting there. It was nevertheless an interesting history lesson which I received from Wynford Vaughan Thomas, but more about that later. The invasion which I actually took part in was in 1982 when a lady from Anglesey took her army to invade London.

Val Williams was a star. No-one could have bettered her for publicity. She not only publicised her hotel but the whole of Anglesey. Her Henllys Hall Hotel near Beaumaris was enormous and the effort to keep it going had to be enormous too, and even though she was struggling with her recent widowhood she wasn't found lacking.

She had all sorts of special weekends on offer, ghost-hunting weekends in the cellars, doggy weekends with the dogs sleeping in little four poster beds, and love-ins where the guests were served with big steak dinners in bed for breakfast.

She had all sorts of special attractions, and then there were her castle-storming weekends when her guests, dressed as medieval soldiers, would join her private army of local desperadoes and rush with ladders down to Beaumaris Castle and storm the battlements. It was this that led to the uprising.

Having written to all the local papers in North London in order to tip them off and invite them to the action, she and her army finalised their plans. These were to go by coach and to visit the pubs she'd selected because of their military or imperialistic names like – The Castle, or the Royal, or the Palace Arms or whatever. I think there were ten on her list and when I say 'visit' them, I mean 'burst in and create havoc!'

Early on the appointed day we set off. It was early morning and the coach was full of sword-carrying soldiers and beautiful girls in Elizabethan dresses with nice tall conical hats and veils. The girls were carrying leaflets depicting in words and pictures the delights of Beaumaris and of Henllys Hall in particular. I was the only outsider, a war correspondent she'd dressed in some sort of tunic and tights. A sight incidentally that aroused some unprintable comments later that day in London when I got to Broadcasting House, but it was a brilliant idea of course. Like I said, for publicity no-one could touch her, but when it came to controlling the weather she hadn't a clue.

As we came into London it started to pour, and by the time we'd found the first pub on the list it was teeming down. It was 'torrential'. In her excitable wonderfully husky South Walian voice our Warrior Queen was shouting - "Come on everybody, all out, come along," and out we went, but not before the coach driver announced that he couldn't wait there because of the double yellow lines, so he'd go round the block and pick us up in fifteen minutes. We didn't see him again. Well not until later that night. He got into a one-way system and he got lost. But anyway, dodging the traffic we rushed across the road and gathered at the door of this first pub.

CBWB 1

Mrs.Williams	"Are you ready Peter ?"
Barham	"The Chief Soldier is about to charge into this pub and ask them if they'll surrender."
Chief Soldier	(Leading the Charge through the door) "Surrender! Surrender to Owain Glyndwr's army! Surrender or suffer the consequences !!"

As anti-climaxes go, this was a big one. The place was almost empty. There was no-one behind the bar and in a corner there were just two customers who looked as if they'd been there all night. As the soldiers rushed in they stared in amazement. A look that turned to absolute horror as Mrs. Williams followed with her girls and conducted them in a fine renditioning of 'All Through the Night'. From their expressions it was quite obvious they thought they'd died and had woken up in a very third class heaven.

It was of course disappointing to find no reporters there, but when the barmaid was eventually found, she said that they'd received no letter. So there was nothing else for it but to hand out some leaflets describing the delights of Beaumaris and bid them a soldier's farewell. Outside we found that it was raining even harder but our leader was in a determined mood. There was no sign of the coach, and after twenty minutes she decided we would have to walk. She had this list of public houses and we were going to visit each one of them come what may.

By the time we found the next one on the list we were completely drenched, but here there was definitely an improvement. Again there were no reporters, but there were five customers here, and as Mrs. Williams conducted her choir I spoke to a very feeble old man.

CBWB 1

Old Man	"Wha's that ? Wha's that all about ?"
Barham	"It's a publicity drive to get you to spend your holidays in Beaumaris, in North Wales you see."
Old Man	"Oh yeah, very nice too."
Barham	"Fancy that ?"
Old Man	(Unconvinced) "Yeah, yeah."
Barham	"They storm the castle in Beaumaris at weekends and that sort of thing."
Old Man	"Oh I see."
Barham	"And they'd like you to come along and watch. Okay ?"
Old Man	"Oh, right oh."
Barham	"Mrs. Williams, it's costing you a lot of money I believe to do this." Mrs.Williams "Oh yes, yes."
Barham	"To bring all these people down to London, how much does it cost ?" Mrs.Williams "About £700."
Barham	"Just to publicise your hotel ? Do you think it's going to be worth it ?" Mrs.Williams "I hope so, yes, I'm sure it will be."
Barham	"How many pubs are you hoping to storm ?
Mrs.Williams	"Ten. Ten different pubs, I'm sure it will be worth it. Everyone is taking a lot of notice of us. We're getting around a lot of people. In the streets people are taking leaflets from us and we're stopping people and telling them about Beaumaris so I think it will, yes."

We only found four of the pubs on her list, but at the last one there was a good crowd. It was lunchtime by then and we got a great response there. Once they got over the initial shock they loved it. It was drinks all round and Beaumaris here we come, and as our route had been planned to pass near to Broadcasting House I was able to fit my piece into the PM programme before joining the others at the Wales tourism office before going off to eat at the London Welsh club.

The BBC could have done with someone like Val Williams, or even a Mr. Micawber, though no doubt his advice would have gone unheeded, and so I have labelled this chapter the 'Inept'. Maybe I should include my own failings in this chapter, but they will come, soon. I promise.

I hope I'm not being unfair but I've often wondered about the BBC. There are always questions over its future. It's such a massive organisation and yet it never looks safe, and in my time I saw huge numbers of redundancies, as always victims of other people's over rated ambitions.

"It's your BBC." they say, (in the manner employed by people passing the buck) and as a fully paid up license holder I've always wondered if the corporation needed to have grown to such enormous and unstable proportions. For instance in the 1950's when 'commercial' television companies were given the green light, the BBC was obviously going to be the poor relation, restricted as it was to an income from a licence fee, but it puffed itself up and 'took on' those enormously powerful companies that had practically been given a license to print money

Its revenue is limited it's true, but the Corporation, with its guarantees of existence should never have become so insecure. If our industrialists, out there in the real world, shared the BBC's privilege of receiving an absolutely guaranteed income, by Royal charter, every year, provided by the public, through a licence fee, enforced by the crown, enshrined in law, they would think they were in heaven. Only the inept would fail.

I don't know what influences were at work again in the 1960's (did they jump or were they pushed ?) but when discussing one particular expenditure I've always thought it was another mistake for the BBC to go into 'local' radio. For some it's been fine, but here again it was a case of 'taking on' a new set of commercial stations that were springing up all over the country, and the establishing, equipping, staffing and maintenance must have cost enormous sums of money, and for what purpose ? When all is said and done, I'm sure most people still regard the BBC as a national institution, and not a corner shop.

However as the years progressed down at my level, my problems were far removed from those of policy. Instead the problem in those last few years leading up to the millennium was trying to get departmental heads in Cardiff to respond to ideas, or even answer letters, or even the telephone. It seemed to some of us that BBC Radio Wales was falling apart.

Alongside our normal duties, we reporters had always been encouraged to come up with new programme ideas and ideas for special features. I'd been lucky to have several of my own programmes and series running, but by the end of the 90's the situation became very frustrating. No-one seemed to be running the place. You couldn't get through to people. For instance, at a time when Radio Wales was striving for publicity, I wrote a 'radio' series of zany comic adventures which I thought could run alongside a number of public gatherings.

My idea was that aspiring writers could come and join in with the writing of them and get themselves launched. I thought it would be an interesting experiment and provide the BBC, and in particular BBC Radio Wales, with much needed publicity, but unfortunately the idea didn't get passed the pilot stage. That in itself is okay. If you float an idea you have to be prepared for it to be turned down, but not without discussion. In Cardiff, where programme heads and organisers are to be found, it was completely ignored, and I still think it's a shame because there is so much comic talent in Wales.

I wasn't alone in thinking this either. Right from the start I'd discussed it with Alun Evans our North Wales Head of Productions and he very supportively let me have the outside broadcast unit to record the first two episodes to see what it sounded like. As I said it was completely ignored in Cardiff so it got nowhere, but we had a lot of fun doing it.

I'd recruited a most wonderfully

enthusiastic amateur cast to play the parts, and to clear the path with the professional actors union they were willing to do it for charity, that is to say – in return for their time and effort the BBC would pay a token amount into the funds of 'Children in Need'. This is the charity the BBC usually supports so well, but it didn't get further than those first instalments.

We recorded them in a public hall in front of an audience, and that - although risky, was essential to my mind. Obviously it needed laughter and although it would have been safer to do it in a studio and use 'canned' laughter, (cheating - they do it all the time) I was determined to perform it in front of a real live audience to see if it really was funny. If that audience hadn't laughed then I would have scrapped it. But we got the laughs alright.

The series was set in the future, and I played the part of a radio reporter at large with his team which comprised of a sound recordist and an assistant, (exactly what I didn't have in real life) and in each episode we were destined to bump into the same bunch of typical 'cartoon-like' figures, traditional stereotypes to match the 'cartoon-like' humour. We had the extremely fat lady, the extremely weedy man, the snooty Englishman, the pessimistic Welshman (Idris my sound recordist), the ridiculous Irishman, and a few others – all traditional British loonies.

For good measure I wrote   eight of these half hour episodes and I got the actors to dress up for their parts, ludicrously, and the audience loved them. The fat lady for instance was a very big hit.

BFG1
Extract from   'The Barham Report'.
Big Gwenda   "Do you remember how we first met ?"
Barham   "Of course I do."
Big Gwenda   "I was on the beach and all those lovely coastguard

boys had to come and rescue me."

Barham	"Well, they had to come and move you."
Idris	"Move her ?"
Barham	"They had to. The tide couldn't come in !"

It was such a relief to hear that audience laugh so much and in no time the cast, drawn mainly from an amateur pantomime company based at Deganwy, were having a ball. They were all just fabulous. Our fat lady for instance, in a gigantic dress stuffed with several pillows, was quite a sight, - a big red faced doll.

BFG1

Big Gwenda	"I always wanted to fly."
Idris	(Sarcastically) "So did Dumbo."
Barham	"Shut up Idris."
Big Gwenda	"I met this pilot and he took me for my first spin."
Barham	"That must have been a thrill."
Big Gwenda	"Oh it was. We did loop the loop, upside down figures of eight, and lots of flip overs."
Barham	"What sort of plane were you in ?"
Big Gwenda	"Oh we weren't in a plane !"

As I said, the stories were set in the future. The Welsh language had been banned but we had a hero, a Welsh freedom fighter in a Red Indian's war bonnet. He was 'Big Chief Die Fighting' and he was our tough guy, whereas little Selwyn, a tiny Japanese boy, was our weedy one. He was hopeless. He couldn't get anything right.

BFG1

Barham	(Annoyed) "Where is he ?"
Idris	"He's still on the roof !"
Barham	"Where ?"

Idris	"I can see his feet !"
Selwyn	(Muffled) "Help, help."
Barham	(Exasperated) "Selwyn ! When I said come down the drainpipe, I meant come down the *outside* of the drainpipe !"
Idris	(Trying to speak through the laughter) "Leave him, leave him."

Wales had acquired a comic German governor, wearing a spiked helmet and a white uniform plastered in silver milk top medals. He was accompanied everywhere by a dreadfully out-of-tune 'umpah' band, and in one episode he was in a train crash.

BFG1

(Band plays and Governor appears out of wreckage.)

Governor	"Oh ! Ah ! Oh ! Oh ! Donna and Blitzen ein Boooondersbank !! Someone will get a slosh in ze Goebles for zis !"
Barham	(Calling up to Governor) "How did it happen Your Excellency ?"
Governor	"The svinehoonts ! I privatised the line, and they've sold the flaming rails !"
Barham	(After laughter) "Climb down this way Your Excellency. Can you get down here ?"
Governor	"Nine, nine, I'm too dizzy."
Barham	"Have you got vertigo ?"
Governor	"What you say ?"
Barham	"Have you got vertigo ?"
Governor	"Vertigo ? I've got ruddy miles to go !"

In one episode we were at a big agricultural show when Big Chief Die Fighting arrived with a rare animal – a cow, and later we found Mr. O'Blarney the Irishman serving meals in a marquee.

BFG1

O'Blarney	(Referring to Big Gwenda) "She's not coming in !"
Barham	"Why not ?"
O'Blarney	"She came in yesterday, sat down and split me marquee right down the middle."
Big Gwenda	(Upset) "Oh."
Big Chief	"What's this muck ?"
O'Blarney	"That's bean soup, Sir."
Big Chief	"I don't care what it's been, what the heck is it now ?"
O'Blarney	(Waiting for laughter to die down) "I've got some nice ham here."
Idris	"It smells awful."
O'Blarney	"Let me see. Well I'm blessed, and I thought it was cured. (Speaking through laughter) It just shows, you can't trust those vets."

I know it wasn't highbrow humour, but the whole point was to provide the chance for listeners to help write further episodes, and although our head of productions in the north was very supportive it had to be sanctioned in Cardiff as I've said, and that's when the long wait began. It was over a year before I even got word of its arrival, but there was no comment, not a word, and it became clear that our hard work up here in the north had been totally ignored. Then in the south they came up with 'Broth.'

Four or five years later a department specially dedicated to producing comedy shows was set up by the BBC in Cardiff and I submitted the idea again. I sent copies of the recordings and several colour photographs of the cast taken during the performances, and of course an accompanying letter explaining the proposed public participation. It's hard to believe I know, but all these years later I'm still waiting for a reply. Any sort of acknowledgement would be welcome. There has been no letter, not even a phone call. Our efforts here in the north were yet again completely ignored.

The sheer incompetence of BBC management not only exasperates broadcasters but most alarmingly, it exasperates the public. I had a phone call one day from a young author – Stephen Gregory. I'd never met him, the call came completely out of the blue, but his name was immediately familiar. The previous year he'd won a most prestigious literary prize with his book 'The Cormorant'. He'd won the Somerset Maughan Award and part of his prize was the opportunity to travel. His phone call to me came soon after his arrival back home. He'd chosen to go to South America and there he'd written a collection of short stories based upon his experiences there, and to my surprise he wanted me to read them on the air.

I naturally thought it was very nice to be asked, but within a few minutes of meeting him I suggested that he should read them himself. They were his stories after all, and I felt sure he could manage it. This he agreed to and we set about cutting a couple of them down to ten-minute slots. Then a few days later we went into a Bangor studio and recorded them. The session went very well and I passed them onto Cardiff, offering to oversee further recordings if they were required. I needn't have bothered.

The days went by and eventually the days became weeks and months, but neither of us had received a single word from Cardiff. I tried phoning only to be told it would be dealt with in due course. I asked for written confirmation of their arrival. None ever came. After six months and several phone calls from the author, he rang me for the last time. "Allan," he said, "Don't bother any more. Just tell them I'll never, ever, do anything for the BBC now that I know how they treat people."

To this day I've never had a reply. Yet another proposal had disappeared into the Black Hole that was BBC Radio Wales.

Out in the real world you don't find many inept people. Most find their right niche, but for some it takes a little time. The Holyhead reserve goalkeeper hadn't found his when I met him. This was one of my first tasks for the World Service, such was the enormity of his 'crime'. The message from Bush House was - "Find that goalkeeper!" But it wasn't easy. He'd gone into hiding. Letting in 37 goals is not a good tally for a season, but for a single match it was thought to be a world record.

I found him on the Monday. It was lunchtime and I found him on a building site. He was sitting miserably under a gaping window in an unfinished house, and when I asked him about the match he solemnly described in great detail how none of them had been his fault. As he finished explaining goal number 37 one of his mates arrived and threw him a bag of chips. They flew right through his hands and out the window.

CHAPTER J.
Jungle survival, Journeys, and Jurassic Park.

If you join the BBC do buy some insect repellent. The BBC might not harbour a greater number of insects than other firms, but you will be 'irritated', and it is a jungle so beware of monkeys in the tent. Don't let them pilfer your best ideas and remember - studios are not as sound proofed as you might think. (Especially if you leave the mic. switched on.) It's like industrial espionage. Many a programme idea has been spirited away only to turn up later with a different coat of paint.

I don't know who invented radio 'phone-ins', it certainly wasn't me, but I did have the chance to introduce them into the UK. It was in the 60's when a friend returning from America told me that he'd heard people in one of the states actually phoning 'live' into a radio programme to say what they thought of it.

This was unheard of over here, and so thinking it ought to have some sort of practical application, I put together a pilot 'request' programme in which people phoned in, between the playing of records, to say what they were looking for and explaining why etc. I got people to phone in asking for all manner of things from books to parts for a clock and a vintage motor car, and then dispatched it to Cardiff. No-one upstairs there liked the idea, but I got a letter from Douglas Muggeridge in London who was the controller of radios one and two, and he didn't like it either ! I think he was worried that someone might come on the air and swear, because he said it might just be suitable for a local station. He must have thought that if there was a sudden swerve away from 'Perceived Queen's English' it wouldn't matter quite so much if it was only heard north of the proverbial Watford.

I didn't pursue the idea any further, but soon the phone-ins were finding their way into every type of programme, made safe by a delaying device that enabled producers to hear what a caller was saying moments before the listener. This gave a producer the chance to cut off any caller who forgot his manners well in advance of making maiden aunts blush, but I soon grew to dislike phone-ins.

They are very good at drawing spontaneous public comments into a programme, and so too now are the E mails and the text messages, but when the telephone is used for a report that's anything longer than a short news item, the result is so 'sterile', so lacking in the essential atmosphere needed to create any sort of picture in the mind. To achieve that you have to have a reporter on the spot - involved with everything going on there, and I believe the over-use of the phone has done radio a great deal of harm. It's done to save money of course , it's cheaper to keep an interviewer locked in a studio than out on the road, but when I heard a town crier shouting "Oh Yea, Oh Yea," on the phone - I knew "The End Was Nigh !"

The same can be said for the practice of asking people to come into the studio to be interviewed. This also saves the reporter burning up motor fuel, but here again the result is a sterile item, and very often a whole sterile programme.

Although the BBC constantly denies that its programmes have been dumbed down, I believe they've been on the slide for a long time, and with the coming of cheaper programmes and a general tightening of the belt, came the gangsters. These were young people coming straight out of college and into production with degrees in things completely inappropriate and using radio, and indeed the BBC, as stepping stones to more lucrative positions. These kids trampled on anyone who got in their way, and this they were allowed to do as long as they cut costs. One cut my travelling expenses. His idea was that whatever mileage I did in a day over eighty miles I could do for nothing. Fortunately this little affair was soon settled (I was usually doing a lot more than 80 miles a day) and he actually didn't last long. I think he went on to rob post offices, but the writing was on the wall and getting clearer.

No doubt the crisis that eventually hit the BBC, and all those other broadcasting companies, over phone - in programmes, and I mean in particular those programmes involved in money-spinning competitions, was a genuine and honest attempt in the first place to generate the prize money, and not a penny more, but it was always likely to get out of hand. You have to wonder if it would have happened a few years ago. In the hands of the wrong people it was always likely to be a disaster.

On the subject of my pet hate, the BBC's obsession with telephone interviews in the 90's grew to ridiculous proportions. To save money on reporter's fuel bills the BBC went to enormous expense equipping the studios with super high-tech telephone equipment that must have cost a king's ransom.

This irritated me so much that on a couple of occasions, as an experiment, I included telephone inserts in a couple of reports that I recorded at home. The first involved a firm that was doing something strange, and having recorded some interviews in their shop with the staff and a few of their customers, I recorded a telephone interview with a director in Manchester, and for the second report I recorded an interview with someone in Leeds but I didn't use the costly studio equipment for either of them.

They were done on my own ordinary phone at home with a button to press if you didn't want to lift the receiver, but it was a perfectly ordinary telephone, and all I did was to hold the mic. close to its little speaker. The result was perfect, every bit as good as on the studio equipment. My questions, and most importantly – their answers, were loud and clear. This I did only on those occasions and apart from some of my closest friends no-one ever realised what I was doing. No-one, not even the sound engineers, ever realised that my telephone inserts were done on an ordinary cheap household telephone because they were just as good.

I enjoyed that, for all the wrong reasons I suppose, but also because it was so much easier. A studio slot didn't have to be arranged in advance, there was no queue to use the facility, and there weren't all those infuriating buttons to press. It was so much quicker. Therefore don't be seduced by technicalities. To misquote a well worn line or two - "While all around are losing their heads, stay practical."

It's amazing how some people's careers depend on their ability to create problems for others, but in spite of all the unkind things you can say about the nation's favourite 'aunt', the sunshine in her public face still shines through, and it's truly amazing how many doors she'll open for you. You only have to say 'I'm from the BBC' and people will let you in immediately, no matter what time of day.

Among so many, many, instances I remember late one night searching for an old engine driver, a very tall engine driver. He'd been on the old Welsh Highland railway before the war and when he was transferred to the Ffestiniog line they had to cut a hole in his cab so he could stand upright.

I wanted his reaction to plans that were being hatched to re-open the Welsh Highland Railway but I hadn't been able to contact him and it was a foul night in the hills near Garndolbenmaen, pitch black and teeming with rain. I could see a light in what I hoped was his cottage across the stream but I couldn't find a bridge, and to add to my problem my torch had packed up. I had to switch on the tape recorder and use the tiny light from the volume meter to find my way across the rocks and onto the far bank. It was a case of holding it inches from every slithery step. Once across however I was soon knocking on the door, and having found that I had the right man, I spoke the time honoured pass words – "I'm from the BBC." He then replied with a big smile, just like everyone does - "That's nice, come in."

Although I loved roaming around wet and wild Wales, producing the occasional holiday feature abroad was a pleasant change and I had some marvellous trips. I had some great working 'holidays' around the UK as well, featuring some of my favourite places like the Outer Hebrides and, as previously mentioned, the Norfolk Broads, but the journeys overseas left me with really special memories.

I travelled alone through Switzerland once in January. You can imagine how deep the snow was, but yes - the trains ran on time, even though one climbed to the top of a mountain, and high up in one village I found someone playing an alpine horn. I was sitting in a café with an alpine guide sitting out an alpine blizzard. We were sharing a bottle of high octane alpine pear juice when the proprietor decided to drag it out from a back room. You should have seen the length of it, and you should have heard it ! It made a wonderful noise to open the programme.

It was on that trip that I skied for the very first time. I was taught by a truly amazing woman, a ski instructor with only one leg. When she was a child on her way to school, she'd lost control of her skis and went under a train. In no time at all she had me following her down a hill – in my suit, collar, tie and overcoat. Afterwards she told me that a friend had asked, "Who was that, was he British ?"

That went very well, as most trips did, but I remember one to Paris that was nearly a disaster. Right from the start I didn't like the way the preparations were going. My new producer said he'd arranged it all with a travel firm and of course they were paying for everything in return for the publicity, and there was nothing new about that. That's how it always worked, but every time I spoke to this travel firm they were hazy on the details, details like where I would eat, and so I took a small emergency stove and a couple of aluminium camping pots.

After you've worked for the BBC for a few years you realise that you have to know how to look after yourself. It was a very small folding stove, about six inches square and an inch thick, and fuelled by solid blocks of some sort of white stuff. The airport staff didn't object, they weren't so fussy in those days, they thought I was just one more happy camper, but as soon as I arrived at my hotel I discovered, just as I'd expected, that no-one had taken responsibility for feeding me.

I set up my kitchen in my bathroom. It was a big hotel, very plush, so I had my own suite, and after trying the stove on a stool immediately under the smoke alarm to make sure I could use it without setting off any alarms, I went shopping.

Each day of course I visited the attractions of Paris. I did all the things that visitors do in that wonderful city, recording all the bits I thought were worth recording, and then later in the week I was talking to a British couple in the bar, and when they realised I was cooking my own dinner I told them it was the regular practice. I just couldn't resist it. I told them that whenever BBC reporters are abroad they always have to cook their own dinners. This really upset the lady. She went off saying that whenever she saw or heard a reporter speaking from somewhere abroad in future she would always imagine the poor soul having to cook his own dinner.

The best trip to Paris though was with a choir in 1982. I was sent with the Fron Cysyllte Male Voice Choir when they were invited to sing at the Unesco theatre and I had to compile an hour-long programme on the visit. It was a fabulous trip. Absolutely fabulous. It was a big choir, over seventy of them, drawn from the Llangollen area, and at that time they seemed to have won every competition going.

It's strange but a really good choir develops something you can't put your finger on. It's a mysterious thing, but to use a modern phrase – they 'click'. They develop a sixth sense, a togetherness that no other group of people seem to acquire. Even when they're scattered around an exhibition hall or a huge departure lounge, an invisible finger will sometimes press an unseen switch and instantly as one, the choir bursts into song like a shell burst. It just happens. There are no preparations. No-one leads off with a word or two to get it going, it just happens as it did in the Departure Hall at the docks in Portsmouth.

The choir was spread out all over the place as we waited to board the ship. Brittany Ferries were in on the act and so we were going to Paris via St. Malo. The place was full. It was late at night, we'd travelled from Llangollen in coaches, we were all tired, but then with no warning, the loudspeakers came to life and a girl's voice announced "Travellers to St. Malo can now board the...." and before she could get any further the choir exploded into song, absolutely filling the whole place with a fabulous barrage of huge strong voices. It was deafening !

"Up with the Jolly Roger boys and off we go to sea,
There's heaps of fun when the Jolly Roger's hung
And the wind is on the lea.
Blow high, blow low, it's off to sea we go".
(And so on.)

They blew the roof off with that – the Jolly Roger song, and you should have seen the rest of the passengers, they looked almost terrified ! They hadn't realised they were travelling with a choir, and you know, choirs are funny things when they're not on stage. They don't look like a team. They're all dressed differently and they're all ages, and they're all shapes and sizes too, but when a big choir hits that first note - 'instantly', with no warning, it can come as an enormous shock. In fact, it's exhilarating!

They hadn't sung on the coaches, which I thought was strange. It was almost as if they were saving it up for later, and when we were on the boat – what a night ! It was a long trip but I don't think many passengers went to bed. The boys of the Fron had a great audience that night, they just took over the ship, and they sang and they sang, with the passengers completely enraptured. It was a gorgeous night too. Through the windows you could see the moon reflected on the sea, and when they softly sang 'Calm is the Sea' you could have heard a pin drop. It was wonderful. There were hundreds of people, perfect strangers, in tears.

"Calm is the sea no wandering breezes disturb the deep,
The twilight slowly darkens o'er us and lulls the world to sleep
And lulls the world to sleep".
(And so on.)

The trip was all to do with a bout of co-operation between the French and Welsh Tourist Boards, and at the theatre the boys knocked that enormous French audience for six. They didn't seem to know what to expect from a male voice choir, but the boys needn't have worried. I've never seen an audience go wild like that, not an audience of grown-ups anyway. They just didn't want them to go. I lost count of the encores. Even when they left the stage they had to come back, and goodness knows what time we got away.

The journey back to our hotel was something to remember too. The singing now, with a fabulous crowd of Parisienne hostesses on our laps, was a celebration, and whoever the Frenchman was leading the way through that brilliant city bestowed upon us a very special honour. We were driven right under the floodlit arches of the Eiffel Tower.

Dinner that night was at a hotel that had been part of a royal palace. It was sumptuous beyond words, and there we dined at separate tables, each holding five or six people. We were all mixed in together, us, the organisers, and of course all those hostesses, and by the end of the main course the boys had found their voices again. Again the singing just erupted. It didn't take a conductor or an accompanist, it just happened as if by magic, even though we were all at separate tables. No-one said "Let's sing such-and-such a song," and no-one said "Okay boys – one, two, three," – It just happened, and it went on happening with perfect precision, perfect timing, without stopping all through the night.

It was a fabulous night, and all night long the waiters came to our tables, time and and time again, with armfuls of champagne, courtesy of various organisations, and I suddenly saw that at the far end of that banqueting hall there were crowds of people coming in and sitting on the floor. These people were clearly from all ranks of life, there were ladies wearing furs, there were kitchen boys in checked trousers, and fat old men smoking cigars. They were all sitting together on the floor, absolutely entranced by this choir. I don't know if anyone in that hotel got any sleep that night, the noise must have been fantastic, I only remember that when we staggered out it was light.

A journey to the French Alps was another particularly good trip. The reporter often goes alone but on this occasion there were a dozen of us, journalists from a number of papers and magazines, and we jelled immediately. They were a great crowd but it was arranged at very short notice, and I arrived in Dover knowing only that it was to publicise activity holidays. The only thing I'd been asked on the phone was "Can you ride a bike ?" A colleague in Cardiff arranged it but forgot to warn me of the rest.

My contact was a representative of P&O ferries and on the phone she told me to bring walking boots.

"I'll meet you on the platform," she said. "You'll know me because I'm a blonde and I'll be holding a P&O brochure," and she was too. As we came out of the station we headed for a brand new Alfa Romeo. "We're taking this one," she announced. We got in and I asked her where we were going. "The Alps," she said, "Didn't you know ?" No-one had told me anything and I asked if she was coming. Her reply was "You bet," and I asked what we were going to do in the Alps. "Don't you know ?" I was asked, and I said I hadn't got a clue. "Oh," she said laughing, "You're going to jump off a mountain with a parachute."

Some of us did the jump, but we did a lot of other things too. It was a great trip, now a goldmine of great memories, like playing games all through the night in a train corridor over rapidly diminishing crates of beer. I also enjoyed driving that Alpha Romeo round those alpine roads. To the alarm of my companions it was just like driving round Snowdonia every day.

The paragliding took a day to learn but I don't remember much about the 'learning'. All that remains engrained upon my memory is the moment when I stepped off the mountain. I don't think I noticed the view, I was too busy concentrating on the strings you have to pull, strings to make you turn this way or that etc. The trouble was, two of them folded the thing up and it was very important not to touch those for a while. I had a microphone attached to me but goodness only knows what I managed to say. All I remember of the landing was that it was a bit bumpy to say the least

Actually I do remember one thing about the Paragliding lessons. I discovered what many people have suspected for a long time. Frenchmen don't have much sense of humour. At one stage our instructor asked if we had any questions, and I asked if it was necessary to bury our parachutes once we'd landed. He didn't understand and stood there shrugging his shoulders

We got up to all sorts of activities out

there including some mountain biking. We were taken with the bikes on a couple of big off-road vehicles to the summit of a mountain where there was only just room for them to park side by side because the summit was so narrow. We should have had the parachutes there. We had to hang on to the vehicles to get the bikes off. It was a glorious view though, and the winter snow was closing in fast.

It was an exhilarating ride down the mountain. It took an hour and it was freezing cold, but we finished up in an empty skating rink at a ski village, clutching huge mugs of hot chocolate. Even before we'd finished them someone was saying "Help yourself to skates," which of course we did, before going off to another superb dinner.

That was a very well organised trip and so too was the one that took me round Wales on a number of trains. This one was organised for me by a researcher, and I wish I could remember his name. He was brilliant. He had someone ready with a story to tell me on every train and platform wherever I was due to stop.

The journey started by going up the single track line of the Conway valley to Blaenau Ffestiniog and later down to Portmadoc on one of the Ffestiniog's narrow gauge steam trains. That part of the journey was done on the footplate, helping to shovel in the coal as I'd so often done on that line. Indeed many of the journeys in that series were done up front in the driver's cabs, but as there's no line now between Aberystwyth and Fishguard I had to do that stretch by bus, and when Wynford Vaughan Thomas heard of it he was at the bus stop in Fishguard to meet me.

Wynford had been one of my favourite radio broadcasters since the days of my boyhood, and it was nice to see him again. He took me up to the house to meet his wife and have lunch, and as we looked out across the bay he told me how the French had invaded Fishguard a couple of hundred years ago, and how they'd turned tail when they mistook some Welsh women on the skyline for British troops. Apparently it was their red shawls and tall black hats that did the trick, and with that having been the last time Great Britain had been invaded we drank a toast to the determination that it would never happen again

He took a great interest in my journey because his father had been a school's music examiner and had travelled all over Wales by train, just as I was doing. As a child Wynford had often accompanied his father, and with great enthusiasm he was telling me what to look out for, especially the Sugar Loaf Mountain on the mid-Wales line.

He was a great broadcaster. His voice was instantly friendly and he presented his reports with the sort of enthusiasm it was impossible to ignore. When Wynford was on the radio you just wanted to listen. What a great teacher he would have made.

I think that was one of the very best features I ever made. It took five days but I turned it into ten episodes. It was certainly very challenging – talking to people as we travelled, with the inevitable comings and goings of people each time we approached a station, and as I have identified earlier, coping later with the ever-changing pace of the train during the many hours of editing. It was well worth doing though. There were so many nice moments. At Llanwrtyd Wells on the very rural 'Heart of Wales' line I got off the train to find the ticket collector was also the booking clerk. Then I found he was also the parcel clerk. He was also the station master, and when I went to the signal box to meet the signalman, he was the signalman too. He was literally the only man running the station, but then I was the only one that got off the train.

Actually that isn't entirely true. I was travelling that stretch of line with a very experienced old railwayman who was now a railway inspector. He'd travelled up from Swansea with me and at one spot he pointed out to the driver and myself an isolated cottage. It was a moment of pure nostalgia.

He told us about the Saturday nights during the war when they were always having to wait there for a signal to change. He said it was always a long time changing and because the woman living in the cottage had a lot of children they used to run a bucket of hot water from the engine and take it up to her for their baths.

It was fascinating to travel so much of the way standing next to the drivers, and from all those recordings I've chosen one little bit to share with you from the Cambrian coastline. It was only the second day and we were heading south from Barmouth, and we'd just crossed the long wooden viaduct over the Mawddach's golden estuary. Driver David Price had been a little quiet, but suddenly he took me by surprise. I'd asked him what it was like to work on that line, and with a deep strong voice he suddenly opened his heart to me.

CBBWB

Mr. Price   "When you see the Cambrian coast you see the
              creation, and I don't think there's an imagination can
              conjure up a vision of that reality. You've got to see
              it for yourself you see, and when you see it at the
              dawn, or when you see it in the evening, you see
              God's creation, and you can't say no more about that
              for the Cambrian coast. I think that pays its tribute to
              it."

It certainly did, but not everyone is quite so struck when they travel by train in Wales. On another occasion, an American woman wasn't in the mood for tributes when she got off a train at Blaenau Ffestiniog. She comes to mind because the reporter often meets other reporters on their missions. Every now and then you have to meet travel writers. These are people from around the world who you hope will write nice things about your country. If they do then obviously it's good for your region's tourism at least, and on this occasion I was meeting a group from the United States at Blaenau Ffestiniog, the town which is surrounded by slate mines and overwhelmed by their towering heaps of grey slate waste.

They'd journeyed up from Portmadog on the little Ffestiniog railway, riding in antique carriages and being pulled of course by an ancient puffing steam train. Normally this is a glorious experience. The scenery on the way is wonderful, but on that particular day it was a bit overcast. In other words it was raining as it so often does in Blaenau Ffestiniog, and all you could see were the dark grey heaps of slate.

I remember this so well. I was waiting on the platform as the train came in. The train stopped in a cloud of steam. A minute or so elapsed, and then the doors began to open, but at first no-one emerged. Then, after a few moments, some of the them stepped warily onto the platform looking bewildered. I approached the nearest one, a blonde woman wrapped in a huge fur coat. "Excuse me." I said, "I'm from the BBC, what do you think of North Wales ?" I think she heard what I'd said but at first she didn't answer, she was too busy looking around her. Then she turned to me with a look of utter dismay, "My God," she said, "They must live on nuts and berries up here."

My series travelling around Wales on trains was so well arranged that if I focus now on another series called 'The Bike Ride' you will see how these things can vary from one end of the spectrum to the other.

The train series didn't start to go on the air until after I returned. I had a couple of days to do all the editing and write the script, but each episode of The Bike Ride had to go on air early next day on the 'Good Morning Wales' breakfast programme. The idea was to cycle down through Wales to Cardiff carrying a tape recorder and a mic.on the handlebars. My task was to talk to anyone I met on the route, but concentrating as much as possible on other cyclists. I was to ask them about the whys and wherefores of cycling, cycling for pleasure, cycling to work, doing the shopping or to keep fit etc.

The peg for this idea was the fact that a bicycle factory had opened at Rhydymwyn, near Mold, and someone thought it would be a good idea for me to produce a report on the place and then ride off on one of their bikes to try it out. The manufacturers thought this would bring them valuable publicity, but there was a snag. I needed to get to Cardiff in four days and only one of the stops coincided with the location of a studio. This was the un-manned studio in a little room under the stairs of a hotel in Llandrindod Wells, one of just half a dozen un-manned studios dotted around Wales, meaning that I had to take the other tapes many miles to studios by taxi each night. Like many a broadcasting exploit this whole idea was what a rock climber would call 'exposed'. If something went wrong there was no safety net to fall into, and it very nearly crashed on the first day.

In order to make all episodes roughly the same length I had to stop in Welshpool on the first night, Llandrindod Wells the second night, Merthyr Tydfil the third night, and then carry on to Cardiff the next day, but even before I got to Oswestry on the first day the gears packed up. Fortunately though I knew there was a good bike shop in Oswestry and I managed to limp into town so they could be repaired.

Actually the gears were so poor they'd bent out of shape and had to be replaced, which was pretty bad publicity for the bike company, but revealing for potential customers because I obviously had to say what had happened, and then during the third day there was nearly another calamity on the way to Merthyr Tydfil.

I'd got as far as Brecon and so far that day I only had one person on the tape. Naturally I was getting worried, but what happened next was a miracle. I was coming down the hill into town when I heard the squeal of brakes behind me. On looking round I saw this young man in a yellow sweater about to peel off to his right. He was going across the road to a school. I quickly pulled out the mic.

CBBWB

Cyclist	(Calling out)	"How do you do ?"
Barham	(Calling out)	"Hey come back!"

Thankfully he did. He swung back and as he did he told me his name was Illtyd Sullivan of Cefn Mawr, and it turned out that he was a teacher.

Cyclist   "Yes I'm just going to take a small cycling group for a little run round Brecon, round the outskirts, hopefully a mixed group of boys and girls in the sixth form. This is our very first outing, it's a new venture, part of their society period."

I was delighted. This was a new angle on cycling. I'd never heard of a school cycling group before, and it was ideal catching him on their first day. He told me he lived near Merthyr Tydfil, and he cycled to school every day, which must have been twenty miles each way. I couldn't hold him up for long but we chatted for a couple of minutes and finding that I was headed for Merthyr he reckoned he'd catch me up after school, and miraculously he did.

It was a very good job too because although I'd picked up a couple more conversations by the time I was reaching my destination, I was still short of material, and with no more than two hundred yards to go before reaching the hotel entrance, I suddenly heard that same squeal of brakes and there he was alongside again.

I can't remember how many people I met over the years who were walking or riding round the British Isles, or riding off to circle the globe come to that. There was a man I met in Pontybodkin who was taking his little son on a motorbike to give a Welsh doll to the Shah of Persia, (I can't remember why) and then there was a man in Towyn on the coast of Merionydd who used to go to Russia on a horse and cart. I should really say horse-drawn caravan. I think he lived in it behind the Spar grocery shop. Heaven only knows why he went so far, and he doesn't seem to have returned from his last trip, but I once had a ride with him down the High Street, but that's standard practice. Producers like you to be involved, which is quite right of course, but on the other hand some do ask for a little too much.

Over-keen young producers can be a particular problem. I had one once (for a few days) who agreed that it would be a good idea for me to go and talk to the timber merchant who lived near Ruthin, who quite amazingly had just bought himself half a dozen Russian Mig jet fighters, but he insisted that the timber merchant and I should go for a flight in one. I pointed out to him that they were still in crates and seeing as we were running a daily programme we'd never have time to unpack one and bolt it together, but no he insisted that this timber merchant and I should take to the sky.

I think that was the only thing I immediately gave up on, and immediately of course we lost the story to another programme that wasn't being produced by an imbecile. On another occasion one insisted that I found a real authority on prehistoric insects when a lady in Caernarvon found one in a small piece of amber. I thought this was going to be another story down the drain, but this time I was wrong.

It was a good story. It was the week that the blockbuster movie Jurassic Park was released, telling of dinosaurs being re-produced from genetic material taken from a pre-historic insect trapped in a piece of amber. Her discovery therefore was a great coincidence, but no this young producer didn't just want a description of the thing and an interview with the delighted lady telling how she found it. He wanted an expert to actually 'identify' the insect! As you might guess, in a place like North Wales experts on certain subjects are often in abundance.

Experts on forests - yes.... experts on mountains - yes.... experts on unemployment - yes.... but experts on pre-historic insects - not really.

I thought we were going to lose this story too. However, it just goes to show that you have to try. Obviously I tried the University in Bangor where lots of experts are hidden away, and someone there put me in touch with the Natural History Museum in London, which I thought was going to be a waste of time as the interview was needed for that afternoon, and an expert in London wouldn't be able to identify an insect from my description over the phone, but this time luck was with us. Not that it appeared so at first. Their palaeontologist Dr. Paul Whalley had retired that week. That was the bad news, but the good news was that he'd come to live in north Wales. "Would you like his phone number ?" I was asked, "He's a world authority on little things in amber."

Dr. Whalley was marvellous. I just caught him and his wife going out of the house. They were going shopping in Bangor and on receiving my phone call they changed their plans and came to shop in Caernarvon. The lady who had bought the piece of amber was Mrs. Miriam Jones. She had a gift shop near the castle and as soon as she showed us the tiny creature in its piece of amber, he knew exactly what it was. We were told that it was a 'Gore Midge.'

CABWB 78
Dr. Whalley (Holding the piece of amber) "Yes, well if you look at it and think about a pine tree, this has run down as a tear-drop of resin, running down the tree so you have almost a tear-shaped drop of resin which would have trapped the insect, and it's like forty million years old, give a week or two."

He even went on to identify a couple

149

more barely noticeable specks as pre-historic ants.

Dr. Whalley   "It's an extremely interesting piece. One or two other bits are ants so you've got ants in your amber and not where they usually turn up".

He said it was a particularly fine piece and it had obviously started off a very long time ago, "Even before me," he said, but I wanted to know if that little midge and his ant friends could have belonged to the dinosaur age. I was thinking of the film of course, but the answer was no.

Dr. Whalley   "This piece of amber originated almost forty million years ago and you were hoping for something about a hundred million years ago. I'm sorry but these little insects weren't sitting on a dinosaur."

Barham   "I see, nevertheless, they could have been sitting on all sorts of interesting things that are no longer with us ?"

Dr. Whalley   "Well it was probably about 35 million years before there were any people around, which isn't bad."

To which Mrs Jones replied, "Suits me," and as a parting gift Dr. Whalley gave us both a piece of paper on which he'd typed out a little poem.

I saw a fly within a bead
Of amber clearly buried
The urn was little, but the room
More rich than Cleopatra's tomb.
         Robert Herrick (1591 – 1674)

CHAPTER K.
Keep going.

You have to keep going. No matter what happens you have to keep going. The programme might be crumbling around you, falling to bits in fact, but you don't tell the listeners, you just don't.

I remember when I was a lad of about twelve, about the turn of the forties and fifties, there was a BBC radio question time programme on the air featuring famous sports people. It was hosted by Alun Williams, and when it came to the Colwyn Bay pier I was there absolutely enthralled with the broadcasting of this live programme. I can only remember one sportsman on the panel but I won't name him for reasons that will become obvious.

The programme seemed to have gone very smoothly and when it finished Alun Williams said to the audience, "Well that's it, what a slick business this broadcasting business is." Over forty years later we were colleagues. The evergreen Alun was still cheerfully on the job and doing it as well as ever. We'd both had a tiring day. We were sitting on the balcony of the George III hotel on the river Mawddach, watching the sun go down over the estuary, and I reminded him of that statement all those years ago. He laughed. He remembered it too. He remembered it well because five minutes before going on the air that evening he was still marching one of the panel up and down the pier trying to sober him up.

Keeping going can be very difficult. One of the most difficult tests for me came one summer in Builth Wells during the Royal Welsh Show. For a couple of years I'd been presenting a weekly programme called 'Points North' which was a recorded programme featuring a miscellany of stories from the top half of Wales, and for some reason the people 'upstairs' wanted us to do it live on that occasion from this big agricultural show, which was far outside our usual patch..

Perhaps it was a feather in our cap to be brought south. If it was they didn't say so, and certainly they didn't say so afterwards, although what happened certainly wasn't the production team's fault. This one was down to that cheerful little band of brothers known as the BBC engineers.

As usual it was going to be an hour long show, and being live it had to be planned meticulously. However, in the end it was saved by a 12-year old boy. If it hadn't been for him the programme would have ended after just five minutes. That week, instead of being produced by Wendy Lloyd I was working with Jack King, like her another good producer to work with. Jack and I had worked together previously on a long running series called 'Country Fair', and on the day before our broadcast from the Royal Welsh he and I walked among the crowds around the ground deciding who to include in tomorrow's programme, and fortunately we had the 12 year old boy with us. This was my son Gareth who decided not follow in his father's footsteps.

Every day thousands of people attend this show. It's on for a week and it's the largest in Wales. There are people showing and demonstrating all sorts of things, and as the plan was for me to interview each of our chosen 'programme guests' at their stands, I was to be accompanied by an engineer who would be re-laying our programme live from a battery powered transmitter on his back. This was common practice, but because of the enormous size of that show ground we had to be careful with the music. We were sticking to the programme's usual format of interviews interspersed by recorded popular music, meaning that I had to introduce a record at the end of each interview, but some of interviewees we'd chosen were a long way apart. This meant keeping the longest records (all played in from a control room in the BBC compound) for our longest 'hikes' as we quickly pushed on through the crowds to the next interviewee.

By the time we'd sorted everything out the plan looked good. On the list we had someone demonstrating a new type of milking machine, someone demonstrating a new fishing rod, somebody breeding miniature cattle, someone campaigning for the conservation of otters, and several others that I now can't recall, except that the first one on our list was going to be a gypsy. She was a fortune teller and she had her colourful gypsy caravan up on a slight rise, and from there I was going to open the programme by describing the scene and telling the listeners what was going on in the show ring. The whole ground was on view from where she was parked, and then of course I was going to have my fortune read before introducing the first record and hurrying off to the next interview. Yes, this was going to be a good programme.

Next day, about half an hour before the programme was due to go on the air, we met in our compound, a grassy area hemmed in by a number of portacabins, and eventually the engineers got out the back- pack transmitter. They fixed it onto somebody's back, unravelled its cable and mic. and gave it to me. Someone on the steps of the portacabin control room said - "Okay Allan give us a few words," and I obliged in the usual manner, "Hello testing one-two-three, one-two-three," The engineer on the steps was talking to someone inside. I could see a couple of them in the window shaking their heads. The engineer in the doorway looked back at us and said "It's not working."

The transmitter was laid on the grass. One engineer suggested casually that if someone had a screwdriver they could have a look inside. Jack was furious, asking why it hadn't been checked earlier but no-one seemed to know, and when a screwdriver was found the back was taken off and we all peered in. It was all very casual. After poking around inside the thing for a few minutes one of them suggested using WD40. By now Jack had his head in his hands and I just stood and watched with a sinking feeling that was all too familiar. It was like seeing the build up to a disaster in slow motion, but then, it was in slow motion, no-one was hurrying, and with less than five minutes to go they declared, with regret of course, that the portable transmitter was dead, and someone ambled off to find a mic.on a long lead.

"A long lead!" Jack was yelling. "How much long lead do you think we need to go to the far side of this show ground ?"! But of course it had no effect. The engineers shrugged their shoulders and went and shut themselves in their control room. They always do that. I looked at my watch. There were now two minutes to go. Someone gave me the mic.on a long lead and a pair of headphones, and feeling numb I put them on while Jack was trying to tell me something. Basically it was goodbye.

As he ran off he shouted that he'd be back, but I didn't believe him. Stupefied I looked down at the cable hanging from my mic. and from the window of their caravan the engineers gave me a thumbs up sign. As usual it meant good luck ! Then a voice surged into my earphones. It was the announcer in Cardiff. He was announcing my death sentence. He was saying "Now we're going over to the Royal Welsh Show Ground in Builth Wells where Allan Barham is there to welcome you." And then came the music. The signature tune to my programme. It was the 'Points North' music I knew so well, well enough to know that in thirty seconds it would fade out and for the next hour I would be on the air with absolutely nothing to to say.

As the music played so the numbness in my head was being rapidly replaced with raw panic. Then suddenly, like a bolt from the blue, I had a life saving idea. I realised that if I ran to the far end of the portacabins I might just be able to see across to the show ring. Something might be going on there ! I could give them a running commentary. Yes ! Yes ! Pulling my cable behind me I sprinted as fast as I could go, but it came to nothing. Halfway past the last portacabin I ran out of cable. I tugged at it, and tugged at it, but it wouldn't come another inch. I was at the end of my tether, literally. The signature tune was fading fast and within seconds it had gone. Points North from Builth Wells was on the air.

Staring at my reflection in the bright green side of the portacabin I said, quite cheerfully - "Good afternoon and welcome to the Royal Welsh Show Ground. There are lots of people here today, my word, yes there are lots of people here today." As soon as I heard myself saying that I was cursing myself. I knew people would now be wanting to know how many. I carried on. "My word yes the place is packed and I'm looking down now on the main ring where there are .... horses, yes horses ..... jumping."

I was now leaning up against the portacabin just making it up. I had no idea if there were horses there or not, I was just describing whatever came into my mind. "Oh yes, that was a nice jump, yes a lovely jump." It was dreadful. All the time a voice in my head was telling me I'd never get away with it, but it was also going through my mind that perhaps there were two rings. In fact I felt sure there might be, so I decided to invent a few more animals. This I hoped would confuse the issue. "There are some dogs there too." I said. "Yes they look very good, and now then ..... are they goats over there ? Oh yes, yes they look very nice too."

It must have sounded absolutely terrible, and I just couldn't see how I could go on, but suddenly I heard the sound of cows 'moo-ing' and spinning round I saw the most wonderful sight. Jack had found the woman with the miniature cattle and was dragging her and two of her tiny cows by their horns into our compound. It was such a relief. I couldn't have been more pleased to see her. I practically knelt at her feet.

As we started to talk about her little cows I noticed Jack was talking earnestly to Gareth, our apprentice. I couldn't hear what he was saying but it turned out that he was asking Gareth if he could remember where we'd been around that huge ground the day before, and if he could remember the people we'd arranged to go and talk to. Fortunately he said he could, and for over three-quarters of an hour he was sprinting through the crowds and literally pulling people up to the BBC compound for me to talk to.

He saved that programme, and then with about ten minutes of the programme left an engineer emerged with the back pack transmitter on his back, signalling with a thumbs up sign that it was now mended, and we rushed off to bag a few more interviews. By then of course our carefully arranged schedule was in tatters as the interviewees had turned up at the compound in any order, and we finished the programme grabbing hold of just anybody as soon as the music in our ear-phones faded out .

The same back- pack transmitter came back to haunt me some time later. Alun Williams had a programme called 'On the Road' in which he visited towns around Wales talking to people live in the street. It was another chat and music programme going out live with records played between the interviews, but as Alun wasn't always in the best of health by then I was sometimes called on to stand in for him.

On one occasion we were in Llangollen and during the planning stage (walking round the streets on the morning of the broadcast, deciding who we might speak to) we accepted an invitation to visit an old mill. The proprietor wanted to show us how he'd converted it into a combined tea-room and museum, but because we knew the portable transmitter wouldn't transmit properly inside such a solid old stone building, my producer decided that I'd have to go in with a mic.on a long lead connected to the portable transmitter outside, and so it came to be.

Soon after the start of the programme we reached the mill. There were four of us, there was my producer and his glamorous assistant, the back pack transmitter man and myself. For this programme the musical interludes were played into the programme from a mobile studio in the street, and relayed through loudspeakers for everyone to hear, even us standing round the corner. We listened carefully and when it stopped I stepped into the building.

At the end of a long passageway the proprietor was waiting for me by a door that he'd jammed open with a wedge to prevent it snagging my microphone's cable. I introduced him to the listeners and he led me on a tour of inspection. He walked very fast, and having to pull the cable behind me I found it very difficult to keep up with him. In fact by the time the cable jammed and I couldn't go any further he'd disappeared. It was the Builth Wells nightmare all over again, except that I did have a couple of old ladies sipping tea not far away. They were terrified but I had to make do with them, and after a few words (I think about what a nice place Llangollen is) I hastily looked at my list of records, announced the next one, and got out of there.

Outside I found that our producer and his assistant had gone on to the next stop but the transmitter man was able to tell me what had happened. A woman had come along, pushed past him, and at the end of the corridor had kicked away the wedge holding the door open, allowing it of course to close on my cable. He couldn't come in and open it because we would have gone off the air, and cursing our luck we hurried off to the next venue, not realising that things were actually going to get worse.

As I said, the records were played into the programme from an outside broadcast caravan surrounded by curious onlookers parked in the middle of the town. This was the usual format for this type of programme, providing the BBC with lots of publicity, and it usually worked very well, but not on this occasion. We had a power cut !

As always the outside broadcast caravan was supplied with power from any nearby shop, and on that day all the lights went out in Llangollen and playing records was just impossible. We could still use the back-pack transmitter because it was battery powered, but we had no music. No music from Llangollen that is, but we knew we could still have music injected into the programme from Cardiff, and so a quick phone call telling them of our predicament got us the music we needed between the interviews, but at such short notice we had no idea what records they were going to use.

You can imagine it became the perfect farce. As I might have said before, we didn't have mobile phones in those days, so our glamorous assistant had to keep running to the phone to find out what was coming next, because for some reason they could only tell her what they were going to play - one at a time. So she spent the rest of the programme running up and down the high street with details of the next record scribbled on a piece of paper. This she held up panting for me to see and announce at the end of each interview. It worked most of the time but not in the fish shop where I couldn't read her writing and I had to think of another couple of questions while they frantically looked for a larger piece of paper. But of course, we had another problem as well.

With the records no longer blasting out into the street from our caravan, the only way we knew a record was finishing was by listening to our own programme on someones tiny portable radio. This was the only way I knew when to start talking again, but as far as I know nobody listening realised we were having any problems at all. That was down to teamwork, essential at times like that.

As I've already said, before getting entangled with the BBC I'd worked in the theatre, but I'd also worked in radio and television plays. Some of these were live and the experience proved to be a good start for presenting live radio programmes. In radio plays of course you read from a script, which is bad enough, but in live television it was very different. In those days before tele-recording it was just terrifying. In the theatre you could occasionally get away with a whispered prompt, but in front of those television cameras there was no chance. The simple truth is that you just had to know your lines, and I'm afraid I find those 'out-take' programmes shown sometimes on television these days quite irritating. In fact I would completely despair of professional actors not learning their lines if I didn't suspect that most of those 'so called' hilarious blunders are done on purpose to publicise the programmes and the actors.

I also remember another edition of the 'On The Road' programme where we had a snag, and that was in Holyhead, where the problem was with low flying aircraft, and often to keep going you just have to adapt to the situation. I often had to feature the various ferries crossing between Wales and Ireland, and I was once aboard a ship run by the 'Irish Ferries' company, and here I met a very serious problem.

I was working alone on a series I was recording at the time called 'A Day in the Life Of.' In each episode I was illustrating the working day of people from all walks of life. I had a lord on the programme one week for instance, and a dustman the next. It was as varied as that, and eventually I thought it might be interesting to spend a day in the company of a ship's captain crossing the Irish Sea.

We wrote to the company and they responded accordingly, and on the appointed day I boarded one of their ferries in Holyhead. In those days the crossing took three and a quarter hours and during the whole of that time there was no sign of my interviewee - the captain. The purser made excuse after excuse as to why the captain wasn't quite ready, but he never appeared. I'd travelled with my microphone on several ships in the past, usually on the bridge, and as it was a perfectly calm and sunny day I couldn't see why there was a problem .

Eventually we got to Dublin and I sat there trying to figure it out. I even wondered if he'd missed the boat, but on the way back I settled on the second best option. I went to see the purser. "How about me calling this week's programme – A Day in the Life of a Purser ?" I said, and his sparkling Irish eyes were smiling immediately. "Oh now sir, that's a wonderful idea." he said. "That is sir, that's what I call the perfect solution." And so he became the star of the show and I didn't ask again where his captain had got to.

I was lucky enough to have quite a few series of my own. 'Summer Holiday' was a good one. That ran for four summers, and for an hour each week I was on the air visiting all the latest tourist attractions, and then there was another that ran during the summer months called 'My Kind Of Town.' That was a sort of 'Down Your Way' produced by one of the best, Alan Stennet who was always very thorough. Then towards the end there was 'Back With Barham', a look back over the years at some of my favourite stories, produced by another favourite long serving colleague Dewi Smith. He had a lively sense of humour and Herbert Williams and Dai Nicholas were good to work with too, like many others who's names have faded, and there were several women I enjoyed working with, but they were always on the move and their names have gone too. So many nice people.

One of the best men I worked for was Bob Atkins who, for just a short time, was our Head of Programmes. On his arrival in Wales he promptly became the only Head of Programmes that I remember to come out of Cardiff to meet the reporters, arriving at my house to present me with a bottle of whisky I might add, and I remember him telling us that weekend about another story of 'best laid plans' gone astray.

Some time before coming to Wales he'd been working on the Esther Rantzen show which some of you will remember on television, and on one occasion they were in a farmhouse filming a talented duck. I honestly can't remember what the duck did, I think it might have done the washing up or the ironing, but it meant them being there all day. As usual with television, it was a big crew and by the time they were ready to go they'd literally eaten the farmer's wife out of house and home. They'd scoffed everything in sight, home-made cakes, gallons of tea and coffee, and heaven knows what else. When at last it was time to go all the equipment was packed into half a dozen cars and they said their goodbyes. Unfortunately, as they reversed across the yard, they ran over the duck.

I had to go and see a few ducks in my time. One had been born in Bangor On Dee with its wings on upside down. It flew okay, but I can't remember now whether it flew upside down or backwards.

There are so many stories I've forgotten. After so many years it all became a bit of a blur, but I do remember where I met the 83 year old foundry worker. He was in Rhuddlan and considering what a hot and dangerous fume-filled place a foundry inevitably is, he was absolutely remarkable. He told me the secret of his long life and good health was down to deep breathing first thing in the morning, and I remember him telling me how he got the job. He lied about his age. He said he was only 63. He certainly knew how to 'keep going' and so did the old boy who was employed collecting the trolleys at a supermarket in Pensarn. He was out in all weather, hail, rain sun and snow and he was 87.

Forgive me please but I feel a list coming on. There was the 70-year old wicket keeper, the 80-year old man playing league table tennis every week for Llandudno Youth Club, the 100-year old man in Ruthin who walked three miles every day with his wife to do the shopping, and the 103-year old woman who was still knitting for charity. She was a jolly old soul who kept slapping my knee, and then there was the 60-year old football referee, and the 83-year old bridesmaid, who, I might add, didn't bother to catch the bouquet. Also there was a woman best-man, but that's another story.

I admire people who keep going. There was David Snowdon - Jones who achieved his ambition to walk up Moel Famau a thousand times for charity, and I remember Reg Tomlinson an old postman of Beddgelert and the schoolteacher Dennis Hoar who both walked up Snowdon over five hundred times, but Dennis Hoar was a tough little man. He was a rugby referee and teacher at a naughty boys school near Llandudno Junction, and on Snowdon he had a most effective way of knocking discipline into those little self-appointed hard men, but more about him later. He'll crop up again appropriately under 'T' for terror.

Snowdon is a killer, especially in winter. It's the cold, the snow and the ice that kills most people. For the Queen's 25th anniversary bonfires were built all around Great Britain, and all were to be lit at the same time to create a network of fiery celebrations. They might have been scheduled for midnight but seeing as the Snowdon one was enveloped in thick cloud and we were all freezing to the core, ours was lit early. There was no chance of it being seen from anywhere and the visibility was so grim I nearly didn't find it.

I started out for the summit at about 10pm and reached the top in just on the hour that night, probably because it was so cold, but I found no sign of a bonfire. I knew that wood for it had been taken up by a helicopter therefore I knew it must be there somewhere, but it certainly wasn't on the summit. The mist was so thick that even with a good torch you could only see about a yard in front of you, but suddenly and quite miraculously, I almost bumped into a small group of people. I think there may have been three or four of them, and without seeing me they past in single file, silently like a line of ghosts gliding eerily past, seemingly semi-transparent in the mist. A few seconds later and I would have missed them, and as I tagged on behind the last man I saw he was carrying large boxes of matches in a plastic bag. "Looking for a bonfire ?" I asked cheerfully and he jumped out of his skin. "Stick close," someone said and eventually we found it on Crib y Ddysgl.

I don't think I've ever been colder than I was that night. I had to work the tape recorder with my knuckles. I'd completely lost the use of my fingers, but the weather can be remarkable in any part of Snowdonia. I was driving home one night, going up the Nant Ffrancon pass when I was hit by stones blowing off the mountainside. It was blowing with a tremendous force and although they remained switched on my headlights were smashed and left looking as if they'd been hit by machine-gun fire.

When it comes to searches in bad weather I think the first really memorable one was in the rolling hills near Llanfair Caereinion. I was sent one day to find an old man who'd taken a disliking to the tap water and was now walking several miles with a bucket to a well in the ruins of his birthplace. I never saw this well, but I did see plenty of snow.

By phoning the village post office (the font of all knowledge when every village had one) I discovered that he wasn't on the phone but instead I was given the number of a neighbour who told me that he'd gone out but he'd be back later to go for his water. This sounded ideal as I could arrive in time to go with him, but there could be a snag. I'd been told he was very elderly. That always means you have to be careful. For some, old age brings problems with speech and hearing, and there is nothing quite so embarrassing as trying to interview someone who is stone deaf. "Is he okay to speak to ?" I asked, "You know being elderly," I added, and the lady at the other end thought for a moment, then she said, "Well yes, he's getting on a bit, but he's alright you know, yes he's alright." So off I went.

It was a difficult journey. It was snowing hard, and when I arrived the neighbour told me that he'd already gone to the well. She gave me some directions, and although the snow was getting deeper I managed to find the farm where she'd advised me to leave my car, and there I found a man covered in snow sitting on a wall. "Can I leave my car here ?" I asked, but he didn't answer. I asked again and still he didn't answer. I took a deep breath. "Do you know where I'll find the man who comes with a bucket to collect water from a well ?" Again he didn't answer, but he did nod. He nodded over his shoulder towards a vast blizzard-strewn icy white terrain, identical in every way to the arctic. He then closed his eyes and appeared to nod off, so I abandoned any further questions (and quite a lot of hope) and set off to search for the man with a bucket.

As I trudged through the snow I was looking for footprints, but it was snowing so heavily now there were none to be seen, and of course with time running short I was worried about getting the car back to the main road, let alone back to the studio in time. The conditions were atrocious, however at last I spotted a figure on a distant hill. Eagerly I hurried towards him, half blinded by the falling snow, hoping of course that it was indeed him, and sure enough when at last I got there, it was a man carrying a lump of ice in a blue plastic bucket.

He stood grinning as I hastily plugged in the microphone and explained who I was, and then I quickly launched into a string of questions – "Why come all this way ? What was wrong with tap water ? Was it worth the trouble ?" – all that sort of thing, but all I got was a big toothless grin. A big toothless grin and some very cheerful mumbles about his brother being up a tree.

I think I was suffering from shock, because I continued to ask the questions, time and time again infact, until in the end I gave up, said goodbye to him, resisted the strong urge to go and see the neighbour, and drove home.

You do need to be fit in order to be a roving reporter. My fitness, once I'd finished playing football, was down to playing in a league badminton team for thirty odd years at Dolgarrog, and if you work for the BBC badminton is an excellent way of dealing with your frustrations. It's fast and furious and the rallies go on forever, and I can tell you that there is a huge difference between the roving reporter and the armchair studio 'presenter'. Time has gradually given this comfortable creature the necessary ability to remain motionless for long periods and acquire a middle age spread, and the only reason it didn't happen to me is that when I had a series to present I usually had to do most of the reporting as well.

I remember on one occasion, when

standing in to present someone else's programme, I even had to be the studio doorman. It was an afternoon I'll never forget. At the time I was presenting 'Points North' as well as working for 'Good Morning Wales' and the afternoon 'Home Run' programme, and so I couldn't spare the time to go down to Cardiff. As a result we did it from the Wrexham studio which at that time was an unattended studio in the attic of an old office block. I say 'we' did it in Wrexham, but actually I was there alone while the production team stayed and twiddled the knobs in Cardiff.

The programme was another in the 'chat and music' form, except that on this occasion it contained more studio guests than taped interviews, and it might have been easy enough to handle if the guests had been asked to arrive before the programme started, and it might have been alright if they'd all arrived together, and it might have been alright if the studio hadn't been at the top of three flights of stairs ! Every time we broke for music I was rushing down the stairs looking for missing guests, dragging them up the stairs, seating them by the mic. and rummaging through my notes before the end of the record.

As Alun Williams said, with tongue wedged firmly in his cheek, all those years ago - "What a slick business this broadcasting is."

The reporter not only has to endure exhaustion but sometimes starvation too. I remember coming out of Barmouth late one night and joining a long queue at a chip shop. I was ravenous but I knew I wouldn't have enough money for a fish, but when I got to the counter I didn't even have enough for the chips.

It was very embarrassing being turned away in front of all those people, and on another occasion, having worked all day down on the Lleyn peninsula, I found myself diverted to Anglesey to interview someone in the Sergeants Mess of RAF Valley. I remember it was an interview with a sergeant who was trying to drum up interest in some form of oriental unarmed combat, and on the way out I found myself passing through a room that was empty apart from a table holding a big dish of sandwiches. They looked so very inviting but someone was coming. From out in the corridor I could hear several voices approaching so I stuffed some of the sandwiches into my pockets and climbed out the window.

Pauline Roberts was good at 'keeping going' in spite of all her setbacks with officialdom. She and a horde of kids were planting trees and flowers around the village of Cemaes Bay, and in the slate quarrying village of Bethesda there was another very good example. Jeff Davies had the Douglas Arms for many years and when metric money was introduced he declared his hatred of it straight away. He swore never to give in to it and, to this day I believe, he still holds a quantity of old money which still changes hands among his regulars.

CBWB 9

(In the Public Bar.)

Barham	"Why do you still dislike metrication ?"
Mr. Davies	"It hasn't done us a power of good has it ? It was a great swindle at the time and now, of course, increasing metrication is swindling people."
Barham	"Do you think so ?"
Mr. Davies	"Damn certain of it."
Barham	"Do you have customers who still understand the old money ?"
Mr. Davies	"Of course we do. I mean there's nothing really difficult in understanding what a shilling is, is there ?"
Barham	"No, but when it comes to, say, three and fourpence ?"
Mr. Davies	(Laughs) "Not many things are three and fourpence now."
Barham	(Talking to customers) "Do you prefer to deal in the

	old money ?"
Customer	"Oh yes, we're used to it."
Barham	"Well, (drinking his pint) it's nice to find an old traditional pub in the real sense of the word, isn't it ?"
Customer	"It is, we can keep up with the traditions you know, instead of doing everything these foreigners want us to do !"

Jeff had a very clever son. From little Bethesda he earned a music scholarship to Eaton. However to keep going - when you're on a roll you just keep rolling, and it's the same in journalism. You find a good story, you use it, and suddenly people are ringing you up with similar stories. Stories like the 'multiple loos'.

They were quite disgusting actually, but to begin with I thought I'd found a rarity when somebody showed me one at a farmhouse near Newtown. I was taken into an outhouse and shown a plank with half a dozen holes cut into it to sit on, one for each member of the family. There were no partitions between the holes for privacy and the holes were situated over a deep trench. I was assured it hadn't been used for many years and I really didn't want to know about any others, but I kept getting invitations

At the time I was working for a producer who had a distinct lavatorial sense of humour and I found myself visiting a number of these relics, and at some I was shown how the 'produce' could be retrieved and used as fertiliser. The blessed things were turning up everywhere, even on the dockside of Port Penrhyn.. This one was very special, it was flushed out by the tide twice a day, and it was built circular so you could actually face the people you were chatting to.

With no queuing one has to admit that they must have 'kept people going' and this must certainly have been true where large families were concerned. They're even found on castle ramparts, whole lines of them. They might have been useful too."Forget the boiling lead, get the Williams family up here quick !"

It's remarkable how some people keep going. Ordinary members of the public who go on cutting the grass verges when the council can't be bothered, or cleaning telephone boxes or railway stations year in year out. Pauline Roberts, the free-lance, free spirit, tree planter I mentioned earlier, took to sweeping the streets at the crack of dawn, and on the purely domestic front I can't help thinking of the two sisters who wrote over twenty-four thousand letters to each other, but then I was always having to keep going.

Late night election programmes, bringing in the news, results and political swings of power from around the country, are only to be expected when there's a general election in progress, but in spite of wide-spread apathy to councillors, some bright spark had the idea of broadcasting another election special for the 'local' elections. Some of us said no-one would listen. Afterall it wasn't as if there had been another re-organisation, but it went ahead and I was sent to the count in Bangor.

I do realise this incident will add my name to the ranks of the 'Inept', but my defence would always be that my career was no more than accident prone. However, statistics were always a worry to me, and so at that election I got the Returning Officer to do my arithmetic. He was very good at it too, and I was able to turn up at the studio with the most marvelous set of notes. Three whole pages of wonderful figures, including all the swings and percentages and things. This was reporting at its very best.

Being late when I got to the studio there was only one other person there, an engineer - Emir, the one with the greyhound, and as we played football for the BBC we first had a chat about our next fixture. Then I went upstairs while he plugged in a few leads. It was a live report of course and before long I had the presenter, the ever-reliable Vincent Kane in Cardiff, coming through 'on air' into my earphones asking me how it had gone. "It's been a very close fight here Vincent." I said, and launched myself into this wonderfully well-informed set of notes and thoroughly boring statistics.

I had carefully numbered the pages 1, 2, and 3 of course, but the only trouble was that half-way through the second page I noticed something dreadful. Out the corner of my eye I saw the number at the top right hand corner was number 3, and not number 2. As I carried on reading I realised that I had the pages in the wrong order. Furthermore it was also dawning on me that all those lovely statistics, percentages, swings and majorities, would no longer make any sense because they now applied to the wrong parties. To put it precisely, it was an absolute mess. It was making no sense whatsoever, but I decided I'd better just 'carry on'.

Coming out of the studio I was feeling sick. Emir met me at the bottom of the stairs. "Finished ?" he asked cheerfully in the hope of being able to lock up and go home. I asked him if he'd heard it. "Yep," he said, and I asked him how it sounded. "Fine, who's playing in goal next week ?"

I'd got the whole thing mixed up and he hadn't noticed, in fact it turned out that nobody had noticed. Nobody realised that those figures didn't make sense, and that was obviously due to the fact that no-one was listening.

CHAPTER L.
Largest and Littlest, Little People, and Lady Luck.

I had to keep a slot for the largest and if you're talking about the largest then you can't leave out the smallest, so let's do it that way round. The smallest house in Great Britain is on the quay in Conway. It measures only 72 inches across and goes back just 100 inches. It's only 122 inches high and yet a man over 6 feet tall once lived in it, and furthermore the last occupants were an elderly couple, who must have got on very well together. They moved out around 1900. It's a lovely little place and you can even have a conducted tour. You can even go upstairs ! We all knew about Margaret Williams's little house, but a few years ago we realised that North Wales also had the smallest post office in Great Britain.

This post office is only as wide as a door, and from the door to the counter it measures only 20 inches. It's just big enough for one person. It's actually Mrs. Bennett's front porch. If it's raining and someone's in there before you then you get wet, and if you have a parcel to post it gets personal. This gem is in the village of Aberangell to the south of Dinas Mawddwy.

CBWB 11

Barham	(Talking to Mrs. Bennett through a screen) "It's a busy post office ?"
Mrs. Bennett	"Villagers yes but passing trade, because I'm off the main road, no."
Barham	"I was going to say what passing trade ? It took me ages to find you."
Mrs. Bennett	(Laughing) "I like it like this."
Barham	"When you're busy I suppose, people have to ..."
Mrs. Bennett	"Queue."
Barham	"Staying out in the rain."
Mrs. Bennett	"That's right, they get very wet."
Barham	"Quite a modern little counter you've got haven't you ? Nobody can actually break in because it has a glass screen."
Mrs. Bennett	"That's right. Originally I didn't have the screen."
Barham	"Well look, I have a parcel here and I'm just wondering how I post this ? My producer told me to take a parcel. I'm not sure what he meant by that. Where do I put the parcel ?"

Mrs. Bennett	"Well the quickest way to hand it to me is through the bathroom window. If you'd like to come round the side I'll open the bathroom window and I'll take it from you."
Barham	"I see. Right, round here ?" (He walks around corner of house). "This is incredible. Now then there's a window here .... oh."
Mrs. Bennett	(Through window) "Hello."
Barham	"And here's Mrs. Bennett in her bathroom."
Mrs. Bennett	(Holding open window). "You can hold my toothbrushes."
Barham	"Right, well here's the parcel." (Passing it to her).
Mrs. Bennett	"Many thanks."
Barham	"What happens now ? Back to the porch and you weigh it and I pay ?"
Mrs. Bennett	"That's right."
Barham	"Tell me, I suppose you have to be careful no-one is in the bath when the post office is open ?"
Mrs. Bennett	"Well it would only be me in the daytime, so there really wouldn't be any real fear of that happening."

She was a nice cheerful lady, and I don't think there's much chance of that post office getting any larger, I hope not anyway, but mighty oaks do grow from little acorns, and sometime in the sixties I saw the birth of a very large oak which became known as 'Iceland'.

The giant food company Iceland grew and grew until it became one of the largest retail chains in the United Kingdom, selling frozen food all over the country from their enormous space-age freezer factory on Deeside. In its earlier days however it was operating from a run-down back street garage in Rhyl, and from there the young proprietors – Peter Hinchcliffe and Malcolm Walker, were selling their products to local hotels. One day, to generate publicity, they froze some fruit juice in a dustbin with a pick handle sticking out the top and declared they'd made the world's largest ice lolly. I was sent to see it and have a lick. If I'd invested a fiver with them that day I might be as rich as them now. However, many years later in 1994, I went to their smart new headquarters to meet them again.

CBWB 8

Barham	"Well you've certainly come a long way. Just how big is your business now, you're multi-millionaires presumably ?"
Peter	"Well we've got around 700 stores now across all of England, Scotland, Wales and Northern Ireland. We've got 17,000 employees, and our company turnover is about 1.3 billion pounds."
Barham	"Did you ever dream that it would ever get this big ?"
Malcolm	"Of course, it was all very carefully planned. (He laughs). No idea really. We just started the business and all we ever said was that we were ambitious and didn't look too far ahead, just concentrated on the immediate problems and just doing everything right if you like. I mean, in as far as attention to detail and quality, and taking a longer term view, the future sort of takes care of itself, and the business has grown steadily. We're not an overnight success, we've been in business together for 23 years and it's just been a very steady year after year increase in sales and profits."
Barham	"You had an extraordinary start didn't you ? You were both trainee managers of Woolworth's ?"
Peter really	"We both worked for Woolworths and we were quite keen to do something as a sideline and we saw a guy on the roadside selling strawberries. He was just about ready to pack up so we bought his stock of strawberries and decided that pitch was important,

position was important, the same as in retailing today. He was on a secondary road in the countryside and we thought if we took his strawberries the next day, which was a Sunday, onto a busy main road on the Horseshoe Pass, then we could probably sell them for more money and sell them quicker than he was doing, and that's what we did the following day."

It's a great story. They soon started to experiment and found that fruit could be frozen. However, a shock was in store. The bosses of Woolworths had heard that two of their staff were selling fruit at the roadside and they didn't like it. The boys were told that this was beneath the high standards of the dignified behaviour expected of Woolworth's personnel, and if they did it again they would be sacked. Well, they needed the money and so they did do it again, and fortunately they were sacked.

Peter "Yes. I think it's quite satisfying that we've got more stores than Woolworth's have now, so yes that really is quite satisfying."

Barham "I bet it is."

I've made a note here . It says 'World's Largest Piano'. I remember it was pretty big but I can't remember now where I found it, but among the largest things - I remember the young man with size 18 feet at Prestatyn, and I once saw 20 people in a phone box, and 41 in a bed, but actually just 3 people in a phone box can be a crush when 2 of them are big fat policemen.

Whenever the time came for a General Election I was often sent with the outside broadcast van to cover the count in Caernarvon. You know how it goes at the declaration, the Returning Officer reads aloud from his notes – "John Smith," and before he can give the number of votes you whisper quickly into the mic. – "Conservative," or Labour, Liberal or who ever, and so on through the list, and then after doing a few interviews I usually had to go on to the event in Denbigh.

There was never any hurry to get to Denbigh. I used to go home for breakfast first. They were always very civilised in Denbigh, never finishing the count until late the next morning, and in those days (before mobile phones) all I had to do there was to get to a phone box, phone in to the election programme (if it was still on the air by then) and give the result. But General Elections, more than any other kind of elections, are fussy events and if you choose to be present in the room when the count is in progress the Returning Officer usually insists that you don't leave that room until it's all over.

On one occasion in Denbigh the count went on so long I was certainly in danger of missing the end of the programme. This was cause for concern because, as I have said earlier, the producer's constant plea with an on-going election programme was always - "Even if there's no result yet - give us something, anything, to keep us going." Nonetheless it took a long time to persuade the Returning Officer to let me out so I could get to a phone, and permission only came with a condition. The result by then was almost certain but he ruled that I could only talk about the different last minute campaigns the candidates had been conducting, and to make sure I didn't jump the gun and pre-empt his declaration, I had to be accompanied by two very large policemen.

Whenever I see that phone box outside the town hall I draw a deep breath, something that was very difficult to do on that occasion. Try it one day. Try going into a phone box and try reading from your notes live into a radio programme whilst being squashed between two big sniggering coppers.

Colin Bowcock was an amazing man. He was a gardener at an estate near Mold who took it upon himself to grow enormous vegetables, like his two hundred weight pumpkin. He finished up with several world records, and then there was an old boy in Rhyl with potato plants over seven feet tall, and another old boy in a caravan at Overton with peas that disappeared into the clouds, and Gwilym Hughes of Dolgellau belongs here somewhere. According to the Guinness Book Of Records he was the world's greatest film fan. He'd assembled a whole reference library on the subject too, and when I saw him last he'd watched over 30,000 films, mostly seen on videos because there hadn't been a picture house in Dolgellau since 1966.

Getting back to physical size though, rather than numerical size, have you ever seen the big oak tree in the Ceiriog Valley? It's not so tall but it certainly is a big tree. Its girth measures 43 feet, and it's said to be the broadest in the land and well over a thousand years old. I don't know if its true, but I was told that Cromwell's troops gathered under it before attacking Chirk Castle. (It must have been raining again). Although it's still in leaf, its trunk is now completely hollow and split in several places. You can actually walk around inside it, and some years ago a farmer put a gate on the widest gap and turned it into a stable for his bull.

Broadcasting house is a pretty big place. The Broadcasting House at Portland Place in London that is. I mention this because it was a good experience to work there. I was still working for BBC Wales but for a year I spent part of every week there working on the 'Checkpoint' programme, but more about that later. It was certainly big enough to get lost in, and so was Bush House the headquarters of the BBC's World Service. My involvement with the World Service meant that I was sometimes there too, and the most remarkable thing I remember about Bush House was the canteen. I'd never seen such a colourful assortment of dishes, dishes from all over the world for the broadcasters of the world.

Broadcasting on the World Service demanded a certain style in your manner of speech. There had to be absolutely no hint of an accent then other than posh English which, being an actor, I could manage. The speed of your speech had to be slower too.   There was in fact a speed limit with a maximum number of words spoken to the minute. The clarity of your voice was important too, essential in fact, but then when I started in this business it was essential on the domestic services too, not like today, but I'm getting off the subject now.

This next bit is about 'little people'. The reporter often needs to interview children but they're not always the best material. They're often shy and only manage to mumble incoherently, and sometimes the little swines just run off. But reporters often need the opinions of children, but unlike the newspaper reporter, who can make sense of a few mumbled words as he scribbles them down, the radio reporter needs words that we can all hear and understand. This invariably leads to a problem that we were never able to solve. Often, with no time to be fussy, we nearly always put the worst types of children on the air, the precocious, the cocky know-alls, and of course the bullies who pushed everyone else out of the way.

One thing is for sure, you can never predict what a child is going to say, and it used to amuse me no end that our city-bound producers, especially in London, never understood the ways of the countryside and the practical minds of country people, or indeed the practical minds of their children.

I remember years ago, a farmer's dog called Bonzo was lost down inside a web of crevices on the top of a mountain called Moel-y-Slates near Trawsfynydd. I was sent on three consecutive days to report on the efforts to get it out, but in spite of what my London producer thought, it wasn't such a rare occurrence, and if the way down between the rocks is too narrow for a man to squeeze through, and crowbars and muscle power can't shift them, then there's nothing that can be done. Anyway, on the third day it looked hopeless. The dog could no longer be heard down there and my producer asked me to go back and ask the farmer's children how they felt about losing their 'pet'. I told him that farm dogs are 'working' dogs, not pets, but that didn't deter him.

He wanted sobbing children.

I knew he was going to be disappointed, and as they gathered round my car I said, "Now children, how do you feel about losing your dog?" They looked at each other but said nothing, and so I asked "Do you miss him ?" and that resulted in a few 'nods', so it looked as if we were getting somewhere, but of course we weren't. They went quiet again, until one little boy declared with shrug "We've got some more."

You can never beat kids for candid judgement. At the performance of a play specially written for young people at Theatre Clwyd I intercepted the first boy to leap from his seat as the curtain came down. "Well young man," I said, holding out the mic, "What did you think of that ?" With a look of absolute disgust he said "Where's the toilet ?"

I did meet some nice families. The Jones family of Beaumaris for instance. I think there were at least half a dozen of them and all but one played in the local brass band. They all played in their tiny sitting room for me once, and the house literally shook with the noise. It was wonderful.

Here's a nice little tape. It's from Anglesey and it's a 'chant' which dates back to goodness knows when. The children here were from a primary school in Beaumaris. They were walking through the town reviving a custom that was once common on the island when children used to go round the farms at Easter, begging for eggs, in Welsh of course.

CBWB 1

Barham   "Some of these children are in Easter bonnets, some children are thinly disguised as rabbits, and they're all clapping bits of wood together like butter pats".

(Children recite their verses.)

"Clap Clap gofyn wy   "Clap Clap ask for an egg
Hogyn bach ar y plwy.   For the little boy on the

177

parish (poor.)

Clap Clap gofyn wy Ac yna'i roi ar y llwy.	Clap Clap as for an egg Then place it on my spoon
Clap Clap gofyn un Wy mawr melyn I mi fy hun.	Clap Clap look for one A big yellow egg for me
Clap Clap gofyn dau Wy I frecwast yn well na chnau.	Clap Clap ask for two An egg for breakfast is better than nuts/seeds
Clap Clap gofyn tri Dau I mam ac un I mi.	Clap Clap ask for three Two for mum and one for me
Clap Clap gofyn way' Sgwni pwy a gaiff y mwya'."	Clap Clap I ask for eggs I wonder who will get the most/biggest."

I'd love you to hear the children of Lixwm Primary School. Their headmaster Brynmor Charles was a 'rock' fan and he turned out some incredible young rock bands. They were sensational with their recordings sounding identical to the originals. Without seeing them you would never know that the eldest was eleven, and also in that age group were those in the remote sea-side quarrying village of Trefor with their famous 'Foo Foo' band, playing their (sort of) comb and paper trumpets.

Now for 'Luck'. We all need a bit of this stuff from time to time, but in Prestatyn there was a man who probably had more than his fair share. He had a lawn full of four-leaved clovers. He didn't know how he'd got them, they just grew there for him. His name was Hywel Hughes.

BBWB 101

Barham   "I suppose you have people coming all the time for these four-leaved clovers ?"

Mr. Hughes   "Oh yes, I've had many letters too, various requests, I suppose I'm just one of the lucky blokes. I'm just lucky."

Barham   "Yes, oh he's just picking one. That's a nice one."

Mr. Hughes   "There used to be such a lot here, but I've given so much away you know."

Barham   "Well what's been happening to you people since you've been collecting your four-leaved clovers ? What about your sister here ?"

His sister   "Well I've had no luck because I've fallen downstairs and broken a chair."

(Neighbours laughing.)

Barham   "Really ?"

His sister   "So I don't think I'll bother any more."

Barham   "What about this lady ?"

Lady   "Well I'm still waiting."

Barham   "And when did you get your first four-leaf clover?"

Lady   "Well about twelve months ago and I'm still waiting."

(Neighbours laughing.)

Barham   "And what about this gentleman over here ?"

Gentleman   "Oh I think I'm very lucky. My car has started first go for the last two years."

(Neighbours say 'oooh')

Barham   "Oh well that's something, yes."

Man   "I had £50 given to me on Sunday, an old aunt of mine gave me £50."

Barham   (To another gentleman) "What about you ?"

Gentleman   "The only time I ever found one by accident was when I was mushrooming, and about a fortnight later I broke my leg playing football."

(Neighbours laughing.)

Barham   "Well I don't know, Mr. Hughes have they bought you any luck ?"

Mr. Hughes   "Oh I won a great big amount on the football coupon a fortnight ago – 85p"

(Much laughter now from neighbours.)

Barham   "I hardly like to deprive you of these four-leaved clovers, I think you need them."

Like I said, everyone needs a bit of luck once in a while. I remember many years ago being sent on what looked like another fool's errand. A film company was shooting part of their production in Garthewin Hall at Llanfairtalhaiarn. I don't remember the name of the film but the Italian director had told the media to keep away. However, the programme I was with at the time 'Good Morning Wales' had a gaping hole in the running order so I was sent to try and get something on it.

It seemed a guaranteed waste of time, but as I drove up the long drive I found an elderly man struggling up the hill so I stopped and gave him a lift. I know this sounds like a parable, but he turned out to be the owner. "Have you come to see them making the film at my house ?" he asked cheerfully. "Yes" I said, "I'm from the BBC." This pleased him no end. "Oh wonderful," he said, "I'll take you in to meet the director."

Swallowing his frustration like a true gentleman, the director accepted me onto the set with every courtesy, and after I'd recorded some of the action, he and some of the cast gave me some excellent interviews. Of course most film directors are wary of reporters. They worry that you will rubbish their story, and of course they're nearly always struggling to keep up with a tight schedule.

When he was filming Macbeth in the seventies, Roman Polanski did all he could to keep us away, especially from Black Rock sands where he had the witches doing their 'Hubble bubble' bit. He'd been upset the day before when he was signing up extras in the Ffestiniog village hall. Someone new to the area, and clearly with experience of the labour market, told them that Polanski was trying to pay less than the going rate, and for a while the little yank disappeared in a seething mass of discontented local men. When he emerged he looked quite shaken by the experience, and his interview with me soon after was terse to say the least, but I needed a snatch of the action and early the following morning I was mingling in the rain with the 'props' people on the beach. With my anorak hood showing only my eyes I was quite unrecognisable, and within half an hour I was standing next to the camera as the witches did their demented bit - "Hubble bubble toil and trouble." (Go back and pay them double).

Occasionally I had to meet people who'd won big prizes, and I remember a marvellous lady in Old Colwyn who'd found the key to winning those competitions you find in newspapers and magazines. The key incidentally was hard work and many hours spent in reference libraries. But in this chapter I can't overlook the unlucky people, like the man who retired at 65 only to find that his wife was expecting twins. Actually he said he didn't mind but I would have fled the country, and reporters too collect their share of bad luck. I took half a dozen people once to comment on a train passing down the line at Amlwch. It was the only train using the line from a chemical works and there was a plan to run a passenger service too, but for just one day a year the line was closed for a maintenance check. You can, of course, guess the day I chose.

For some people, bad luck is a permanent way of life. Of these I remember several, especially one who reckoned he was the unluckiest man in Great Britain. He came to live in Barmouth from Peterborough, and when we learned that he always spent friday the thirteenth tucked up in bed just to keep out of harm's way, I was sent to find him.

This cheerful but chronically short-sighted man became familiar around Barmouth in his extremely thick glasses, but his bad luck was something that he revelled in. He was always telling you how, on several friday the thirteenths, he'd walked through plate glass windows and fallen off things and how, when he was on the buses, he'd wrecked two cars and a van in one day, even though he was only the conductor. It seems that his bad luck used to spread like wildfire, and on one occasion he was walking alongside a river when five passers-by fell in. In fact it was this concern for others that prompted him to stay in bed every friday the thirteenth. His name was Bob Renphrey and this is an extract from that first time I met him. I'd managed to contact him by phone and when I got there the front door was open, so I ventured in.

CBBWB
(Climbing stairs.)

Barham   "He assured me on the phone that he always spends friday 13th in bed so I'm making my way up the stairs ..... presumably there's a bedroom here somewhere .... (Barham calls to him) Mr. Renphrey, where are you ? .... Ah, I think that was a faint reply."

(Barham knocks on a bedroom door).

Mr.Renphrey   (Faintly) "Come in."

Barham   "Well this seems to be the room. (He opens door) Here he is sitting up in bed. Hello Bob, there you are I've bought you a newspaper."

Mr.Renphrey   "Thank you very much, more money saved."

Barham   "I don't know if you've seen any papers today, you've really been in bed all day have you ?"

Mr.Renphrey   "I've been in bed since before midnight last night and I shan't move until tomorrow morning."

Barham   "Do you mind if I plonk myself down on the bed here ?"

Mr.Renphrey	"Be my guest."
Barham	"It's very comfortable anyway."
Mr.Renphrey	"Oh yes I like my comfort."
Barham	"You've got a tea making machine on the far side there, telephone on the pillow next to you, so you're in touch with the outside world ?
Mr.Renphrey	"Well the outside world is in touch with me."
Barham	"People are ringing you up then during the day, asking how you are ?"
Mr.Renphrey	"Yes I've had several people ring me up thank you very much, wishing me happy friday 13th,like I do for you."
Barham	"And on the bed here you've got a couple of cats. Just for luck ?"
Mr.Renphrey	"Yes, well there should be three actually but we've just had an accident. Next door's dog attacked one and I had to send for a friend to take her to the vet."
Barham	"Oh dear."
Mr.Renphrey	"Friday the 13th. Even in bed I'm in trouble."
Barham	"Where's your wife ? I hope she didn't mind me coming in like that, it's just that the door was ajar."
Mr.Renphrey	"I told her to leave it ajar because she's taken the dog for a walk on the beach."
Barham	"Oh I see, well now then, how long have you been spending every friday the 13th in bed ?"
Mr Renphrey	"Well since about 1979. This will actually be the eighteenth time."
Barham	"Is it worth it ? Is it … I mean, you're so accident prone ?"
Mr.Renphrey	"Oh definitely. I actually stay in bed for the safety of others."

Other people certainly did need protecting from him and it wasn't only on friday the thirteenth either. On one occasion the local pantomime producer (farmer Tony

183

Turner, who obliged marvellously whenever you needed a moaning farmer) very unwisely tried to exploit his fame. A lot of people came to see him, but the scenery collapsed and it landed on everybody else but him.

He then moved to Rhyl and for a while he helped the boatmen, singing a cheerful little ditty every day on the promenade -

"Have a boat-ride by the sea-side,
Give yourselves a thrill,
Have a boat-ride in Rhyl.
Come along children,
All the kippers you catch you can keep".

Wonderful. For a while it looked as if this change of location had lifted the curse, but it wasn't long before he was in deep trouble again. It was coming up to a general election and he insisted on helping the Liberals.

I have one more entry for this chapter. He was a young man, a teenager actually, who I can't make up my mind about. I initially thought he was lucky, very lucky, but on the other hand perhaps not. Because his father taught at Colwyn Bay's Penrhos College he was taught there too, but it was a girls school. He was the only boy among 299 girls. So what do you think ? .... No, perhaps not. Not with his father there.

CHAPTER M.
Money, Monsters, and Mavericks.

In the sixties a man in Llandudno called Richard Williams was printing money. He called it Welsh money and he stayed out of prison simply because his Bank notes were technically known as 'promissory' notes. Printing his own notes was clearly designed to make him a fortune but they were perfectly legal and negotiable. He'd worked in a Bank so he knew a thing or two about money, and I was so taken by the idea that I bought a couple to keep for curiosity's sake.

BWB13

Barham	"I understand this is perfectly legal, but is your money legal tender ?"
Mr. Williams	"No. Our Welsh pound notes are not legal tender, neither for that matter are Scotch pound notes, even in Scotland which surprises most people. What legal tender means simply is that if I owe you a debt and I offer to pay you in terms of legal tender money, then you must take that money, whether you like it or not, whether you have confidence in it or not, and if you don't take it, then the debt becomes null and void. Our notes are both legal and negotiable and they are obviously of interest, but there is no financial advantage in using them."

It boiled down to the fact that you could accept them in payment or accept them in your change, or even accept them in your wage packet if you wanted to, but you didn't have to, and if you did accept them you'd probably get stuck with them ! Nobody was obliged to accept them from you.

Far superior to Mr. Williams' Welsh money was the Wrexham groat. This was the currency of a local economy in Wrexham which was similar to several others that sprang up around Britain, mainly I think in the 1990s. I was told the idea came from Canada and was known as Lets, which stood for 'Local Exchange and Trading System'. Basically, people who participated exchanged goods and services without parting with a single note or coin of the realm. Instead they either did a straight swap with others in the scheme, or they paid each other in 'groats' drawn from a book like a cheque book. As and when they ran out of groats, they then had to do some work for other members in order to earn some.

It was ideal for people who provided services, and the members I spoke to were available for a whole variety of things from babysitting to plumbing and dressmaking to decorating. The scheme was held in shape by an administrator, and to the surprise of a lot of people it was perfectly legal. It seemed to be a cheaper way to buy goods and services, and there was no VAT involved, but that's enough on the subject of money. We'll turn now to monsters.

Moving around his patch the reporter can come across several. My favourite two were splashing around in the water. One was swimming around in Bala and the other was in the sea at Barmouth.

Tegi, the Bala monster (named after the real name of Bala Lake – Lake Tegid) hasn't been reported recently, but he was particularly active in the 1970s when several people saw him, including the late warden Mr. Dewi Bowen in 1978. I regarded Mr. Bowen as a reliable witness. I couldn't imagine him making it up when he told me he was looking out of his office window when he saw this 'thing' travelling across the lake. It's a big lake, and at nearly five miles long it's the largest natural lake in Wales but, and here's the surprise, Tegi is a 'mini' monster. Everyone who sees it describes it as being about eight to ten feet long, and some say it's like an upturned rowing boat but, big or small, it still sounds very strange.

CBWB 15

Mr. Bowen   (In his office) "Well this is where we were, sat having a cup of tea, and I happened to look out of the window onto the lake and there was this 'thing' whatever it was, about eight feet long and travelling rather slowly right across the lake. It was only about 200 yards away from the foreshore so I had quite a good look at it. There would be about four or six inches sticking out of the water. My immediate reaction was to dash out of the office, jump in the car and arrive at the spot where this thing should have come ashore. Having got there, there was no sign of the thing."

On another occasion another eye witness was a Mr. Rowlands, a local greengrocer. He was fishing from the shore with his cousin. They saw it coming towards them, following one of their lures into the shallows.

CBWC 8

Mr.Rowlands "The thing I told my cousin was - John we'd better wind in, in case we catch it. I wouldn't want to catch the damn thing !"

Barham "How would you describe it ?"

Mr.Rowlands "Well it had a big head, as I say about the size of a football. It had two glaring eyes which were looking at us. We had obviously attracted its attention with the spinners, and it came in towards us and looked at us, and then turned slowly and went into the deep. But at the time we were very frightened."

There were another two men I met who'd had a similar experience. They were fishing in a rowing boat when suddenly the big broad shiny black back of something 'sleek' came out of the water and swept past them so close that they rowed to the shore as fast as they could go! When I met one of them again several years later he told me that neither of them had ever plucked up the courage to go back on the lake again. I met him the day the Japanese came to look for Tegi.

It was in 1995. They were filming all round the world searching high and low for monsters and they arrived in Bala with a submarine on board a huge lorry. They were working for a Japanese television programme, but after a couple of days they gave up because once below ten feet the peat content of the water made visibility as poor as Loch Ness. Quite 'inscrutable.'

There's an interesting angle to the story of the Bala monster. One man who'd seen it on several occasions when walking the dogs first thing in the morning was convinced it was a seal. He said it used to stick its head out of the water and was obviously a seal, but when I contacted the main UK research centre where they study seals, I was told the furthest record of any seal being found away from the sea was ten miles up the River Ouse. That river is very slow running and deep, but the River Dee, which runs to the sea from Lake Bala, is sixty miles long when you take into account its hundreds of twists and turns, and as well as being a fast flowing river, it also goes over weirs.

But even this angle has a twist to its tail. Many years ago the 'military' was involved in some very secret research on the lake, and according to some of the locals they were using 'sea lions'. However, as seals and sea lions are not partial to remaining submerged for years on end, it's not likely that Tegi's related to that episode in the lake's history, and lake warden Dewi Bowen would tell you that Bala could well harbour something genuinely strange and rarely seen because, after all - look at the Gwyniad.

I went out in a boat with him once to net some of these lovely silver fish. They live very deep down, and when you cook them they smell like cucumbers. They're delicious, and they're an amazing relic from the Ice Age. They're found nowhere else in the world, so if something as rare as that lives in Llyn Tegid, why not something a little bigger ?

In 1975 something strange was turning up in the sea around Barmouth. It was seen by several people including a couple who were sailing past the town, and there were even reports of strange footprints in the estuary sand. I went one morning to the old wooden bridge over Penmaen pool where a clearly worried toll keeper told me that something had been nudging the timbers all night (Can you imagine that ?). But the only people who'd actually seen it at very close quarters were very young.

Three or four little girls were walking along the north end of Barmouth beach when this 'thing' leapt out from behind some rocks almost scaring them to death ! I can't remember the name of the girl I spoke to that night, but some years later I met another of them. Joanne Jeffs was visiting her parents and she remembered the incident very well. (Not surprising really.)

CBWB LS

Joanne   "Right, I can remember its strange shaped body. It had a flat body with a hump on, and a long neck, and it just sort of glided into the sea very quickly. It moved at an amazing pace. It was quite a size from where we were, it was quite a large sized animal whatever it was."

Today we're told that the Barmouth monster may no longer a mystery. Marine biologists are fairly sure that it would have been a Leather Back Turtle. They're not often seen around our shores but the description the girls gave seems to fit, and they are certainly big. One that was washed up dead here some time later was six foot long, seven foot across – flipper to flipper, and it weighed one ton.

Those little girls definitely had a fright, and I know it happened a long time ago but Joanne is amazing, she still goes swimming there ! But apart from driving a 50-ton Chieftain tank one day (and being told by the instructor when I reversed over a hump, that I'd gone over my car) I didn't come across many more monsters.

The one in a quarry pool near Mold was intriguing. It was quite frightening really because although no-one had seen it, there was no doubt that it was there. It was lurking in a pool sixty foot deep at Alltami, abandoned by a quarrying company and taken up by members of a fishing club. Delighted by their acquisition they stocked it with nice placid carp and roach, but before long something was finding them very tasty. The horrified members started to see evidence of their £11,000 investment float to the surface in the shape of blood stained heads and tails.

I arrived on the scene to meet club bailiff John Davies, and finding him peering into the water I asked him what he made of it.

GRMB 7

Mr Davies   "I wouldn't go swimming here, put it that way, because the amount of fish that's gone from here, and the size of the fish that have gone from here, and the tackle I've used to try and catch it - is unreal. I've lost baits with it, hit into it, lost it, gone, finished, tackle gone, everything."

Barham   "So you've hooked it, whatever it is, but it's just been too strong, too big for you to pull in."

Mr Davies   "Yes. Thirty five pound wire trace with two 0 trebles, half a mackerel to a 28lb line, and gone."

I wondered if perhaps some - one just might have slipped in a pike to stir things up a bit, but he said it was just too big, and when Alan Gee turned up he too pursed his lips and shook his head.

Mr Gee   "I've been down here bailifing when we've had one of the top carp anglers on the lake and I watched him for thirty five minutes getting dragged all over the place. I don't think it even realised it was hooked to tell the truth. It just kept swimming and swimming, and there was nothing you could do."

The club secretary, Jim Howard was one of those counting the cost , and like everyone else he too was shaking his head in bewilderment because he'd hooked it as well.

Mr Howard	"We've lost 60 to 70 prime roach between a pound and two pound in weight, and it isn't due to natural wastage or anything like that, it's purely down to this predator or whatever it is in our water taking big chunks out of their backs and biting their heads off and tails etc."
Barham	"What's it like to have it on your line ?"
Mr Howard	"The adrenaline really runs, it really does. It flows. You just don't know what you've got. We just don't know what it is, because no-one yet has seen what it is on the end of the line.
Barham	"Bit scary isn't it
Mr Howard	"Very, very, very. You know one day, this person, who ever it is, one of the carp anglers with all the good equipment, he's going to get – say a 40lb line, and then the thing maybe comes to the surface, and you'd be scared out of your wits when it comes up !"

I checked out this story again only recently and it's still a mystery. The quarrying company have reclaimed the pool and half drained it. No-one was able to fish there anymore and I was told the monster was never ever seen.

It's quite apparent that some monsters can be elusive, very elusive, shy even, but the one at Capelulo near Penmaenmawr can be found very easily on or around 6th December, and at that time of the year at least, he certainly isn't shy. This one actually has a name, it's 'Grampus' and strange as it may seem he's actually a restaurateur. He was born in Austria and once a year he enjoys 'inflicting' his diners with a little Austrian culture. As he laid into his guests, beating them with a big stick and a length of chain, I spoke to his wife Judith.

ABWB 34

Barham   (Shouting above noise of monster raving and roaring
            and people screaming) "Judith, don't you think it's
            rather a strange thing to do, for him to go round
            whacking your customers ?"

Judith   (Also shouting) "Well they all come back every year
            for it to happen again."

They do too. People book a year in
advance to get thrashed at Christmas. They start off by having a
nice traditional Austrian dinner, and then they receive gifts from St.
Nicholas. The trouble is, according to Austrian folklore, a monster
called Grampus has to have his chance to beat up all those who've
been naughty during the year, and of course he thinks that's the case
with everyone.

To begin with we saw him coming
down the street roaring like a lion, then he pressed his face against
the window. It was hideous, and before anyone could close the door
he burst in and started to attack everyone in sight. I was alright. I
was hiding behind his wife who was trying to point out to me an old
gentleman with a long white beard.

Judith   (Still having to shout) "We have St. Nicholas here
            who is saving them from themselves, so he's not
            taking them away to hell, so we've got a mixture of
            pagan and the devil figure and the Saint – St.
            Nicholas the forerunner of Father Christmas who is
            protecting everybody who has been good."

If he was supposed to be protecting
people he was an absolute dead loss, they were all getting beaten up.

Barham   "He's the gentleman in the robes and the long white
            beard ?"

192

Judith   "That's right yes and the mitre, he was the Bishop. He was a real person who came from Turkey about 900 years ago and became the Saint of children because he was very good to people with lots of children, so by the time he'd got to Austria he was becoming quite a well known figure being good to the poor."

In spite of him attacking his customers, I wouldn't describe Freddy Pigler as a 'maverick', not even an eccentric. His portrayal of Grampus is purely theatrical and only strictly seasonal, but the true 'maverick' does his own thing and goes his own way every minute of every day, and he would never dream of wearing a monster's mask . I've met many mavericks. I think these people are optimists in the main who cheerfully believe that no-one is going to notice their peculiar behaviour or attitude to life. Of course people do notice, but as most people are too polite to say anything, the maverick thinks he's getting away with it and his unusual behaviour continues unabated.

However, not being paid to be a shrinking violet, I did once feel it was necessary to point out to a man who was hoping to attract Britain's best young tennis players to his training camp, that the courts he'd built might have been better if they'd been built on flat ground. I really thought this was worth pointing out, but to be fair there wasn't much flat ground where this particular maverick lived, being on the side of a mountain, and anyway it turned out that he had a reason for building them on a slope. He firmly believed that it was a mistake to get young people too accustomed to perfect facilities.

He obviously had a point. Youngsters do expect too much these days, but on the other hand his courts did look rather weird. One went downhill steep enough to double as a ski slope, and the other sloped sideways with a dip in the middle that made you feel seasick just looking at it let alone play tennis on it. That one at least was a grass court, but in every sense of the word

– a long way from Wimbledon.

This true maverick was truly marvellous. He was an official Lawn Tennis Association coach, he was well known by the hierarchy of the LTA, but he had no faith in their coaching manuals, and his amazing optimism was absolutely typical of so many mavericks. He actually thought he could persuade 'well heeled' tennis mad parents from around Great Britain to uproot their precious sons and daughters from their 'A'-level studies (he wanted them at that age) and move them to Wales to study at a mainly Welsh-speaking comprehensive school in Caernarvon, and sleep at his hill-billy tennis centre – in a caravan. Naturally when he told me of his plans I thought they were crazy, but what turned out to be even more crazy was that before long it was happening. It didn't follow through exactly as planned. Several aspiring young players arrived to be coached by him, but they played most of their tennis on the courts at school, where soon an indoor tennis centre was built

Incidentally, next time you're chatting to your own particular tennis idol before he or she jets off to the next Grand Slam via a luxurious mansion in the sun, you might like to mention that this game that has brought them vast riches and world-wide adoration, was invented at a house near Ruthin. The house (one of those large ones standing in acres of manicured parkland) is Nant Clwyd Hall, and there's a plaque there showing where the very first court was marked out on the lawn in 1873 by the owners – the Nayler-Leylands and their friend Major Walter Wingfield.

He'd adapted it from some other sort of game played indoors, and before long lawn tennis was being played at several other houses in North Wales, including Ruthin Castle and further afield in Beaumaris Castle. Infact, it caught on so fast it wasn't long before the 'All England Croquet Club' took it up and organised a tennis championship just 4 years later at their place near London called Wimbledon.

I can't help wondering what sort of ball they used, but what really puzzles me is the name the Major chose for the game. He called it Spharistike. According to a very large dictionary in my local library it appears to be Greek for 'skill with a ball'. I don't know who campaigned to have the name changed to tennis. Equity probably. Appearing in a blazer and white flannels at the french windows and asking - "Anyone for Spharistike ?" just wouldn't have sounded right at all. And come to think of it, neither would - "Any-one for skill with a ball ?"

The word 'maverick' describes a wayward beast that can't be fenced in, and I noticed that many of the mavericks I met had taken to the open road. No fences for them. Take for instance the lady who was walking around Britain visiting Gas showrooms. They made a change from stately homes, and then there was the Dutchman touring Britain on a tractor.

BRL 8D
Dutchman   "I tour your country on a tractor. I go everywhere. I do it for charity, and I do it for a bar of chocolate. A wager."

He was towing an ancient caravan behind his tractor, and having parked them both on Llandudno's promenade with no apparent concern for local by-laws, he commenced to 'blast' a handful of bewildered on-lookers with a selection of tunes on his trumpet.

I think it's right to say that he was a real Dutchman, but Betty Lucking wasn't Dutch. She just pretended to be, and although she was only putting on an act like Freddie Pigler, I can't resist including her among my mavericks. She was a Midlands Guest House keeper at Benllech Bay and she did her Dutchwoman act around the Anglesey womens institutes. This was a truly remarkable act. She was a star, and when she came onto the 'Points North' programme she wouldn't let me get on with introducing the programme until she'd shown me her clog dance.

195

Seeing as the programme had started she was something of a handful, but this woman was unique. She'd spent some time living in Holland and she just thought that Dutch women in their white caps, aprons, and enormous great wooden clogs were hilarious. Fortunately the good-natured Dutch are not touchy about such things.

BWB161

Barham	(Introducing the programme) "It's time now for Points North."
Woman	(Repeating Barham's words but in Dutch).

(Programme signature tune starts. Woman starts to clog-dance. Sig tune fades. Woman continues to clog-dance.)

Barham	"Yes it's time again for Points North, and this week …. this week …. erm, excuse me (speaking quietly aside) do you mind, just for a little while." (Clog-dancing stops, then starts again). No, no hang on !"
Woman	(Stops clog-dancing "You not like my clog-dancing ?"
Barham	"Yes it's very nice, very nice."
Woman	"What's the matter ?"
Barham	"Later, later."

The Right Honourable Dowager Countess Chetwynd of Arthog was nothing less than a real life 'Margaret Rutherford' and was another who could cause a stir with her chosen attire. This old girl was undoubtedly my favourite from that wonderfully mad world in which I found myself. She lived alone in a great house overlooking the Mawddach Estuary called Arthog Hall, in which I can only describe as 'carefree neglect'. She had a finger in every pie, she bred Welsh Mountain cobs, and she still had an Aston Martin tucked away in the garage, which wasn't surprising because in the twenties she used to race at Brooklands.

The first time I met her was when she was campaigning to stop a firm called Rio Tinto dredging the estuary for gold, and after that battle had been won I met her on several occasions. On one occasion I had to go and see her because one of her ponies had won something notable, and upon phoning her to arrange the interview I was told "Bring your wife this time dear boy and first we'll have lunch". I knew what to expect, but my wife didn't. I let her think it was going to be a smart affair but within five minutes of arriving Christine was stirring the soup.

As anticipated we were having lunch in the kitchen, a huge dingy back of the house black dungeon hung with chains and cluttered with old meat cabinets and old bare top wooden tables, and while our host clattered pots and plates around us, Christine's job was to stand at the great stove stirring the soup while I laid cutlery out on one of the tables, and yes of course it was great fun. The old girl was fabulous.

We were doing a television piece for a change with her that day, and after the crew had arrived and we'd done our bit, the five of us, her ladyship, Christine, the camera crew and I, sauntered off down a path to a roadside cottage where her boyfriend lived. Christine and I had already met Captain Louis Cutbill a few years earlier because of his guide book for tourists – The truly amazing 'Captain's Guide.'

This old Royal Artillery man was as extraordinary as his grand neighbour and they made a perfect couple, I hope in every way. He was easily typified, he was of the 'Noel Coward' variety. He spoke with an extremely well cultured voice which was so painfully 'over-the-top' for his choice of environment. Further-more his way of dressing always had a touch of the artist about it, but he was always polite and seemed to be very kind hearted, and I suspect that he rather enjoyed being so very much out of place living on the edge of a small Welsh village.

In contrast to his neighbour's mansion, the Captain's abode was tiny, but in we all went that winter afternoon for what was going to be a 'quick one' but no-one wanted to be quick that day, the company was too good, and our piece wasn't needed until after the weekend. Some of us were sitting on boxes, others on the floor, and one thing led to another, and then one story led to another, and all I remember now was that it was one of the best afternoons I ever spent at work, and Christine drove home.

Let me read a few lines to you from one of the 'Captain's guides.' They charted walks, places of interest, tea rooms, round robin car rides, beaches of course, and although his descriptions were essentially brief and penned in an extraordinary form of cryptic fantasy, his appetite for mischief was clear to see. He pokes fun at the very people he was writing for – the tourists; the 'Charlie Rhinos' as he described them. At the Swallow Falls he refers to the coach loads of tourists in the car park. - "A top tank park, endless stream in/out mighty English troop transporters, battle cries 'toy lights'! 'Ices !' midst jolly jostling throng, dart, hover, helpful yellow/blue uniformed advanced patrol. (AA and RAC)."

The words 'toy lights' meant 'toilets' and, as you might have guessed, this was his way if mimicking the Londoners, and for just one more example of this man's kaleidoscopic language I'll turn to this page where he's directing tourists to take the mountain road from Dinas Mawddwy to the lakes of Bala or Vyrnwy. He writes, - "Mountain hair balding adventure. Wiggy ! Wig ! Hell fire path, one in four sheer unfenced precipice ledge road. Beware near bottom tight S-bend. Recommended kit spare clutch, spirit revivers. Uncle George silenced, Auntie Mable too."

I am sure that when his readers met him they must have been amazed that such colourful language could have come from a type so refined and reserved, but across the road his neighbour was exactly what she appeared to be. As they say today – with her you got what you saw. She was a full blown bustling maverick with a loud voice and all the exaggerated gestures to go with it. I don't remember seeing her slap her thigh, but I'm sure she could have done to great effect. I did however see her go through her filing system. On another day and on another story, she said - "I've got a letter I must show you" and I followed her into her study. It was a big room at the front of the house. I think it might have been a sitting room once, but now it was practically bare, except that the carpet was littered with letters. There was a reason for this, the carpet was the filing system.

"It's here somewhere." She said (several times) and she proceeded to stop and pick up letters right left and centre, discarding them over her shoulder almost as quickly as she picked them up. She was amazingly quick for a sturdy figure of advanced years, and as she made her way round the room it looked as it if was snowing, the air was so full of letters gently falling to the ground. By the time she'd reached the far side of the room they'd settled back on the carpet, and walking back over them she declared that the damn thing had disappeared and we went back into the kitchen to put the kettle on again.

On one occasion this remarkable lady was invited to a dinner party by another titled lady who lived in the area, and not being eccentric this one advised her to dress up for the occasion as some very smart people were coming. It wasn't until they were all leaving the table that the host noticed that beneath the long dress, her guest from Arthog Hall was wearing her wellington boots.

Across that lovely Mawddach estuary, there was yet another maverick. Major Bill Tilman was the image of my father. I drove down to meet him soon after he'd got back from sinking another boat. He was still wearing the holey blue jumper he'd been rescued in, and puffing away at his pipe he found it difficult to understand why anyone should be interested. After a distinguished war service he'd sailed and climbed mountains almost everywhere, and on that occasion he'd hit an iceberg in the Arctic. Friends who'd sailed with him always said that he had an alarming attitude to safety, and one day Lady Chetwynd rang me with a request. "Allan will you please do something about that silly old fool Tilman. He's going to the South Atlantic next. There will be a whole bunch of young fools with him and he'll kill the lot, for God's sake stop him." I told her that I didn't really think I could, and of course I didn't even try, but she was right. Some weeks later they sailed and were never seen again. Just what he had in mind we might never know, but they disappeared somewhere in the South Atlantic, on the eve of the Falklands conflict.

This next one we do have a recording of. She was another elderly titled lady, but this one was slight of build with a wicked twinkle in her eye - the good one that is, not the glass one.

Lady Margaret Williams Wynn of the huge Wynnstay estate at Ruabon was a maverick and a real mischief of the first degree, but in the opinion of the law this 83-year old lady had been involved in so many road accidents she couldn't be allowed to drive another yard until she passed a test. When she'd started driving over sixty years before, tests hadn't been thought of, so I was sent to 'discuss it' with her. "Oh yes, do come," she said on the phone, "We can go for a drive and you can show me what I have to do in this test." I tried to explain that she couldn't go out in the car, but she laughed at that. "Oh not on the road, we'll drive on my estate," she replied, and thinking that was all we'd be doing, I said okay and turned up just after lunch at the front door.

Working for the BBC you always go to the front door, even when visiting a mansion, and after her maid had served us bone china cups of coffee in her sitting room we ventured out to where another servant had parked her car. As soon as she jumped in and gleefully grabbed the steering wheel I knew I was in for it. It was only an old Rover but we shot off at such speed that I was sure that she must have tinkered with the carburettors.

In that first hundred yards it was obvious she was attempting a lap record. In the second hundred yards we were up on the grass verge, and in spite of hitting my head several times on the roof, this was in fact a blessing in disguise. It gave me the excuse to suggest that we stopped and started again, and mercifully she agreed. "As you drive off carefully," I said, "I'll start the tape running." She nodded. It was clear the nod came with a measure of reluctance, but at least I'd won a reprieve.

CBWB 15

(Car starts. Car jerks forward several times)

Barham   (Diplomatically) "Oh dear, a bit of kangaroo petrol."
Lady Margaret "Ah yes."
Barham   "Shall we try a three-point turn ?"
Lady Margaret "Yes, whatever that means."
Barham   "Ah well that's something you'll have to do in the test."
Lady Margaret "Well you see I don't know any of these things."

(Car slows down. Stops. Reverses.)

Barham   "Pull round to …."
Lady Margaret "I'm just trying to see where the road is."
Barham   (Alarmed) "Not too far back! Hold on."

(Now stopped close to a tree.)

Lady Margaret "No."
Barham   (Diplomatically) "We nearly landed in the nettles didn't we ?"
Lady Margaret "Oh."
Barham   "Pull round to the left."
Lady Margaret "To the left ?"
Barham   "Yes."
Lady Margaret "That way ?"
Barham   "Yes, avoiding the …"
Lady Margaret "Round here, round here do you mean ?"
Barham   "That's right avoiding the kerb on the other side. (Car manoeuvres), there you are, you're round."
Lady Margaret "Now where would you like me to go, up there ?"
Barham   "Oh I think you've gone far enough, don't you ?"

(Taking no notice she accelerates quickly.)

Barham   (Quickly) "You're on the grass verge (lots of bumps), oh (sounding relieved) that's better.(Regains composure) What are you going to do in order to pass this test ? Are you going to engage a proper instructor ?"

Lady Margaret "Oh no I don't want to, er, boast or anything like that but you know, I've never found it difficult driving, never in my long experience and, er, I think I can generally say I'm a safe driver. I think I probably do react quickly, but you see I'm not really a fast driver."

Barham "Do people perhaps say you shouldn't be driving at 83 ?"

Lady Margaret (Chuckling) "I think some people think it's rather wonderful."

Barham "I notice you're not wearing glasses ?"

Lady Margaret "No."

Barham "You've got perfectly good eyesight ?"

Lady Margaret "Very good eyesight. Perfectly good eyesight, even though it's only with one eye."

Barham (Sounding concerned) "Go on.?"

Lady Margaret (Looking now at the reporter instead of the road) "Well, when I say one eye, this eye was injured when I was 19 in a hunting accident."

Barham (Sounding worried) "What about hearing ?"

Lady Margaret "Who ?"

Barham "Hearing."

Lady Margaret "Hearing ? Oh my hearing's very good."

She went on to tell me how much she relied on the car, and I couldn't help laughing to myself when she complained that Ruabon was a couple of miles away and the buses only went every hour. But on the other hand, perhaps she might have travelled on a bus. She would have been so out of place, but I'm sure she had it in her if necessary.

Back in her sitting room with another delicate cup of coffee balanced on my knee, I faced more questions about the driving test, and for some reason I mentioned 'starting on a hill.' She raised an eyebrow. "Oh," she said, "Do you have to do that ?" I told her she probably would, and she put her cup straight back on the coffee table. "Let's do it." she said, and not realising what I was letting myself in for, I agreed. We went through the rear of the house this time and found the car in a back yard. I naturally thought we were going to find a hill on the estate but no, we got into the car and immediately shot off in the direction of a gate that led out onto a public road, and hearing shouts coming from somewhere behind I looked in the mirror and saw the figure of a manservant racing after us. He was left choking in a cloud of smoke.

I turned to her and told her that she wasn't allowed out onto a public road, but that only made her laugh. "Oh we won't be long," she told me, "There's a lovely hill in Ruabon." And there is too. At the bottom of this hill we swung round in a tyre-ripping arc and stopped at the opposite kerb. She was clenching her grip on the steering wheel now and looking eagerly at the hill ahead, and I was feeling ill. I could see the headlines already in the newspapers – 'BBC man assists Banned Driver.' I was sure I was going to get the sack, and it was a feeling that intensified minute by agonising minute. As she started to rev. the engine I closed my eyes, she was going for it, she was reving the engine like fury, and before long I was choking on the stench of a red hot clutch. Then suddenly we were off and we raced up that hill. At the top she turned to me and asked in triumph "Well, do you think I'll pass ?"

What a lady. Sadly I don't know if she ever passed her test. She died a long time ago now. I only know that if I had the chance I'd just love to go for that ride again with her.

Lady Olwen, the last surviving daughter of the early 1900s Liberal Prime Minister Lloyd George (the Welsh Wizard) was another old driver. She hadn't been banned, but I had to accompany her on a drive because at the time there was a move to have elderly drivers re-tested, but she was quite competent and was only chosen for the feature I think because of her fame.

I met her several times I'm pleased to say. The first time was when the television series came out in the 1970s portraying the life and times of her father, and she was very upset about it. She told me what a wonderful father he was, and how we were all wrong to see him as a womaniser, and she didn't like the way the family home had been depicted either. "My mother would never have had ornaments like those on the mantle shelf," she groaned, adding "Why didn't they ask me ? And those curtains ! They should have asked me."

Whenever I hear the beautifully haunting theme tune of that series I always think of her sitting at her home in Criccieth telling me how unnerving it was to see her father again. Philip Madoc's portrayal was so brilliant.

I have another very special memory of her too. On one occasion the Liberals were holding their Welsh conference at a hotel near Criccieth, and of course she'd been brought along. For them she was the treasured icon, but after coming to the door for a group photograph (with a swarm of politicians jostling to stand next to her) she suggested a walk around the garden, and like a shot a dozen or more offered their arms, but either because she didn't want to show favour to any individual or she was sick of them all I don't know, but she turned to me instead. Naturally I hadn't offered my arm but she reached across to me and took it.

I've never voted Liberal but I was very proud of that honour. We had such a nice chat once again as we walked slowly around the garden, followed every step of the way I might add, by a pack of deeply disappointed party members, all eager to grab her if I let go. But I had no intention of letting go of her. And who'd have thought, when I was a lad, that one day when

204

I grew up I would rescue Lloyd George's daughter.

I had a good share of lively aristocrats in my patch. Lord Langford, who was always waging war on bureaucrats – planning officers and taxmen in the main, once started a society to save the half-crown. He also had his shirts re collar-ed and cuffed, to rile the taxman in some way, and then there was the Marquess of Anglesey, who was very active with great wit and gusto in supporting worthy causes. They were the liveliest of the bunch, and of course they both had mansions to maintain. Lord Langford faced a huge task with Bodrhyddan Hall, but opened it to the public and amazingly got it back on its feet, and eventually the National Trust took over Lord Anglesey's Plas Newydd.

Yet another great warrior who fought planning officers to a standstill was Clement Beretta, a self-taught architect and serial builder of Rhosneigr. By the time he'd used up all the ground he could lay his hands on there in the village, he tried to go underground. According to his plans the front of each house would have been visible, but the rest would have been laid back into the hill with a skylight dome on top of each to let in the sunlight. He was obviously ahead of his time and I have to say I do admire builders with imagination, and they're not all men either.

One lady especially stands out in my memory. Up in Cwm Croesor Bronwen Naish 'builds' with the same hands that play the double bass. I'm talking now of an internationally acclaimed musician who could turn her hand from music to laying bricks and mortar and then go off to America with her saw to win the ' World's Best Musical Saw Player' Award.

The mavericks were always great fun. People like Brian Taylor for instance who built a tree house. He was an artist and board game inventor who lived near Ruthin. One of his games was called 'Two-nil.' It was about football and it involved a lot of shouting, which wasn't surprising. He enjoyed shouting. He had a very loud voice and playing it with him up in his tree house was deafening.

With his shock of curly black hair he reminded me of Dennis the Menace, (in fact I'm sure he was wearing a red and black hooped jumper) but actually it was his laughter I remember most. It was like the maniac laughter of someone who'd won the lottery, but I also remember all too well that the tree we were in was swaying violently. It was extremely windy that day. As for his game, he'd told me that you had to get the right letters to spell the word 'goal,' but I wasn't paying much attention. With the little tree house lurching from side to side I kept asking myself the question I so often asked – "What the hell am I doing here ?"

BWB 2V

(Wind howling. Door bursts open.)

Brian Taylor (Shouting) "The door's blown open again !"

Barham (Shouting) "I'll close it before the cards get blown away, it's bad enough with the window open. How high are we up here ?"

Brian Taylor (Shouting) "About thirty feet. (Laughing wildly) This interviewer daren't look outside !"

Barham "No I'm keeping my back to this window, and the tree's swaying around a bit I might say, right, deal the cards."

BrianTaylor (Enthusiastically) "We'll deal them eight to you and eight to me."

Barham "Right okay."

Brian Taylor "There we go." (He deals the cards).

Barham "Right, I'm looking at my hand here, hiding it from Brian of course. I've got a blue G and a blue O."

Brian Taylor "It's my turn first !"

Barham "Oh is it ?"

Brian Taylor "Yes it is, I've got a goal already !"

Barham "You haven't have you ?"

Brian Taylor "A white goal. (Shouts) Goal !!"

Barham	"Oh good heavens, I've only got a blue G and an O."
Brian Taylor	"Now you've picked the red card up and you'll have to kiss me or something." (He laughs madly now dealing 'forfeit' cards).
Barham	"I'm one-nil down already. Why is it called Two-Nil ?"
Brian Taylor	"Because that's the game, first person to two goals wins."
Barham	"Oh I see."
Brian Taylor	(Laughing wildly, then becomes serious) "Can you feel it wobbling, the tree ?"
Barham	"Yes"
Brian Taylor	(Laughing even more wildly) "He's not listening folks, he's getting very worried."
Barham	(Inaudible)
Brian Taylor	(Still laughing wildly) "Okay folks, we're about to fall down ! He's just thought it now, what the hell are we doing in this gale ? (Still laughing crazily) Playing Two-Nil of course!!" (Continues to laugh wildly).

A much quieter builder was Mark Bourne, first of Machynlleth and later of Corris. He built lovely miniature Italian architecture in concrete to compliment his hillside garden, but he also built ruins from time to time. I especially remember his quarter sized Greek temple at Machynlleth. It was big enough to walk through, and it was complete with fallen pillars made chunk by chunk in a dustbin.

Mark used to write some very nice articles for the Cambrian News, and while I'm thinking about Corris I have to remember our friend and his neighbour. Tom Heaton, the lanky old cockney Cambrian News photographer was a special constable, and was known among the local cops as the 'Sheriff of Corris.' In the nicest way possible, this Londoner stood out like a sore thumb in that part of the world. It was always a pleasure to meet up with him on a job. We saw a few cafés in our time, usually on wet and miserable occasions, and his cockney humour would always shine through like a great dollop of sunlight.

I wish I could bring all these people back for a party. What a night we'd have. They were a tough bunch, resilient perhaps is the word, and none more so than Doug Arnold of Tal-y-Cafn. He was an old soldier, a founder member of the SAS who went to their reunions no matter where they were held on his push-bike, staying overnight in what he called the roadside 'Hiltons'. These weren't actually hotels, they were bus shelters.

He was getting on in years but he used to hike up into the mountains of the Carneddau two or three times a week to look after a mountain refuge hut. This had once been a shepherd's tiny refuge on Foel Grach but in more recent years it had saved many a hill walker from freezing to death. It was only a rough stone building with a corrugated roof, but he kept it tidy and replenished it with a few essentials. He'd leave a poppy there for Armistice Day and he kept a visitors book there, and he even pinned up a few festive cards at Christmas. It was a long way off into one of the most wild road-less parts of Wales, but this old boy was as tough as nails. Nevertheless that didn't prevent him from believing in fairies. It was a very spiritual belief.

CBWB4N

Mr. Arnold   "To me the little people are always up there waiting for me to arrive and I like to think just occasionally, just occasionally I've made contact with them, and I don't mean on a Friday night coming back from the pub."

Barham   "Yes, you spoke of the little people last time."

Mr. Arnold   "I honestly believe that the little people are there working for us and again they will help us."

Barham   "In what way ?"

Mr. Arnold   "Well yes there have been times when I've wondered which way to go, and then I've seen something, a little footprint, I've walked towards it, and when I've got there the footprint isn't there. It was just an impression that I got and that has proved to be the right road. Now I honestly believe that there is some other form up there which is willing to help us if only we would accept it, and I was brought up with fairies. We had fairies at the bottom of our garden I'm sure."

Barham   "Where was that ?"
Mr. Arnold   "Isle of Man, a good Celtic upbringing you know."

I was often up there on Foel Grach, and once with my dog on Christmas Day. It was snowing hard and in the refuge hut I found a couple who were planning to stay the night so we shared a bottle of wine and the little Christmas cake I had in my rucksack. It was a very pleasant afternoon but when Cindy and I left it was late and now very dark. It was also snowing harder than when we'd arrived, but the dog found our way down.

A few years later the County Council took the roof off the refuge hut so that no-one could use it, and when people complained, these people who are supposed to maintain the natural beauty of the National Park, left a 'roadside' aluminium workman's hut in its place, and not only was it an eyesore, it was thoroughly unsuitable. Anyone going in to shelter from a blizzard wouldn't have been able to get out because the door opened outwards. It's a very lonely part of Snowdonia up there and anyone trapped in freezing conditions would have been in serious trouble. When at last more pressure resulted in the old refuge hut being restored it was re-built with the interior divided into small, dark and impractical halves. It was ruined.

Another favourite tough guy was the old chemist in Buckley. His name was Jim Bentley, a real enthusiast who became so enthusiastic about the town's brick and tile making history that he literally dug himself into it. The last time

I saw this old boy he was trying to dig through an old tunnel that had been filled in many years before. Actually I don't think he ever finished it, but I loved his enthusiasm. All the time people were telling him that it was too dangerous, but he wanted so much to reach the end of that tunnel.

The last real maverick that comes to mind was quite remarkable. For this one I had to go up onto the flat roof of the Wellfield shopping centre in Bangor where he was flying his kite above the offices of the North Wales Arts Association, with whom he'd had an argument. No matter how eccentric your mavericks are most will display a remarkable degree of enthusiasm. None more so than this one. He didn't appear to be oriental, but he said his name was Dr. Feng, and he was so excited with his kite that he never took his eyes off it once as he danced around trying to control it. This he managed to do quite well most of the time, except when I stood on his string, but to be fair he was quick to admit that he wasn't the best kite flyer in the world. In fact, he said that he was only the second best kite flyer in the world.

CBWB5

Barham	"You're having a bit of trouble with your kite, Dr. Feng ?"
Kite Man	"Yes, well at the moment the wind is proving a testing time, but as you see the kite is flying
Barham	"I see. Oh dear, I'm standing on your string. I do apologise.(Ducking to avoid diving kite) Why exactly are you flying your kite here ?"
Kite Man	"Well basically what I'm doing is a flying picket if you'll pardon the pun, against the North Wales Arts Association. Basically, I was not considered fit to be even called for an interview, and I find this a little strange given the fact that I'm considered to be the number two kite flyer in the world."
Barham	"How can you be the second best in the world ?"
Kite Man	"Well I always think that in the world there's always

	someone better than you are at what you do, and I think that's a fair and civilised way of looking at things."
Barham	"So you haven't actually competed in a big world competition and come second ?"
Kite Man	"Kite flying is not about competition, I really think it's the best form of occupation for the soul, and it's something that is universal, reminds us of man's civilisation and humanity. (Now getting very excited) Oh just look at that! Look at those people enjoying it. I'm enjoying it, but I must stay in control ! Look at that pulling. Don't you think that makes a lovely sight against the sky ?"
Barham	(Not really impressed) "Yes".
Kite Man	(Now ecstatic) "Look at that, isn't that nice. Oh, oh, this is flying picketing at its best I think, and most cheerful."

CHAPTER N.
Newspapers.

People who inhabit the media world, whether they work in newspapers or magazines, radio or television, all feed off each other, pouncing on each other's stories as soon as they appear, unless of course they're all at the same trough that day and feeding on the same story. Those occasions I always enjoyed. I liked the occasional company of my fellow reporters. They were good company every one of them, but those gatherings started to fall away when editors began tightening up on their budgets and newsmen were chained to their desks and their telephones. Then, with phone bills cheaper than petrol bills, came the drop in standards. A reporter trying to see what's happened on the phone is always going to make mistakes.

As I said, to start with I did occasionally come across other reporters but as time went by that became a very rare event, and you know, it's a lonely life being a radio reporter. Newspaper reporters usually had a photographer with them and obviously television reporters had their cameramen and sound recordists in attendance, but in radio you're on your own.

A lot of things have changed, and certainly radio reporters are not on the road as much now thanks to the direct public link of the mobile phone, text and e mails, but this chapter is about newspapers, and the voracious appetite newsmen have for snapping up each other's stories. There's no harm in this, once a story's out anyone can have it, but when it's the reporter himself that gets gobbled up, as opposed to the story, it stings. Reporters are always telling people there's nothing to worry about having their names and photographs splashed across the pages of a newspaper, but I can tell you it's the very last thing they would wish upon themselves, and of this I have personal and painful experience. Rarely have I been quite so embarrassed, and for that reason I am approaching its recall with caution.

First I will explain that at the BBC, and particularly in radio, we somehow or other fell into the habit of fabricating April Fool's day reports. I remember someone reported on a scheme to put anti-glare lenses into the eyes of young salmon before they migrated so they could find their way back, swimming back to Wales in a predominantly eastern direction towards the rising sun. A lot of people believed it too, and for one particular April 1st broadcast I got a friend to pretend he'd just won a contract to supply a French restaurant with worms to make up for a shortage in France of edible snails. I told the listeners that the French had discovered that worms from Wales were just as tasty, and believe it or not a lot of people believed that as well.

My imaginary worm exporter was an old friend Chris Woolfenden, who for some reason chose to emphasise his strong Lancashire accent and accompanied me out into his garden armed with a garden fork and a plastic bucket. I'll play this tape for you because he was just brilliant, absolutely brilliant, unprompted, unscripted, and straight off the cuff, and of course we performed it absolutely straight faced.

ABWB13

Barham	"Look, look there's one."
Mr. W.	(Digging) "Oh aye, aye that's a big'un."
Barham	"Yes. What sort of worms do you have to have ? That looks like a common or garden worm to me. That's alright is it ?"
Mr. W.	"Aye, ordinary earthworms, the bigger the better."
Barham	"I see, and do you eat them all ? Every part of the worm ?"
Mr. W.	"No, only the flat bit."
Barham	"The tail on the end ?"
Mr. W.	"That's it, that's it."
Barham	"Yes, I see."
Mr. W.	"Yes you cook 'em, in a special sauce. A special sauce. Only known to a French chef. He's in Paris."
Barham	"I see, he asked you to send these worms over to him ?"
Mr. W.	"That's right."
Barham	"How did you meet him ?"
Mr. W.	"Well it were down at Grimsby near Cleethorpes. French cricket championships."
Barham	"You play do you ?"
Mr. W.	That's right, aye, aye. He plays, he's good too. He's only got one leg."
Barham	"Oh, he must be good then. Yes. He's using worms if I understand correctly because they're running out of edible snails in France ?"
Mr. W.	"That's right, that's right yes."
Barham	"And he's found that the tail of the flat end of an

	ordinary earthworm is just the same as an edible snail."
Mr. W.	"Aye, aye."
Barham	"Have you tried them, have you been over there to try them ?"
Mr. W.	"Aye, aye, aye I've tried them."
Barham	"What do they taste like ?"
Mr. W.	"Horrible, but they seem to like ours, the ones from Wales. They seem to be the best. It's something to do with the rock formation here. They're pre-Cambrian. Rocks are pre-Cambrian. Aye, aye."
Barham	"Good gracious me. I wonder what effect it has on the soil ? You haven't gone into that ?"
Mr. W.	"No, no."
Barham	"How do you get them to Paris ?"
Mr. W.	"I send them off in jars with lids on, but with holes in the lids so that they can breathe. Aye, they've got to arrive alive you see."
Barham	"They're not eaten alive are they ?"
Mr. W.	"Oh no, no. No, they're popped into boiling water like lobsters."
Barham	"Do you have to have a permit to export Welsh worms ?"
Mr. W.	"Aye, aye, you have to have a licence, form G68/N or something."
Barham	"Who issues these licences then ?"
Mr. W.	"Post Office."
Barham	"Could I get one of these licences ? If I was to start up in opposition to you ?"
Mr. W.	"Oh no, I've got the sole rights in this area, but I was quick off the mark you see."
Barham	"You certainly were, yes."
Mr. W.	"Well it's the early bird that catches the worm ain't it lad ?"

Barham   "Oh I suppose it is, yes."

I enjoyed doing April Fool reports. It was refreshing to let your hair down, to have a whole day's licence to tell enormous lies, to invent news and facts instead of reporting on them, but one year I fell hook line and sinker for someone else's. This was when I turned up in someone's newspaper and was made to look (with total justification) the complete blockhead. Falling for their story was marginally understandable, (at least marginally I would claim) it was after all a very good story, but..... not realising it was April 1st was beyond any kind of excuse.

It was 1993 and the North Wales Weekly News printed a story about a man who'd been wandering along the beach at Rhos-on-Sea. The tide had gone a long way out and at the water's edge he'd spotted a fossilised footprint in a rock. It sounded very convincing, (and I might add the fake photograph also looked convincing) and the report said a Professor Rolf O'Pail had identified it as the footprint of a dinosaur !

Like I said – a 'good story', but had I been a bit more sensible I might have realised that - not only was it April 1st, but Rolf O'Pail was an anagram of April Fool. Instead I blundered straight into it, and the following week's edition of the paper carried an even better story about the BBC reporter Allan Barham who'd rung up their news desk to arrange an interview with the beachcomber and Professor O'Pail.

Now here's an interesting question, what's the difference between a reporter and a journalist ? I don't know. At various times the BBC called me both a reporter and a journalist, but my Auntie Olive once told me that in her younger days she'd gone out a few times with a reporter. "He was ever so nice," she said. "Then he became a journalist and he was horrible."

CHAPTER O.
Occupational Hazards, the Occult, Overtime, & Opportunism.

On balance the radio reporter will not have a comfortable ride. The wet nights will certainly outweigh the sunshine and the hard roads will always be longer than the sandy beaches. Also, every now and then the reporter will encounter the 'occupational hazard' and the most uncomfortable I came across was meeting 'Mr. Smelly'.

This title was bestowed upon him by common consent among the population of his home town, and in the hope that he's now a reformed character I won't name it, but suffice it to say that it was a city and he was said to be barred from every one of its public houses. It wasn't surprising either. His stench was genuinely gruesome and due entirely to the fact that he had an overgrown passion for garlic. He claimed the stuff had helped him recover from an accident and he was now wanting to tell everyone to eat it by the sackful. It must have been pouring out of every pore in his skin. Nevertheless he really did want to tell everyone about it, but the snag was his wife.

I was surprised he still had one. She was dead set against him drumming up any sort of publicity, and when I found his phone number she shouted something into the phone which I took to mean "Come anywhere near my house with your microphone and I'll slaughter you." But her man was determined. A few minutes later he rang me back, and in a whisper he told me to come in an hour's time when she'd be out. It didn't work. When I rang the bell she leant out of an upstairs window. I didn't get the boiling oil or the molten lead, but the screeched abuse and the blood-curdling threats were certainly enough to prompt a tactical retreat as far as the gate, and when she showed no sign of ending the barrage I got back in the car and drove round the corner.

Hoping she was still upstairs I rang the number again. He answered it and I told him I was round the corner. His reply came in the faintest of whispers. "Give me five minutes." As he put the phone down I heard him call out "Wrong number dear," and soon he was with me.

It was a mistake. I regretted it as soon as he got in the car. He stank to high heaven ! It was ghastly ! It was unbearable ! I couldn't stand it, and with no diplomatic bearing whatsoever I told him to get out and I recorded an interview with him on the kerb. Even so, those few moments he'd sat in my car contaminated it for weeks !

When thinking of occupational hazards you will find some have gone straight into the chapter reserved for things like 'terror', but I remember I had an early warning of what might be in store for me soon after starting with the BBC. In comparison with some of the things I endured in years to come this was of mild concern, but whenever I drive along the Wrexham by-pass I think of it and cross my fingers in the hope that the concrete plug isn't yet ready to plunge down the hole.

When they were building this fast stretch of road they came to a mine shaft and their method of putting a plug into it was raising a few eyebrows. The shaft was half full of water so the road builders added a few chemicals to freeze it, and then they laid a floor of concrete on top of it. The hope was that the concrete would hold against the sides of the shaft after the water beneath had melted, and I was lowered in a bucket to jump up and down on it.

Those minxes of the Penrhos College for young ladies, the 'St.Trinnians' of Colwyn Bay, gave me a hard time once. In the best traditions of British 'slap-stick' they set themselves up as Coast Guards with a high speed rescue boat, hoping of course to capture sailors, but they couldn't have thought much of me. They took me a mile off shore and dumped me overboard. They said they'd come and find me later, which they did, at last. Then they let me drive their boat, and what a boat!

Good advice for any reporter is 'keep

your mouth shut' but of course that is quite impossible for the radio reporter, especially when working with a producer who's hoping to get him poisoned. Actually some of it wasn't bad. The alligator meat was quite tasty but whenever someone , even vaguely, connected with the business of producing food and drink comes up with a new product the reporter is obliged to sample it. It makes no difference how revolting the concoction is, or how untrue the culinary claims may clearly be, the reporter is still required to swallow it. You first swallow what's said about it, and then you swallow the thing itself. And then, and only then, are you allowed to say 'Yuk!'

When it comes to a broadcast where you have to eat or drink something there are many producers who believe the actual act of 'swallowing' is an essential element of sound broadcasting. It's true, the sound of food and drink gurgling down the gullet sets the scene for such encounters, but from time to time it gives rise to some pretty disgusting noises as reporters strive to make the act of swallowing loud enough to be picked up by the microphone, but one of my most memorable tasting sessions came my way during the postman's strike of 1970. A jolly old boy in Ffestiniog had been beavering away behind his garage and petrol station for donkey's years producing bottles of liniment oil, but as with all other mail order businesses, he was now stuck with the stuff.

It was an old family business which had been started by his father (or grandfather) many, many years earlier, using a secret formula given to him by a passing tramp. They called the stuff 'Morris Evans Oils' and every bottle packed a pong you could smell for miles. If you've ever played a contact sport like football and suffered a few bruises you will know the sort of smell I'm talking about, the sort of stink that's constantly found in every dressing room, only this stuff was worse and the claims on the label were astounding. He told me a swig or a rub down with this stuff would cure you of anything from eczema to lumbago, sore throats, rheumatics, piles, and even flat feet !

I remember that afternoon so well. He certainly enjoyed it, but then on this occasion he had a real live victim to pour his stuff into.

BWB 2

Mr. Evans — "Yes that's called the 'Morris Evans Cattle Oil' – 'Horse Sheep and Cattle Oil.' We've been supplying some of the leading circuses like Sangers Circus, Fossett's Circus, Bronco Bill and them, and football teams. We've supplied Everton when they won the English Cup, we've supplied Liverpool too, Cardiff City, yes."

Barham — "Would you say your oil is as popular today as it was in years gone by ?"

Mr. Evans — "Well yes, because of the quality I suppose of the oil, and the old generation I think, they're coming back to the old medicines you know these days. There's a lot of new things on the market now and they're coming back to nature, the lemon and so on you know."

Barham — "And do you use it ?"

Mr. Evans — "Yes I take it for sore throats, anything like that."

Barham — "Do you rub it on your throat ?"

Mr. Evans — "No I take a few drops on a lump of sugar."

Barham — "Well, I thought it was solely for rubbing on ?"

Mr. Evans — "Oh no you can take it on a lump of sugar, it's quite safe. Would you like to taste it ? It's not very nice mind you."

Barham — "I don't suppose it is. (He takes a spoonful) Oooer! You can't run a car on this stuff can you ?"

Mr. Evans — (Laughing) "Oh no you can't."

Occupational hazards can include ladies too of course, and once I had to get into one's bath. She was complaining that the council estate had been fitted out with baths that were too small, and true enough they were. They were okay on length, but they were so narrow anyone with an 'X' rated pair of hips would never have got out again. Not that she had that problem. She was slim and very attractive. No, she didn't have broad hips or a big bum, but she did have a jealous husband. Not that I was alone with her. That day again I was working in my role as reserve TV reporter and I had a whole television crew squeezed into that little bathroom. Apparently though when her husband sat down to his dinner that evening and I came on the screen sitting in her bath, he blew a fuse. Next time I met her they all had new baths and she had a new husband.

When you're 'physically' involved with your stories, you're bound to get into trouble sometimes. Mostly they're minor skirmishes, like spending a day working with an award-winning coal man and dropping coal on a bad-tempered woman's driveway. That was in Amlwch, but then on the other hand the hazards can be a little more dramatic. Forest fires for example. They can provide tremendous radio drama, but forests are normally big places and to capture the moment you have to get right into the action. This is where you get the terrifying 'roar' of the fire and the shouts of the fire fighters.

In 1976 we had a particularly big one. I was driving home from Bangor late one night and as I came up to Lake Ogwen I saw the distant sky had turned orange. It was clearly an enormous fire close to Capel Curig, and as I got there small groups of people were hurrying into the forest carrying anything they could find to beat the flames, even shovels and brooms, but this blaze deep in the heart of that huge pine forest was in no mood to be stopped.

Grabbing the tape recorder from the boot I joined them, and in silence we hurried up a stony track by torchlight towards the glowing sky and the muffled roar which lay over the ridge. As we drew near, and the air became thick and stifling, so the noise of the inferno grew louder, and somewhere to our right we could hear the frantic noise of chainsaws and the crash of trees falling as men, completely unseen in the darkness, were trying to cut a fire gap. Then as the roar of the fire grew louder and we rounded a corner we found ourselves looking into hell on earth. With our faces lit up by this vast blaze we stood staring at the scene. As far as we could see the forest was ablaze in a blinding swirling orange confusion of flame and smoke, and yet amidst this inferno there were people - people running and stooping here and there to beat wildly and hopelessly at it, but the task was enormous, thousands of trees were ablaze and the noise was incredible !

I did my best to describe it all into the mic then ventured further in and I recorded a few words with some of the beaters as they beat at the undergrowth, people of all types, ordinary people, men and women, as well as forestry workers and soldiers too, red in the face and all drenched in sweat, but no matter how hard they worked it was clearly a losing battle. Everything, trees and undergrowth, was ablaze, and with the fire raging all over the place, spreading behind them and back into areas they'd already covered, there came an amazing sight. A sight that looked, not unwelcome, but absolutely ridiculous in the middle of a forest. Very slowly, a big red urban fire engine was trundling into view, pitching and rolling laboriously along the rough track, with a weary looking crew gazing out of the windows wondering where on earth they might do something useful.

They were creeping along so slowly I was able to open the door and climb in, "Where the hell do we start ?" the driver asked, and after a while they decided to turn off onto another track where there were no beaters. Here they decided to go into action, jumping out to beat at the undergrowth, but the trouble with those forest tracks is that they combine in a tangled web to form a 'maze' and I couldn't help noticing this particular track wasn't very well worn. I suggested to the driver therefore that it could lead to a dead end. This was an important point because already the fire had cut us off by crossing the track behind us and was now surging up into the overhead branches.

Leaving the others to carry on beating, the driver drove off to see if the way ahead looked promising. He drove off quite slowly but he came back very quickly. It was a dead end, and our drive back through the flames was memorable to say the least.

Even in a situation like that there's usually something to give you a good laugh. Soon after I left the firemen to continue their 'tour', I came across an army officer yelling into a radio set – something we used to call a 'walkie-talkie'. He was furious, absolutely furious ! He was standing next to a little wooden post bearing the outline of a fish showing the way to a lake, and in the midst of all that chaos, with people running in all directions, he was shouting his head off. "You (something,something) Fool ! I told you to meet me here at the this sign with the (something,something) fish on it !" He was raging on and one, but I didn't like to tell him there were several of those little signs in the forest.

It was absolute chaos, but when I drove a couple of hours later round to the Crafnant end of the forest it was a lot calmer. A fire engine stood in the dark pumping water from the lake and following the hose, length after length for a very long way, I caught up with local people struggling to carry extra lengths up to the firemen.

For the sheer noise and activity, fires take a lot of beating for radio atmosphere and there were several I will always remember. The Asda fire in Llandudno, the blaze that destroyed the tubular railway bridge over the Menai Straits with its disastrous wooden interior, and several other forest fires, like another in the Gwydir Forest not far from Geirionydd. Here the fire suddenly turned back on us with a rush, and as with the other big fires, my recording of that and all the firemen yelling to each other "Everyone out !! Get out !!" was cut into so many programmes it eventually disappeared.

Covering fires provides deserved publicity for the fire brigades. On that occasion near Geirionydd it was day time and a couple of policemen were at each entrance to the forest stopping people from going in to help, which was ridiculous, and I was just turning away to go round the corner and climb over the fence when a County Fire Officer arrived in his car and ignoring the policemen threw open the door, called to me and took me right up to it.

When the action is out of sight you have to climb fences. It's no good waiting down the road for news. Newspaper reporters can do that if they want to, but photographers, cameramen and radio reporters have got to be there where it's happening. You've got to be in the midst of it all, and this even applies to riots and demonstrations, and as I think I've already said, it's safer on the inside. On the edge you'll get hurt. Get into the middle and stay there where you'll get all the noise, shouting and cursing that you could possibly wish for.

This lesson was never more clear than at the farmers riots in Holyhead and there was very nearly another riot in Holyhead when a ferry strike clogged up the town with cars unable to get into the harbour. After several days with people, and understandably fractious children, literally camping out in their cars, things were turning nasty and on the Saturday morning a huge crowd gathered outside the offices of the ferry company.

I got there just in time to see a company spokesman emerge to read a statement, and when he'd finished reading it without a single word of hope, a stone came through the air and smashed a window. That did it. The whole crowd surged forward. They were on their way in ! But suddenly a woman's shrill voice could be heard above the uproar. It was so shrill that everyone stopped to listen. She was going on and on and on – "You (something, something) - You (something, something)" she was screaming. "This young lad here was getting married in Dublin today, but thanks to you the wedding's off !" For a moment no-one moved. There wasn't a sound, and then another voice piped up, a man's frail little voice, an Irish voice straining to be heard from the back, and what he said completely squashed the uprising. He shouted, "And to be sure, he should thank his lucky stars."

It was wonderful. There were people, who'd been furious a moment ago, who were now collapsing, just rolling around and clinging onto each other. The riot was off the boil, and within ten more minutes the crowd was disappearing and heading for the pubs.

I mentioned the police a few lines back, and although I never got coshed with a truncheon I was chased once by one of their Alsatians. With some consideration I must add, they fitted me up with a specially padded jacket, but it was still terrifying. Take my advice, if you're up to no good and the copper has a dog don't run. Just don't run.

It was at the Anglesey Agricultural Show and I was there to attend the Police Dog Handler's demonstration and offer myself up as a victim. Not actually my idea of fun you understand, and not an experience I would recommend, but someone in Cardiff thought it was a splendid idea, and as soon as I was introduced to the snarling brute I knew I was in for it. (The dog wasn't very nice either.) "Okay," the policeman said with a smirk, "See if you can get to the far end of the arena." and with the crowd baying for my blood, I was told to get going. "Go on," the copper said, "I'll give you fifty yards start."

It was the stuff of nightmares. The crowd was loving it, and suddenly they were yelling in delight and I knew without looking back that the dog was on its way. It was like being in a Roman arena. I was running as fast as I could, and although I was panting hard I could hear it coming ! I could hear its 'hooves' pounding the turf getting closer and closer, and then 'crash' - it hit me and I fell under its weight. In a flash the growling beast was on top of me, its foul smelly fangs were viciously biting into my padded arm and its wild gleaming eyes were glaring into mine.

"Don't move." the policeman shouted when he'd caught us up, but there was no way I was going to. Those ivory fangs biting into my arm were only inches from my throat.

A reporter's occupational hazards usually come in single bites (if I can put it like that) but occasionally they can come in a continuous stream. Almost certainly because of my reputation for being gullible I was invited in the late seventies to spend a year with a weekly programme called 'Check Point'.

This was a London-based Radio Four programme that chased after villains. It was fronted by a New Zealander by the name of Roger Cook, a very large guy who looked like a rugby 'All Black' but regularly got beaten up by the villains he was chasing. I was being invited to stand in for him because he was in hospital. Someone had thrown him down the stairs, and seeing as the previous week someone had run him over, I wasn't all that sure that I wanted this job.

My reluctance was further enhanced when they told me I'd be confronting these people single handed, as Roger had done. I wouldn't have a body- guard or any sort of assistant with me. "You're out there on your own," they said, but they were very persuasive. "Stay with your Welsh programmes but join us for three days a week, just for a year, and you'll enjoy it." And I did. For a year I travelled the length and breadth of Gt. Britain sticking a microphone and a string of awkward questions under the noses of every conceivable crook and con. man. Banging on their doors, shouting through their letter boxes, confronting them in car parks and walking unannounced into their offices or warehouses, or wherever I could find them

Each week started Monday at 10 am at Broadcasting House in London, *THE* Broadcasting House in Langham Place just off Oxford Street, and there a team of researchers would decide who I was to go after. It was enjoyable, but yes you went off and worked completely on your own in those days, and even when Roger came back we were never sent off together. We each had our own story to cover and left the building to go our separate ways. On the whole I was very lucky, and I don't think he came to much more harm that year. I only had a few scuffles when they turned nasty but of course you had to hang on to the tape recorder, and the practice was to go in with the tape running and just get what ever you could and get out again.

It was certainly an interesting twelve months. Much of the time we were responding to letters from the public, and many of our targets were fraudsters while others were involved with straight forward theft, and there were some very strange experiences too.

One week I went to find a mail order con-man that our researchers had traced to a flat in Southport, but when I reached the top floor I found someone else had beaten me to it. There was a hole in his front door big enough to walk through, so I did. Inside it was like the Marie Celeste, no-one was there but every room had been ransacked and in the kitchen there was a meal for two on the table, half-eaten. Later I found another address he'd used in town. This time there was a decorator working there and on the front door mat I found a pile of letters. Some contained cheques which we were able to return, while others contained letters from people wanting to know why their goods hadn't arrived.

Another unusual story came to light up in Newcastle. I was searching the discos every night for a charity worker who'd 'forgotten' to hand over the money he'd collected. He was a building worker and he'd been touring Britain with his stunt - disco dancing with a hod of bricks on his shoulder. I'd worked on the building sites as hod carrier so I knew what a strange sight he must have made, but we were told this guy danced with a couple of buckets at his feet for people to throw money into.

He said he was doing this to fund a London hospital, but he'd disappeared with the cash. He'd danced with his bricks in several towns and had last been seen in Newcastle on Tyne, but I found him eventually in a village several miles north of Newcastle. Naturally, like all the others I caught up with, he wasn't pleased to find somebody from the BBC on his doorstep and half an hour later it finished up with a promise from his girlfriend that he'd pay up by the end of the week. I don't know if it was quite that quick, but before long we got a nice letter from the hospital to say they'd received the money.

In most cases we were dealing with some really nasty characters who obviously thought they could help themselves to anything they fancied, and it was irritating to see how easily some of them side-stepped the law, but how they squirmed when confronted with a microphone.

Another strange, and rather surprising case involved representatives of a local council and a double glazing firm. There was no crooked dealing going on here, just neglect. It was at Fareham near Southampton, where three very badly handicapped brothers lived in a house right next to a motorway. Originally it was to be demolished when the road was built, but when it was realised they couldn't be expected to settle in a house they didn't know, it was allowed to stand. They'd all grown up there and they were truly disabled. One I remember could only crawl along the floor, and the most able bodied brother was the one who was blind. He was the breadwinner, keeping chickens and producing eggs behind the house.

Because of their plight they were initially delighted to be able to stay put, but the noise from the motorway passing so close to their windows was driving them mad, and it had been found that their disabilities entitled them to double glazing. This of course would cut down the noise level considerably, but guess what ? Two years later- it still hadn't been installed. All this time later I can't remember what the problem was, but it was tied up with the cost, and it was very satisfying to hear that just two weeks after I got it on the air the glaziers had been and done the job at last.

That year we won an award. The big

one. We were awarded the 'Sony Radio Award' and we had a 'grand do' at the Saville Club in London. It was a great occasion, a big dinner, and truly a night to remember.

I enjoyed my weekly trips to Broadcasting House. Cardiff's B.H. is pretty imposing but it's modern, it hasn't got that ingrained glamour of Langham Place. Walking around those corridors in London made you feel and sense the presence of so many great broadcasters and the great programmes of years gone by. Programmes we used to enjoy so much before television reared its greedy head. For me that was back in the days when I got hooked on the 'wireless' as a boy just down the District Line, playing soldiers on smouldering bomb sites and watching dog fights in the sky.

They say London's broadcasting house is haunted, but I didn't see any ghosts while I was there, but in Wales ghosties and ghoulies are always coming out of the Celtic mist. In a cave on Llandudno's Great Orme for example there was evidence that suggested that devil worshippers were gathering there, while in another cave poems were found crammed into crevices. I saw them there, and I met a man once who swore he'd entered one of the cliff edge caves to find it lit by candles, even though there was no-one there.

Talking of the Great Orme reminds me of a cave rescue I was involved in one night with a good friend, news cameraman John Reay. I'd had a phone call from the newsroom telling me that someone was trapped in one of the copper mine tunnels by a roof fall, and although rescuers could speak to him through the rubble it was a race against time because the tunnel entrance was on a ledge close to the water's edge and the tide was coming up.

Driving round the Great Orme I came across John climbing over the wall. Close to some vehicles he'd spotted a rope dangling over the cliff and was preparing to climb down it with his camera and a battery-powered light slung over his shoulder. So I took the tape recorder from the car and joined him, and eventually we got down to this ledge and in the moonlight we could make out a very narrow tunnel with 'noises' coming from it.

We could hear voices booming from inside and things being pushed around. It was a tiny, very low-roofed tunnel, and within a few feet of crawling in I came up against several rocks and someone's hobnail boots. It turned out to be a policeman laying on his stomach like we were, and several other rescuers ahead of him were passing rocks under their bodies for the policeman to kick back as far as he could, which by then was my head.

It wasn't long after John and I joined in this game that a great muffled cheer broke out ahead of us and we guessed it was coming to an end. We backed out of the tunnel followed by a half a dozen others and were soon recording the victim's joy at being released. His nickname was Billy Bones I remember, and of course he was very pleased to be out of there, and as the others climbed up the rope John and I sat at the water's edge in the moonlight and ate a chunk of my birthday cake, which I happened to have stuffed into my pocket. It's a nice memory. As for the cake, you never know how long you're going to be out on a story like that.

Billy Bones belonged to the Great Orme Exploration Society, set up the explore the Orme's old copper mines, and by finding 'prehistoric' workings and prehistoric tools they've re-written the history books. They've proved that early man went much further than scratch the surface for their minerals, but recalling tales of the occult as I was a while ago, reminds me of a very strange story concerning a little church at Trelystan not all that far from Welshpool. This is where I went one day to meet the devil.

According to local 'knowledge' he lives there in a small wooden box locked away in a cupboard. The strange thing is - I remember going there, and I remember somebody opening the cupboard and taking out the box, I remember it very well, but I can't remember who showed it to me, and more to the point, I cannot remember whether or not the box was opened. This is quite baffling and I've pondered over this for a long time. Opening the box would have been my quest, but did we open it ? I honestly don't know. It's as if that part of my memory has been erased. It really is very odd, and on top of that – the tape has disappeared.

The letter 'O' is also for overtime. There's a lot of overtime if you're a reporter, and for me in my day it was unrewarded. Many a time I've worked right through the night and often in atrocious weather for the breakfast programme Good Morning Wales, and I've very often slept on the studio floor with wet clothes drying on the radiator. Even the unmanned studios were always warm and you can't beat BBC carpets, they're really soft, but one Christmas morning I set off all the alarm bells.

Very late on a very dark Christmas eve I'd hiked up into the mountains to a wild area known as Cwm Eigiau to find a gang of people in an old shepherd's hut who wanted to see a Christmas morning sunrise. (Not the refuge hut I mentioned earlier, but something similar.) This was for a Radio Five programme and we were going live into the programme through a large and bulky new-fangled battery-operated radio-phone link. (Yes, we were approaching the mobile phone age). The morning dawned with a wonderful 'West Ham' claret and blue sky, and to my surprise the radio phone worked perfectly, but it wasn't to be.

Some sort of international incident somewhere in the world cut us out of the running order. Instead they asked for a recorded piece to play later in the day, and with the recording made and all the Goodbyes and Happy Christmas's said and done I hiked back to the car and drove off to Bangor, being the nearest studio. As it was Christmas Day I had to use the unattended studio, but once inside I needed to visit the toilet in the main part of the building. That's when a new invisible beam picked me up and activated all the alarms. The noise was terrible and at the same time it signalled a break-in at the home of my old pals the Chief Engineers who were at home just sitting down to their Christmas dinners.

Actually, in an effort to stop the police arriving and arresting me for breaking and entering, the first thing I did was ring the police station. I said "I'm sure everyone living around here can hear these alarm bells, but I'm just ringing to say it's okay. I work here, I'm not a burglar." I might have been though. "Okay," the policeman said "That's alright, Happy Christmas Sir," and he rang off. I almost wished I'd brought a transit van.

Reporters need to be like poachers on the football pitch like I used to be. Opportunism more than skill will net many a goal, and 'opportunism' rounds off this chapter. In a nutshell, if you see the making of a story – just do it.

Sometime in 1971 I needed to see a psychiatrist. (Not surprising really). He was Dr. Dafydd Alun Jones who lives on Anglesey, and when I knocked on his door there was no reply. The reason for my visit isn't clear all these years later. It might have had something to do with a big new road project which was alarming people, but when I went round to the back I found a much better story in the offing. I found him kneeling on the ground next to a whole line of chickens lying fast asleep. Nothing strange about that you might say, except that they were lying on their sides. I thought they were dead, but no they weren't dead, he'd hypnotised them.

"Come and have a go," he said, and of course I did, switching on the tape recorder right away. Here was an opportunity not to be missed - a psychiatrist hypnotising chickens.

BWB 67G
Dr. Jones   (Catching hold of an un hypnotised chicken and
                 holding her wings by her sides.) "You lay her on the
                 floor on her side like this, on her side on the floor,
                 and you put her head on the ground in line like that.

You gently hold her head down, then you draw your finger away from the beak, like that."

I watched him fascinated as he slowly ran the point of his finger through the gravel, drawing a straight line away from her beak.

Dr. Jones	"If she's a good subject, which most hens seem to be she'll just stay there."
Barham	"Wonderful ......well there we are, completely still, lying on her side."
Dr. Jones	"I've got hold of her legs now, practically turning her over on her back .... you see ?"
Barham	"All twisted up."
Dr. Jones	"All twisted up ...... ah, and now, she is only now just getting up."
Barham	"Yes she's broken from it now. Do you think anyone could do it ?"
Dr. Jones	"Oh yes, I've been treating a little lad with asthma and I'm doing it with hypnosis, and when we use hypnosis for therapy I explain it as a purely mechanical thing with nothing particularly mystical about it, and I showed this little lad how to hypnotise chickens. Here now, you do it this time. You put two fingers like that on the nape of her neck, right ?"
Barham	"Hmmm"
Dr. Jones	"Then you draw a line away from her back as I did."
Barham	(Laughing) "She won't bite me will she ?"
Dr. Jones	"No they're very old hens these."
Barham	"It's not causing a sort of temporary paralysis is it ?"
Dr. Jones	"You're not pressing hard are you ?"
Barham	"No, no."
Dr. Jones	"See what she does when you let go now, gently ... ... there you are, she's lying quietly on her side."

Barham   "Do you think I've really hypnotised that chicken ?"
Dr. Jones   "Something has brought her into a bemused state.
            She just lies there. We could have several of them
            laid out in bizarre positions flat on their backs." (He
            chuckles mischievously).

                              He's never been allowed to forget that
interview. Apparently when it went on the air it landed him in the
pages of a satirical magazine, and he told me very many years later
that it was chastening to realise that he will always be remembered
among his colleagues for being able to, at least, hypnotise chickens.
                   I have to admit that hypnotists on the
radio are very much like conjurers (with or without a tunnel), but we
had quite a few hypnotists on the air, and one in Abergele was
offering his services to enlarge ladies breasts. He advertised this
service in the local paper but no-one turned up on the day I was
there. (Typical). And on the subject of ladies breasts I remember a
man in Caernarvon inventing a device for measuring them, and
whilst on the subject of opportunities to be 'grasped' I must
remember to tell you about the earth's crust which was a very
strange story indeed.
                         I'd been told on a couple of occasions
about odd noises coming sometimes from underground among the
long deserted lead mines of the Gwydir Forest. I lived on the edge
of that forest but nothing came of those rumours until one day I was
up there collecting gravel to patch up my drive. I was hoping the
lead content would stop weeds from growing on it, but anyway as I
filled my buckets a couple of young and studious looking men
arrived in a Land Rover, and instead of asking me what I was doing
pinching gravel, they stopped and chatted about the weather. They
were hoping the rain would keep off because they were camping
out. When I asked them why they were visiting an old lead mine
they told me they were often there. "Why ?" I asked, and soon
realised I'd found the source of the lead mine noises. "We're

scientists," one said, "And we're working at the bottom of an old mine shaft." And to my amazement they told me in the course of the next few minutes that they were checking on the rise and fall of the earth's crust."

Seeing as this sounded very strange, seeing as I never thought that it went up and down at all, I told them I worked for the BBC and they agreed to an interview. I was running short of time though because I was due in the Bangor studio that afternoon and I put it off until I returned later. It was dark when I got back, and as I searched through the trees for them I was beginning to wonder if the story I'd been told was true, or whether they'd actually be there. But after a while I could make out the glow of a camp fire and soon we were sitting by it.

I have often wondered about this story. They showed me how they'd built a shed over the shaft and they told me how they could monitor their equipment from inside this shed, but they also told me that the equipment was too sensitively balanced to take me inside. Instead I conducted the interview by their camp fire, and what they told me just amazed me. They told me that in that area we all went up and down twelve inches every time the tide came in.

CBWB 4

Scientist	"Okay, the force of gravity that occurs between the sun and the moon and the earth, as the sun and the moon rotate, in respect of the earth, this attraction causes a bulge which travels around the earth synchronous with the sun and moon as they travel around."
Barham	"I know, the sun and the moon have an effect on the tide, it's tied in with that ?"
Scientist	"That is the tide. The gravitational attraction is the tidal force."
Barham	"Now does that mean that this, this bulge in the

	earth's crust rises twice a day with each tide ?"
Scientist	"Yes. Every 12 hours and 29 minutes the bulge travels, or the bulge is seen at a particular point on the earth."
Barham	"And approximately how much do we all go up and down here above the Conway Valley ?"
Scientist	"A foot."
Barham	"A foot !! ?"
Scientist	"Yes."
Barham	"As much as that ? Now, is it in fact more here than elsewhere ?"
Scientist	"This particular part where we are now is very large indeed mainly because we have what is called 'ocean loading' and that is caused by the Irish Sea. This is one of the largest tidal areas in the world."

For the 'would-be' reporter I can't stress strongly enough to take your chances as soon as they appear. Don't ever let an opportunity pass you by. I did once, it passed about 12 inches from my left shoulder. In my defence I can only say that it happened a little more than a year into my career and so I was still a bit green, but it taught me a lesson and I swore that I would never let it happen again. Furthermore I was so disappointed with myself that I've never told anyone until now. I certainly didn't tell my producer.

It was on the eve of the 1969 Investiture of the Prince of Wales at Caernarvon Castle. As I was coming out of the castle I almost bumped into the organiser of the whole show – Princess Margaret's husband Lord Snowdon. I was there to report on the last minute arrangements for the following day. My report was going on the air the next morning, and here was the organiser himself hurrying up the steps towards me, and I didn't stop him. He even nodded to me and yet I didn't stop him. He looked as if he was in a great hurry but all I had to do was switch on the tape recorder and say "How's it going?" But I let him pass by and how I regretted it !

I met some great opportunists, and among the more unusual opportunities they exploited there was the trap door in the floor of the Woolpack Inn at Pandy in the Ceiriog valley, through which you could 'fish' in an under floor stream, and not far away there was the house with back garden fishing in the tunnels of an old silicon mine, but I'm digressing.

To round off the earth's crust story, they went on to tell me that they were there for the last time. Their work was finished, but my curiosity persisted. Some months later, on a restless day off, I went with a torch to have a look round. The quite substantial shed they'd built over the shaft was still in place, untouched and securely locked, but I knew of a tunnel further down in the forest which might lead through to the bottom of that shaft. I'd often rummaged around in the old mines of Gwydir, having been introduced to them many years earlier by Aneuryn Hughes, my first mate in Trefriw, and I knew this was a possible way in.

With the passing of time the entrance was well concealed now by trees and undergrowth, but once inside the going wasn't too bad. The tunnel was lofty enough to walk through upright and after only one awkward bit and a couple of junctions I found something interesting coming into view. The beam of my torch was showing the way ahead was blocked by iron bars, and in the deep shadows beyond them I could make out a brick wall. I'd seen iron bars and brick walls in gold mines but never in lead mines, and as I got nearer I saw that someone else had been there before me.

Set into the iron bars was a gate and although it was secured with a hefty padlock, the bars around it had been sawn through presumably with a hacksaw, and it was now standing ajar. Furthermore, I could see now that there was a door in the brick wall beyond, but someone had smashed through it. The door had been covered by a sheet of metal but this had been torn almost completely away, and so I went through the bars and found I could have gone through the hole in the door as well, but I didn't, I could see enough. The beam of my torch was showing a scene beyond that door of utter destruction. It was an area wider than the tunnel I'd come down and it was a huge jumbled mass of what seemed to be twisted metal frames and broken pipes, and huge chunks of white polystyrene, and lots of things that appeared to have been basins, all smashed to bits with more broken basins and pipes hanging from the walls. Someone had done a very thorough job of getting in and destroying everything down there.

CHAPTER P.
Pets, Participants and Politicians.

Forgive me please for skimming over these pets, there were hundreds of them, far too many for 'B' and Beasts alone and most gifted by far was man's best friend. There was the dog that climbed trees and barked poetry, and another that closed doors as well as opening them, an ability that should be genetically engineered into all domestic animals, especially children. But as you might guess, the spotlight usually fell on the professionals, the singers in particular. It's marvellous how the handler's grip tightening on the nuts of a warbling canine can so efficiently produce even the highest notes, but among the carefree amateurs, little Pip a Denbigh terrier, needed no manipulation.

This little scamp sang for the sheer joy of it, especially when it was time for 'Neighbours'. As soon as he heard that all too familiar signature tune come on the telly he'd come trotting in from the garden and sing along with it. He loved it, and he must have liked Australians because he adored Frank Ifield. He'd sing with any record by Frank Ifield, and he also loved male voice choirs, especially the Welsh ones. He loved them all except the Pendyrys. Whenever his owner played one of their records he walked out in disgust. I saw it happen. Sad but true.

Another terrier you couldn't help admiring was the one at Tyn y Groes. Fred was a hardy little soul. No matter how bad the weather he went to work every morning on his motorbike. Standing on a box behind his master, and with his arms round his master's neck, he made a marvellous sight with his ears pinned back by the slipstream and his cheerful little eyes gleaming through his goggles.

There were other dogs I didn't take kindly too. There was the snarling brute who insisted on accompanying his master to the pub every evening, and every time threatened to tear him to bits if he tried to touch a second pint, and then there was the landlord's dog at a Coedpoeth pub who ferociously drove everyone off the premises as soon as it was closing time. This he did on the flimsy excuse that it was time for his dinner, but at an inn called the Lion at Gwytherin they had a very different problem.

Here the problem was a cat, the sort most of us know as a lion. At first it was only a big kitten, but by the time it grew up it made sure no-one else got near the fire. Strange to say, customers started to drink at home. He looked magnificent of course stretched out on the hearth rug, but with him watching you from a half closed eye and swearing under his breath, I for one certainly didn't fancy stepping over him.

I lost count of those cases where one species was fostering another species. There was the Great Dane that was feeding a gang of pumas, and so on and so forth. I remember a Boston terrier rearing orphaned lambs, but dogs especially do like to work. They love having a job to do.

There were several dogs that collected glasses in public houses, and I will always remember Trixie an Alsatian in the Anglesey village of Llanerch-y-medd who worked as a petrol pump attendant. She didn't actually put the petrol into your car, but she was very good at taking the money, and if you really needed change, she brought it out to you in her mouth. It was always wet and slimy of course, but I didn't see anyone refuse to take it. On the other hand, I suppose the dog who could lay claim to the greatest achievement must be Major, the St. Bernard that established Manchester United.

I was told this remarkable story in 1973 by the dog's owner, a Mrs. Partington. She was a friendly old soul in a wheelchair who invited me to come up in her lift and have coffee with her one morning so that she could tell me this tale of long ago when she was a girl, the daughter of a Manchester brewery owner. She told me that this enormous great cuddly stray bounded into their garden one day and it was love at first sight. He swept her off her feet, dumped her on her back, and licked her face all over. But her father wasn't having it and advertised for the owner to come forward. The man turned up but claimed he couldn't afford to feed the massive thing. "You have him," he said, but her father was unmoved until the man said that he was so poor he was having to give up running his little local football club. "Take the dog and the team," he said, "You'll have fun with the lads." And eventually father gave in, reluctantly acquiring a big dog and a bunch of unwanted hooligans.

The old lady said, with such longing in her eyes, that this dog brought such happiness to the family. They had wonderful times supporting the lads, and then one day father threw a stick for the dog and as it landed it dug up a smudge of something white, revealing that just under the surface there was salt, and because of that they got even richer. With the profits from beer and salt they moved further up the social scale, and more money was spent on the football club, improving facilities, paying for better players, and eventually re-naming it – 'Manchester United'.

People can be barmy with animals. We all know how smelly goats are. I remember a woman who took hers to bed. She's dead now, and then there are the bird lovers. Birds range from nice little twittery creatures to hideous monsters

239

that cause reporters to cower in corners. Take the huge and gruesome beast Sam Barnes kept tethered in his front garden. This was some sort of eagle from a remote part of the world where it was said to have killed a forestry worker, and if you made the mistake of sitting with your back to the open window, it would bound in, block out the sun and sniff at the hairs on the back of your neck .

Sam Barnes was one of my favourites. He was a large and very loud Yorkshireman with a big Yorkshire accent to match. He reckoned his pet was twice the size of a Golden Eagle and it had been given to him by a sultan somewhere for saving a relative from drowning.

Several times I was onto a story that involved Sam Barnes. I always enjoyed my visit to that topsy-turvy house where he lived on the Pwllheli promenade with his daughter Amanda, but my favourite recollection of him was when he was playing a practical joke on the organisers of the European Veterans Athletic Championships. He was well known in the athletics world and he'd just caused a sensation in the British Veterans event by entering an old friend in the 60 yards dash. Now he was going to enter him in the European event.

Sam's old friend was very old, and nothing like athletic. I only remember his name was Dave, but poor old Dave was pitifully thin and well – just very elderly. Nevertheless, although he didn't say much he was as game as his mischievous mate, and I persuaded them to come out onto the promenade for a training session.

This tape shows what you can do with an idea when people 'participate' and the rest of this chapter is dedicated to some of those people who could see what I was trying to do – taking a story and bringing it to life. None of them were actors but every one of them deserved an Oscar. As always with all these off the cuff 'dramatics', this was completely unscripted and performed with perfectly straight faces.

The scene – a sunny morning on the

Pwllheli promenade. The focus – two elderly men. One tall, authoritative and athletic. The other, very elderly, very thin, terribly fragile, and wearing shorts and a running vest.

BWB17

Mr. Barnes	"This is how we hype him up you see, before the event, because he's nervous. You have to relax David you see, yes."
Barham	"But is it important for him to lie down on the promenade ?"
Mr. Barnes	"Yes to think nice thoughts you see, with his muscles relaxed you see and he's breathing deep and he's counting, and he's going off now you see."
Barham	"He's falling asleep isn't he ?"
Mr. Barnes	"Yes he's falling asleep, that's right, that's the idea. See that's relieving his tension you see. That's relieving his tension and I'll just give him a minute or two like this and his nerves have gone you see, and I've blocked his ears up so he can't hear the guns banging and authoritative officials and what-not, and then I get him up to start you see."
Barham	"I see, so have you had enough rest now David ?"
David	(Weakly) "Yes, fine."
Mr. Barnes	"And he's coming to now. Yes, yes."
Barham	"Can he get up on his own ?"
Mr. Barnes	"Yes he can get up on his own. I'll give him a bit of a lift from behind you see."
Barham	"Give him a lift, there you are."
Mr. Barnes	"The trouble is, his shorts keep coming down."
Barham	"Right okay, so what's he going to do, 60 yards isn't it ?"
Mr. Barnes	"Oh yes, yes."
Barham	"They call it the 60 yard dash. ?"
Mr. Barnes	"Oh yes. They call him Dave the Dash.(Speaking to

	the athlete) So this time you're doing 60 yards. Round that shelter and back again, and stand facing the shelter 'cos you're going that way you see. You see. We don't want you running into the sea and cooling off. No, so I'm counting down now."
Barham	"So he's got him facing the right way now."
Mr. Barnes	"Three – two – one …. Off !" (David staggers off towards the shelter). "There you are, there you are, look at that action, just like a duck you see, just like a duck (shouting) 90 degree arm action David now. But he has to keep putting his hands down to pull his trousers up. Notice how they fall down ?"
Barham	"Yes, (concerned) he didn't really get off to a very fast start did he ?"
Mr. Barnes	"No, no that's another of his problems you see. His feet sort of spread out like a duck's."
Barham	"You've got a lot of work to do."
Mr. Barnes	"Oh a lot of work to do on him, yes, but he's coming up now, (looking at stop watch) let's have a look, see how many seconds have gone."
Barham	"What's it now ?"
Mr. Barnes	" ….35."
Barham	"What's the world record ?"
Mr. Barnes	"For sixty yards it's 8.6."
Barham	"Seconds ?"
Mr. Barnes	"Yes, seconds, yes, yes."
Barham	"Well he's coming in now …."
Mr. Barnes	"He's coming back now and he's up to 50. Come on, keep going (shouting) right through, right through."
Barham	"Well done."

(Elderly runner returns panting).

Mr. Barnes	"He's broke the electric tape you see."
Barham	"Yes, very good. Is he getting faster ?"
Mr. Barnes	"Oh yes, sometimes he does, yet it all depends, if he

	has the wind with him or behind him or what-not."
Barham	"That's right, yes, yes."
Mr. Barnes	"Yes, if he's in his strip or has his pipe in, and things like that you see."

It was probably putting that sort of thing on the air that caused the run-down in my career. I won't say ruined it because I enjoyed it, but as a younger generation with little sense of humour filtered into the BBC's chain of command there was less fun, colleagues spoke increasingly of tension, and many reporters were reduced to nothing more than 'fact quoting robots', but there was no way I was going to change.

It seemed that the new breed of producers resented the reporter's freedom to travel the open road and share with the listeners their enjoyment of a good story. All they wanted was more and more sad and miserable tales of woe brought to the microphone by reporters showing no personality, and I couldn't accept that. I never shared their moronic view of journalism or indeed of life. To many only bad news was worth covering. Instead I carried on doing it my way, but it wasn't easy. Those young people took themselves and their jobs so seriously, and really my greatest fortune was the 180 miles that separated me from Cardiff.

It reminds me of something the television reporter Michael Buerk wrote in his book 'Lost For Words.' He said "My enjoyment of the BBC has been directly proportioned to the distance I've managed to put between me and it, and you know, the furthest away you are, the more control you have over what you choose to do and how you choose to do it."

On the subject of 'participants' though, over the years I enjoyed the help of so many. One of my earliest efforts to breath some life into what otherwise might have been a life-less interview must have been getting the local councillors of Machynlleth to stand in a group under the arches of their town clock and sing Happy Birthday to it. "Happy Birthday dear clock, happy birthday dear clock," .... etc. etc. This did actually make them sound a bit silly, but that really wasn't my intention and here and now I will say "Sorry councillors." But it did show how proud they were of their clock, and rightly so. It's magnificent. In fact whenever I pass it I sing "Happy birthday dear clock." I can't resist it. (It still makes me laugh !)

There were so many 'participant' episodes, and on one occasion I remember taking doctors and nurses, and some of the hospital office staff too, on a climbing expedition up their main staircase. This was at Bodelwyddan and this one came out pretty well. They'd been encouraged to use the stairs in order to keep fit, and in keeping an account of their climbs they were comparing their efforts with climbing mountains. We all pretended to hang on to ropes and climb to the summit, huffing and puffing, while someone (sharing the oxygen bottle) explained to me the physical benefit of regular exercise. It was fun and it illustrated the point.

Sometimes participants would volunteer in quite large numbers. When a fence was laid across the Rhydymwyn football pitch to define a new pipeline the team was naturally upset, and so I got them to arrange a match in which a member of each team carried a pair of step ladders. Seeing them line up to go over the fence every time the ball went over the half way line was wonderful, and I had it filmed for television news, but television people take themselves too seriously and it wasn't well received.

Thinking of that ladder episode reminds me of one of the old 'Carry On' films. When the savage hordes in that classic - 'Up the Khyber' were rushing to go through that little gate in the Khyber Pass, I was there interviewing some of the cast, in particular Terry Scott and Charles Hawtry. It was filmed on the lower slopes of Snowdon's Watkin path, and incidentally the gate is still there.

Some of these exercises were hard work for my participants, like the next one which has always been a favourite because I can still see in my mind's eye this very tubby middle aged man bouncing up and down on a pogo stick. Infact I can still see his big red cheeks getting redder and redder.

In the days of 'It's a Knock-Out', that great BBC television series in which towns competed against each other in spectacular and wonderfully silly outdoor games, Colwyn Bay needed a lady in their team who could bounce up and down on a pogo stick. They were going to be up against tough international opposition but unfortunately she was proving difficult to find because she needed to keep bouncing up and down for a good ten minutes, which was going to be very tiring of course.

When they put out a somewhat tongue in cheek SOS I was sent to report. No lady had yet come forward, but they did at least have a pogo stick and their trainer, a very large mayor's chauffeur, a retired army major by the name of Fred Wilson. While I interviewed the team manager - their Director of Tourism, I got the chauffeur to bounce around for a few minutes.

STR 12

Chauffeur	(Calling out numbers whilst bouncing up and down) "1! 2! 3! 4! 1! 2! 3! 4! 1! 2! 3! 4!" (repeated continuously).
Barham	"I'm standing outside the Civic Centre here in Colwyn Bay and the team coach major Fred 'Tiger' Wilson is trying out the pogo stick, bouncing around us at the moment, and I'm going to turn first of all to Mr. Leslie Shepherd the Director of Entertainment in Colwyn Bay and team manager. Mr. Shepherd, what qualities should an international pogo stick jumper have these days ?"
Mr. Shepherd	"She's got to be tremendously fit. A girl of this kind has got to be an athlete, someone with willpower to

	practise for hours on end with complete dedication."
Barham	"And how far have you cast your net ?"
Mr. Shepherd	"Well I can truthfully say the world. We've sent telegrams and letters all over the place to try and get somebody who is really good at this form of sport."
Barham	"Can we just have a word with …."
Chauffeur	(Stops counting. Panting) "Oh my god yes."

(Staggers off pogo stick)

Barham	…. "With Major Wilson. What will this young lady have to do exactly ?"
Chauffeur	(Still panting) "Well, apart from having to balance on a pogo stick and ride it, it means she's got to be able to hop forward and back, she has got to remain balanced stationary for some time. She's got to be physically fit as well, my God!"(Still panting.)
Barham	"Will she be up against very tough opposition ?"
Mr. Shepherd	"Very tough, very tough. Some of the continentals are pogo stick mad you know, even kids go to school on them, and I'm told some of the factory workers hop to work on pogo sticks."
Barham	"Good gracious me. I've heard of going to work on an egg but that's ridiculous. Can I hop off to the studio now if I can borrow the pogo stick.?"
Chauffeur	"Yes you do that. Right, hop off. (With feeling) Go on Hop off !"
Mr. Shepherd	(Collapses in a fit of laughter).

You never know what people are going to say of course, but many were brilliant, like the worm catcher, and others like Sam Barnes, but here's another genius. He's another old friend – Phil Duncalf, one of my old badminton partners. I thought he'd be good, but not this good.

It was another April 1st spoof when a lot of anti-shooting protests were in the news, so I got him to play an old military type with a rich plummy accent shooting everything in sight. We went out into his field with a gun and he just made it up as he went along, but he was so good my producer didn't dare put in on the air.

RWR16

Barham	"Lovely day isn't it ?"
Colonel	"Beautiful, yes beautiful."
Barham	"Yes beautiful. When this gentleman, Colonel Humphrey Jones Bagshott retired from the army and came to live here in the Vale of Clwyd, he made sure that he got himself a good reliable shotgun."
Colonel	"Yes, this is it here."
Barham	"You made sure that you had a shotgun because, as I understand it, if the rumours are correct, you use it quite a lot don't you ?"
Colonel	"Oh yes, yes I do rather. But you see, you didn't get these birds sitting outside your bedroom window in London, making this silly dawn chorus. You just get some industrial noise which of course you can put up with, but here in the country you find that there is a terrible raucous cacophony all the time. Well, I had one the other morning, a red breasted fellow, I don't quite know what it was but I shot it."
Barham	"Yes, a friend of mine actually rang me because … in fact... what's that there ? …. (bang, bang),...Ah..... what was it ?"
Colonel	"Got it anyway."
Barham	"Yes, yes some little bird."
Colonel	"A blackbird I think."
Barham	"Yes, well they do make a bit of noise I suppose."
Colonel	"Oh yes, and thrushes too, damned things."
Barham	"But are you aware that several people in the locality are disturbed by the fact that you are shooting so

	many birds ?"
Colonel	"Oh nonsense, nonsense."
Barham	"It was said anyway, that you shot a duck a couple of weeks ago. Is that right ?"
Colonel	"Oh yes, that was the next door neighbour's duck. Quacking it was, so I shot it."
Barham	"Well people do shoot wild ducks but that was your neighbour's duck."
Colonel	"No, can't expect me to shoot wild ducks, can't get after those. But we can't stand this raucous cacophony every day."
Barham	"Hmm"
Colonel	"So someone has got to do something about it."
Barham	"Yes."
Colonel	"So I shoot them you see."
Barham	"The duck of course was on your property was it, when you shot it ?"
Colonel	"Well nearly. It was on the boundary on a hedge you know."
Barham	"On the periphery ?"
Colonel	"On the periphery, yes that's the word I was looking for. My word ! I think I can see something ! What's that moving there ?"
Barham	"I think it's a tractor isn't it ?"
Colonel	"A tractor ?"
Barham	"Let it go past."

(Tractor passes).

Colonel	"Look! There it is, I can see something moving in the bushes. Can you see it ? (Bang, bang). Did I get it ?"
Barham	"Err …… well whatever it was it's fallen out of the bush."
Colonel	"What was it ?"
Barham	"Have you done a lot of shooting in the army ?

Colonel	"Oh yes, well of course even as a schoolboy of course, I used to go to these fairgrounds to shoot these little ducks going up and down on the fairground things. I used to be fairly good at that. Daddy of course bought me a gun at an early age, of course I've always been keen on shooting. I like now to shoot things that move you see."
Barham	"I suppose in the army you were only shooting at targets, things that didn't move ?"
Colonel	"Well except for a short period of time I was in Malaya and then I shot a lot of monkeys in the trees. Good sport these monkeys. Used to kill few. Twenty I had in one day all by myself, and that was with a hand gun."
Barham	"Surely the RSPB, the Royal Society for the Protection of Birds...."
Colonel	"I know, these peculiar people."
Barham	"Aren't they right in trying to protect bird life ?"
Colonel	"I'm going to have all the trees down next weekend anyway, the whole lot, all coming down, they're a habitat for birds you see, can't have it. Cutting all the trees down next week."
Barham	"Why don't you go back and live in the city ?"
Colonel	"Well it has been suggested by quite a few people actually, but I like it here, if it wasn't for the noises you know. I quite enjoy it here."
Barham	"You've got some splendid views."
Colonel	"It's glorious isn't it, beautiful, Mr. Barham. The sun is shining and it's glorious. What better than to go out and kill something ? Makes you feel as though it's good to be alive."
Barham	"Yes, I suppose soon we'll be hearing the first cuckoo of spring won't we ?"
Colonel	"No I don't think so lad, shot him yesterday."

One day in the 'eighties we got a report saying that the Council in Llandudno was thinking of giving up its deckchairs because it appeared that hiring a deckchair was something of the past, and so I had to go and interview the deckchair official. This I decided to do standing next to a great stack of them on the prom, while I also endeavoured, quite unsuccessfully, to hire them out to passers-by.

You never know how things are going to go with a stunt, and this one was going badly. No-one was showing any interest until a lady came by with her husband and I realised immediately that I had a 'star' to work with. I don't know who she was, and I don't know whether she really was a cockney, but she sounded like one, and 'cor blimey' she certainly saved my bacon.

BWB 24

Barham	"Can I offer you a deckchair only 20p for halfa day?"
Passer by	"No thank you."
Barham	"I didn't realise it was so difficult.(Couple approach.) What about you, would you like a deckchair ? I'm not doing very well."
Woman	"They're a bit shabby aren't they ?"
Barham	"Sorry ?"
Woman	"Look, look they're a bit shabby."
Barham	"What ?"
Woman	"Your deckchairs."
Barham	"Really ?"
Woman	"Don't you think so ?"
Barham	"Yes, they're just a bit faded, it just goes to prove we get a lot of sunshine in north Wales."
Woman	"It just goes to prove you should have a better cover on them. You've got to make 'em glamorous."

Barham	"Well what about this one over here madam, a red and white striped one. And over here I've got a green and white striped one."
Woman	"I'm sorry that don't go with my colouring."
Barham	"Well what about green and white ?"
Woman	"Well, green and white is more effective."
Barham	"Look, look, let me just put it up for you. Now hang on, look .... I'm sure you've got a minute if I just ... hang on .... If I can just get this backrest down. Look here ...oooh... that's it. There we are. Right. How's that madam ?"
Woman	"That's not right."
Barham	"Yes it is.... hang on ....I've got my foot caught" (he wrestles with deckchair).
Woman	"Do you want me to ...."
Barham	"I've got my foot caught in it. Right... ah .... how's that ? Right.(Woman sits). Comfy ?"
Woman	"Oh I only want Tom Jones, I'll be well away."
Barham	"You only want what, sorry ?"
Woman	"Tom Jones."
Barham	"What for 20p ?"
Woman	"Well I'll have him for 40p, I don't mind."
Barham	"I'll sit on your lap if you like ?"
Woman	"Oh I don't think so. Can you sing ?"
Barham	"Of course I can."
Woman	"All you've got to do is take your trousers off, stick out that chest of yours."
Barham	"Yes, yes ?"
Woman	"And give 'em a little bit of you know .... how's your father."
Barham	"You wouldn't like to take on this concession would you ? Letting out these deckchairs ?"
Woman	"I think I could do a better job than you. How long are you down 'ere flogging these things ?"

Barham   (Gloomily) "The rest of my life if I'm not careful."

One of the world's greatest tennis players was one of my participants. It was at the opening round of the Men's World Championships just before he won the first of his Wimbledon titles.

Strange to say, during the seventies this big world event opened two years running at the Deeside Leisure Centre at Queensferry near Chester, and my producer wanted me to find out what it was like receiving a world-class fast service, a stunt agreed to by the organisers for the sake of publicity. Understandable really. Industrial Queensferry is hardly the hub of manicured lawns and cucumber sandwiches, so I took along my tennis racquet and little white shorts, changed with the world's most famous players, and went out on the court in front of about 2,000 people.

They were still applauding a match that had just finished and my guardian – the organiser, introduced me to one of the contestants, a very fierce looking foreign giant who was supposed to meet my request, but this is where it went badly wrong. He'd been expected to win but he'd lost, and instead of shaking hands with me he stormed off court with the organiser chasing after him. With his victorious opponent, umpire and ball boys all gone too, this left me standing there alone. The crowds simmered down after a while and then fell silent. It was very uncomfortable. They were studying me.   Soon they were whispering. I could hear them distinctly asking each other "Who the hell is this ?"

Maybe I should have included 'embarrassment' in Chapter E. There were plenty of embarrassing moments, and this was one of the worst. As the agonising minutes ticked by and the whispers turned to titters, I once again began to feel like Norman Wisdom. I felt so 'lost' and 'abandoned' so I started to walk around a bit, practically dragging my racquet behind me, and very quickly the titters turned to laughter. One guy pointed to my tape recorder and shouted "What's in your box then, your sandwiches ?" Then at last the organiser returned with someone in tow, a young lad in shorts carrying a racquet, and he was introduced to me as a Swede by the name of Bjorn Borg. But being twelve months before he won the first of his several Wimbledon singles titles, his name meant nothing to me. We shook hands and I was told he would send me down a few serves.

So, finding a big voice, I told the crowd who I was and what we were going to do. This amused them even more, and laying the microphone down beside the court I shouted a few words of introduction in its direction, and then shouted to my opponent that he could commence.

The crowd loved it.   He had me running from one side to another, but he wasn't serving fast. He'd misunderstood and instead he was spinning each serve first one way and then the other. I'd played tennis for most of my life but I'd never seen anything like this. I was shouting a commentary across to my microphone and of course we were entertaining the crowd at the same time, but it was so difficult to even guess which way the balls were going to bounce. But then, I had that sort of match winning luck that all great players need from time to time. From one of my returns he smashed the ball into the net. The cheers were deafening. I'd won a point ! It was obviously a good time to stop, and I ran up to the net and consoled him.

The wonderful thing about that incident was that he was about to start his match.   In fact his opponent had arrived on the scene as we returned to the umpire's chair. There can't be many players who would have a joined in with a bit of fun like that moments before starting the match.

The Australian player Ken Rosewall was a pretty relaxed kind of guy too.   The night before the tournament he was due to arrive in Chester by train and I was sent to wait for him at his hotel opposite the station. His plane from

Australia had been late arriving, the fog delayed the train from London, there was no food on the train, and he arrived with his wife after midnight. It had obviously been a dreadful journey.

I introduced myself as he signed in and he said "Okay I'll be down in a minute," and as he went upstairs I settled down in an armchair thinking that it was going to be a long wait. But I needn't have worried. He came down immediately and recorded a really nice interview, telling me all about the tournament, who was going to be there, and anything else I wanted to know. I've never forgotten that. All the way from Australia, hours late, hungry, jet-lagged and a nice interview. A lesson to us all.

Politicians come next. These are the easiest people to interview. Among the biggest names among them I interviewed Margaret Thatcher on the eve of her moving into number ten, and whether they're prime-ministers, cabinet-ministers, or mere back-benchers, they will submit to your microphone like martyrs, like faithful messengers happy to be shot. It's extraordinary. For you it's a day off. The issues are clearly defined, the selection of questions is obvious, there's no need for background noises, no need for atmosphere, and you can be as awkward and argumentative as you like, they just 'beam' at you, and at the earliest opportunity come back for more.

In 1997, by way of a change, I indulged in a spell of role reversal. I contested the Conwy constituency for the Referendum Party. It was a protest party to try and bring about a referendum on the hated EU, and it was well worth doing, and among the lessons I learnt is that a lot of people think an election is horse race. They have to be on the winning side. They say "You're absolutely right, but it's no good voting for you because you can't win."

CHAPTER Q.
Queer Ideas.

It's difficult to know where to start on these. Queer ideas come in every guise and I'm afraid the best ones emanate almost entirely from men. They come in a variety of sizes too, both in concept and content. When it was proposed in the nineties that Criccieth should have a harbour with a wall built out to the castle rock, I found that soon after the First World War the village's most famous son, David (Prime Minister) Lloyd George, had been thinking the same thing, and had been willing to provide an instant harbour wall by scuttling a couple of old warships there.

If you know Criccieth you will know it's a pretty little place, and the rusting hulks of a battleship or two would have provided an interesting addition to the picture postcards, but when it comes to the other end of the size spectrum and the inclusion of the opposite sex, Pat Evers Swindel of Pwll Glas has shown that an artist can use anything as a canvas. Her party piece has been to paint on cobwebs, several layers of them, and very nice her work is too. Something in the cobwebs appears to glow through the paint.

There was another lady artist I remember, her name was Pat Ballard and she picked up something of a dirty habit. She took to sitting up to her ankles in mud for hours on end, like one of those military artists of the first world war, only she was painting pictures of dirty great engineering projects. The A55 tunnels were among her collection, but usually feminine attempts were on a smaller scale, like the girl in the Flint area who made paper from porridge. However, people in this category can also be musical. Take the man in Rhosneigr who drilled holes in his bamboo settee and with great enthusiasm turned it into a flute. He might have gone far, but it was awkward to carry.

DG47

Inventor	"All you have to do is bend over and blow in here."
Barham	"Good gracious."
Inventor	"It's great." (Plays Bluebells of Scotland furiously).

I like inventors. Some do it quietly and inconspicuously whereas Paul Morris of Coedpoeth went in for the spectacular. Can you imagine a garden shed coming up the street on wheels ? Or a garden gate ? Paul you see, turned everything into bicycles.

AC3B

Barham	I'm with two of Paul's children at the moment, and I can see you've got your bikes so you're a real cycling family aren't you ?"
Child	"Yeah."
Barham	"Oh hang on, here comes your dad. I can see the shed coming up the road now. (They all laugh). This is remarkable. It's on three wheels. (Knocks on door). Can you hear me in there Paul ?"
Mr. Morris	"Ching ching hello."
Barham	"Ching ching ? Haven't you got a bell ?"
Mr. Morris	"I haven't got a bell, I pretend."
	Barham (Laughs).
Mr. Morris	"Not many garden sheds have bells."
Barham	"Well I suppose not. (Dog barks) Oh you've scared the neighbour's dog now. Can you climb out of this?"
Mr. Morris	"I can ..... ooh! .... Ow! .... It's difficult, very very difficult."
Barham	"What on earth made you make a bicycle out of a garden shed ?"
Mr. Morris	"I haven't got a clue really. I suppose sheds are pretty immobile things most of the time, so I wanted a mobile shed."

He said that he'd made all sorts of bicycles and we walked round to the back of the house to see some of them. The first one I spotted had been a garden gate. Now it had a seat, two wheels, and a pair of handlebars of course.

Mr. Morris	"Well if you've got a garden shed you need a garden gate. I don't think much escapes being bicycle-ised."
Barham	(Laughs and points to a miniature bike) "How big is that ?"
Mr. Morris	"Fifteen inches high to the seat and it's got a ten inch wheelbase."
Barham	"And I see you've got a reclining bike that you can lie back on, but what's this 'winged' bike with a child's bike mounted near the handlebars ?"
Mr. Morris	"That's called Heaven Sent."
Barham	"Do you ever go far on these bicycles ?"
Mr. Morris	"No, only to work, which is just over a mile away."
Barham	"You don't go in the shed do you ?"
Mr. Morris	"No not as yet. It's quite heavy and it's up quite a hill."

This good lad sometimes auctioned his bikes for charity, and another funny bike I came across in the Wrexham area was called the 'Snaark' and this was special because it was a 'family' bike. It had four seats, two in the front and two at the back, it had a canvas roof, and it was about the size of a family car. But this 'car' used no petrol or diesel because it was purely pedal powered, with pedals situated in front of every seat. It was created by the Eastwood family of Bwlch Gwyn who used it for family outings and going to church, and they were very willing for me to go for a ride with them, as long as I did my share of the pedalling.

Father was in the front steering, with mum alongside with the baby on her lap, while I sat in the back with five-year old John, who had to pedal as hard as we did.

F91E

Mum	"Oh yes, it's more than he dare do, not to pedal now."
Dad	"Stand by to change gear."

My only worry was having a large lorry come round the bend behind us and squash us flat, because at the most we were only doing about 15 miles an hour. Nevertheless I loved all those queer ideas, and when I said they come in a variety of guises, they do, but they can also be found in all walks of life.

To state the obvious, farming is a pretty 'down to earth' business, but how about the Anglesey farmer who was trying to prolong the useful life of his ewes by fitting them with false teeth, or the Anglesey farmer who bred bald sheep? After many years of selective breeding they had only a little covering of wool, but he reckoned the price of wool didn't warrant the bother of keeping them free of problems or indeed the effort of shearing.

With farmers at least there is always a reason for queer behaviour, but how would you fancy licking an ice cream made out of sheep's milk ? That was somewhere on the Lleyn Peninsula, and I'm afraid that was something else I had to swallow. Seeing sheep go through such a tiny milking parlour was a strange sight, and the two-ton rubber whale was a strange sight too. That was being used to teach people how to re-float whales that had become stranded in shallow water.

That was a good idea, but all to often I saw good ideas wiped out with the stroke of a bureaucratic pen. The motor car tyre nest for lobsters and was one. No sooner had maverick fisherman John Povah chained a few tyres together and dumped them into the deep off Rhos on Sea, a sea monster in the shape of 'Officialdom' reared its ugly head above the waves and made him remove what a lot of us thought was a brilliant idea, but animals too can be awkward creatures.

In Beddgelert, the residents of that

beautiful Snowdonia village, famous for its floral awards and a dead dog, once held a 'Wild West' week to attract more tourists. This for Snowdonia was a very queer idea, but it attracted a few cowboys and Indians, who sat in wigwams smoking various stuff in peace pipes, and during the week they did all the things they were expected to do, like getting thrown out of saloons and shooting each other, and at the end of the week the local lads who'd organised it, staged a grand rodeo. At least, they were going to.

At the appointed hour I joined the crowd alongside a field close to the village centre and watched with high expectations as the cowboys set about the task of rounding up the horses. It was certainly worth coming for. It was very entertaining. For half an hour we watched them running from one side of the field to the other. Those horses just didn't want to be caught, and as far as I know, never were.

One of my favourite queer ideas was for a decimal clock, and I've wondered sometimes if this was a bit too clever to be classed as a 'queer' idea. It was the brainchild of someone in Deganwy, and I realised that talking to him about it opened up a whole new way of seeing time. Not that he was alone of course, people have always been meddling with it, and I've met plenty of people who'd like to keep to British summertime, but this man had gone one step further. He'd made a clock that would be decimal and therefore give us only twenty hours in a day. I spoke to him where he had it on display at the Conwy Visitors Centre.

BBWB 27

Barham	"Well Mr. Williams, it looks like a pretty ordinary clock. The face is round, it's got two hands, an hour hand and a minute hand, but I see the hour hand only goes up to ten, not twelve."
Mr. Williams	"With everything as they are, with everything being in tens, we've got feet and inches we've forgotten about, and even we've got the pounds and pence that

	we've forgotten about. Children today don't know

we've forgotten about. Children today don't know nothing about them. So now really, would be the time to get everything into tens."

Barham "It looks a bit strange though doesn't it, because according to your clock midday would be 10 o'clock, ten noon."

Mr. Williams "Yes it would.

Barham "You've written to the Prime Minister I believe ?"

Mr. Williams "I'm hoping to get a reply from him because it has been two or three months since he had the letter."

Barham "Perhaps he can't find enough hours in the day, and you'd do him out of four more ! You're talking about a 20 hour day aren't you ?"

Mr. Williams "Yes, but there are 72 minutes in the hour."

Barham "Right I see, okay. You've got a card up here on the side explaining the idea. I see, you've got 100 sets equals 1 minute."

Mr. Williams "Yes, well that's because I've divided it up into 100 equal parts."

Barham "So you're also planning to do away with the seconds and have 100 sets of them in a minute ?"

Mr. Williams "But they'd still be there because you can't go beyond 1,440 minutes to the day."

When I spoke to the onlookers they weren't too impressed, and I stood aside as he tried to win them over. He was trying very hard.

Mr. Williams "It will be safer for your children, because as things are now, you send your child out to a shop and you tell him to be there and back in a quarter of an hour, while at the present time it's a quarter of an hour and its only fifteen minutes, where it would be, in my time, or in this time, it would be eighteen minutes.

They need it to cross the road and go to the places and come back."

I still need extra time to work that out. But here's a good one. A real queer one this is. Every now and then the Mayor of Beaumaris has to climb over a roof. It's only done once every seven years and if the tide's in he also has to swim for it. That comes later, but he starts at the edge of the sea by throwing a stone as far as he can into the Menai Strait so as to claim that much of it for the town, and then he and his posse of dignitaries march off to an isolated house where a ladder is leaning against the house, and he goes over the roof.

On the one occasion that I was there to meet him, the Mayor was Councillor Stan Zalot, and very impressive he looked too.

BWB 95

Barham	"The Mayor looks very smart indeed in his official chain, but at the moment he's not really behaving with a lot of Mayoral dignity I must say that. I'll try and give him a call because he's up there on the roof of this house – 'Mr. Mayor ! (crowd cheers) – Mr. Mayor ! What are you doing up on that roof ?"
Mayor	"Claiming the boundary for the town of Beaumaris."
Barham	"Is it really necessary to climb up onto the roof ?"
Mayor	"It certainly is because half of this building is in a different parish."
Barham	"I see. Alright then. ….. Well he's right up on the very top of the roof now, I'll go round the other side and see if I can have a word with him when he comes down. (Walks round the corner). There's a ladder over this side as well and he's ready now to come down this other side. His name is Mr. Stan Zalot and I think this marking of the boundary, this ancient boundary of Beaumaris, only happens every seven

	years. (Mayor comes down ladder). Well done Mr. Mayor."
Mayor	"Thank you very much."
Barham	"Very good, now tell me, tell me more about this, this is all to do with old boundaries isn't it ?"
Mayor	"Yes. The Charter of 1533 I think it is, I'm not 100% certain of the date. It was the old boundary of Beaumaris that was perambulated by the people of the town and for every building and area of ground that was within the boundary, we could charge rates and taxes, etc. etc."
Barham	"And I suppose this house lies right on the very boundary ?"
Mayor	"Smack in the middle of it. So half of it is in Cwm Cadnant and the other half is in Beaumaris."
Barham	"Tell me though, wouldn't it have been easier to go in through the front door and come out through the back door ?" (Crowd laughs).
Mayor	"Well that's the way it's been through all the centuries and that's the way it's going to stay."

Good. I like old traditions, but this one gets queerer by the minute. After climbing over the house the Mayor and his mates hurried off to a road junction where they sat an old lady on a throne in the middle of the road and crowned her 'Queen of the Crossroads'. The Mayor placed a garland of wild flowers on her head, gave her a kiss, and then marched on to 'wade' under a bridge with the prospect of getting wet again later walking round the end of the pier if the tide was in. But first he had to go to church. This was Llaniestyn Church, and here the Mayor saw to it that a party of schoolchildren carried sods of earth into the church on their heads. Don't ask me why, I'd completely lost the plot by then.

CHAPTER R.
Races, RAC, RAF, Rescues, and Red Tape.

Wales is a good place for unusual races and some have been quite glamorous, like Llandudno's Waiters and Waitresses race along the Prom. ("She's well out in front") with runners carrying trays, crockery and glasses, whereas at the lower end you have the snail races.

D514

Barham	"What's your snail called ?"
Little girl	"Cedric."
Barham	"Is he going to win ?"
Little girl	"Yep."
Barham	"Is he fast ?"
Little Girl	"Course not silly."

I've seen some very strange races, and competitions too. A local orthodontist, Richard Parkhouse beat the train once going from London to Edinburgh on his motor bike, then broke the record for riding through every county in mainland Britain. Working out the shortest route was fascinating, and so was 'worm -charming'. This was a competition in Wellington, Shropshire,where you had to induce worms to the surface by sticking various implements like forks into the ground and 'wiggling' them about, but my favourite among the races were always the donkey derbys. I used to love it when the galloping donkeys – driven on by their eager young jockeys, spotted someone eating an ice cream and they all piled up in a heap wanting a lick. On the other hand it was difficult to beat the spectacle at Lake Vyrnwy when the tandem races were held there. A twisting road surrounds that beautiful lake, and as you might know tandems go very fast. It was like the TT races on the Isle Of Mann.

Another excellent race, but one rarely run, was the Welshpool 'Race the Train' race. This was an event where runners set off from Llanfaircaereinion to beat the old steam train to Welshpool. It was very evenly matched because the train took a less direct route and stopped as usual along the way, so when road and rail came together for the last mile, a great climax was assured. They used to have something similar on the Tal y Llyn line but the runners finished nowhere near the train, whereas at Welshpool, another of the little re-borne steam railways of Wales, you could actually see panic on the runners faces as they pounded along - the hooting train gradually coming up behind them, getting closer and closer !

The RAC rally can be a good radio spectacle of course, with the sound of cars roaring past and drenching spectators with mud. I've had quite a few wet and muddy nights covering that event. That was often the case with 'Good Morning Wales'. The programme went on the air each day at breakfast-time so if something went on all night you stayed with it until morning. But one year when I was working for an afternoon programme, I was able to cover the RAC rally as it progressed during daylight hours for a change, and on this leisurely occasion I spent the morning checking the over-night positions on the phone before driving down to record the inserts as they hit Dolgellau.

As I approached that nice little grey stone town I saw all the flags flying around an area they'd prepared next to the cattle market, and at the gate a very friendly marshal allowed me to drive straight in and park next to some of the large vans belonging to the various teams - loaded with tyres and things. It was perfect. I got out the car, and mingling with mechanics in smart team overalls, I asked when they were coming through.

"About half past two mate." One of them said, and to further gen up on positions I asked who was likely to be in the lead and so on. I then went and sat in the car and read my newspaper.

It's quite remarkable, but in all those 32 years I never ever learned to recognise the peril of seeing everything go smoothly! It was a lovely day. The sun was shining, and I had half an hour to spare. I was parked right in the middle of it all, and I was perfectly prepared. I had the intro script already written, and all I needed now was a few moments recorded with the leaders – find someone famous, followed by an organiser giving a few more details, and then just finish on lots of noise as they shoot off on the next leg. Easy. Lovely. A nice restful day.

There wasn't much in the paper but the time gradually slipped by. I had another cup of coffee from the flask and sat watching them stacking tyres and rummaging through tool boxes until, with the time now a quarter to three, I sauntered over to one of the mechanics.

"What's the hold up ?" I asked.

"What hold up ?"

"When are they arriving ?"

"Who ?"

"The drivers, you know the competitors."

"Oh no mate," he said, "They don't come here, they're on the other side of town !"

"What !! ?"

"They stopped by the Cross Foxes pub."

"What !! ?"

"They'll all be gone by now. This is where they come if they need repairs."

I flew to the car, rammed it into gear, ran over the marshal, raced out the gate and up to the Cross Foxes and caught the last one. I only got him because he'd got lost. I don't know who he was, he was a driver I'd never heard of and haven't heard of since.

Getting back to a studio on time is often the most difficult part of a radio reporter's day, and can result in you taking part in a race of your own. I really must have led a charmed life when I think of the way I had to drive. I think the worst experience was on a mission in France trying to catch a train from Marseilles. It was in the dark, in the rush hour, in the pouring rain, and for over sixty terrible miles I had to hang onto the dim rear lights of a French lunatic who knew the way. Thanks to someone mislaying the tickets we were very late, and that race against the clock was absolute madness.

One of the worst blood pressure experiences you can have is being caught in heavy traffic while on the radio you hear the programme start ! Perhaps I've said this already, but it really is infuriating. You hear the signature tune come on and you hear the presenter say something like - "Hello, in today's programme we have news on the latest inflation figures, we have news of ferry cancellations, and Allan Barham has been.." and you find yourself shouting "You fool, I'm not back yet !"

Returning from the South Stack lighthouse one day I pulled onto the Mona airfield to quickly cut out a few chunks of tape. (Remember ? It's called editing.) As usual the gate was open because it's shared between a local flying club and the RAF who use it as a spare landing strip. It was rarely busy and it was a good place to get off the road. It was raining hard that day and very soon the windows steamed up, and I remember a vehicle passing. It was going towards the gate and I took no notice, but I should have done. He not only closed it but he locked it too. As soon as I wiped the mist off the windscreen I saw it was shut and locked with a gigantic padlock.

I jumped out of the car hoping to lift the gate off its hinges but it was built in a way so as not to lift off its hinges. The time was racing by and I was trapped. I tore round to the control tower and banged on the door. No reply. I tore round to the flying club hut and banged on that door. No reply there either, and so I raced round the runways desperately searching for another way out and eventually spotted a gate at the bottom of a very steep grassy slope. This one did lift off its hinges and I drove down the bank, through the gate, across a field, through a farmyard scattering chickens everywhere, and at last out onto a country lane with a pack of barking dogs chasing me off down the road.

I'd often sped along those runways in aeroplanes, but doing it in a car was exhilarating. I had an MGBGT then but it would never have matched Owen Wyn Owen's 'Babs', but then nothing, even today, would match 'Babs'. She was a 20-foot long monster powered by a deafening 27-litre aircraft engine, and in the 1920s she'd broken the world land speed record on Pendine Sands by reaching 171 miles an hour. When Owen had finished restoring her he tried her out on those runways at Mona and she did 80 miles an hour. It would have gone faster but he couldn't get it out of first gear !

Owen of Capel Curig was a very skilful restorer of old cars, but before he could start on this one he had to dig it up. While making another attempt on the record in 1927 it crashed and killed the driver Harry Thomas of Wrexham and the car was buried there on the beach. It was a wonderful piece of restoration and it must have been rather frustrating for Owen not having an RAF runway long enough to try it out properly, and it was with the RAF that I had one of my most frustrating experiences. It was sheer agony. I can't describe it in any other way. I warn you, if you've got blood pressure, don't read any further because on the Richter scale, this blows the roof off.

Health warning.

Reading this can seriously damage your health.

All my life I've had dogs that I have loved dearly, but in the eighties I had a dog that was pure 'evil. She stole, she kept bad company and stayed out late. Cindy was by far the worst Labrador I've ever come across. Our previous Labrador 'Toby' came with me on every job, always sitting up front with me, he was always interested in where we were going, and only fell asleep on our way home, snoring and leaning against my shoulder.

Cindy on the other hand was a bitch who showed no interest in anything but herself, and when she started roaming the streets all night I made her too come to work with me. Of course it didn't occupy her mind, she just curled up on the back seat and slept all day. When I let her out to pay a penny she'd slink off, and one morning she slipped away from me at the Valley RAF station.

I'd really been looking forward to this visit. It was just before Christmas, and at that festive time of year the RAF always flew a hamper of food and drink in one of their helicopters out to the lighthouse keepers on the Skerries, which is a nasty outcrop of rocks off the north coast of Anglesey. They'd done this for years and always took a party of journalists with them, but now it was coming to an end. This was either because the light was going automatic or the RAF was running out of fuel, I can't remember now, but this was going to be the last time, and for one reason or another I'd never been on this trip. Now at last I had a place booked on the helicopter. This, I repeat, was a trip that would never be repeated, and I was looking forward to it very much. The invitation said 'Gather at 10.30 am. for Christmas drinks in the officers mess', and this I did, and what follows is the nightmare account of how the events of that morning unfolded, one agonising step after another.

I arrive at twenty past ten. I let the dog out to pay a penny. Dog wanders behind bushes. I follow. Dog gone.

I search everywhere, shouting her name, trampling over flowerbeds and pushing through hedges. Twenty-to eleven dog turns up.

"Where the hell have you been ?" I ask, she says nothing, just gets in the car without a word.

I go into officers mess. I know it well but unusual, no-one around. Enter room on the left. It's empty but I hear the laughter of several people coming from a door at the far end. I go to open it but it's locked. A voice on the other side shouts

"Come round the other way."

I go back to the entrance hall and go the 'other way'. Soon I find a room where there are empty glasses on a table and cigarette ends smoking in ashtrays. Outside a vehicle starts up and drives away. I go to the window and see a mini-bus disappearing round the corner.

It's now a quarter to eleven. I quickly leave and run to the car. The dog's on my seat. It doesn't want to move. It gets shoved over and I drive off to the reception building at the main gate. I know where the helicopter base is, it's 22-Squadron and it's on the other side of the runways, but I need clearance.

At the reception building there's a queue. None of them are reporters. I wait in line and the time ticks by. At the window hatch at last I tell the corporal who I am and why I'm there. I say that I need to go to 22-Squadron. He looks dubious. "Got an ID ?" he asks. I've not been asked this before. I rummage through my wallet and produced my BBC identity card. He looks as it. "Should we have you on a list ?" I explain that they should. Eventually, with visible reluctance, he gives me a visitor's badge and hurriedly I clip it on my lapel and go towards the car.

"Oi !" He's shouting from the window. "Do you know where you're going ?" he asks. I nod, "Yes 22-Squadron," I say. He shakes his head. "No, it's different this time. Don't go there. Go through the barrier here, straight on, follow the road round, take the second left, then right, straight on and first left." I stand looking confused, so he repeats it. Still confused I run to the car.

I happens again. "Oi !" I turn to see him pushing a plank through the window. "You've got to take this," he says. I go back amazed and take hold of it. It's a plank with 'Visitor' written on it. "Put it across the top of your dashboard," he says and slams the window. I look at it in disbelief. I've never been given anything like this before. It's enormous. It's a plank.

I carry it to the car. I feel like a

joiner. The dog's on my seat again. It yelps as the plank lands on it and it crawls into the back. I shove the plank onto dashboard and get in. I can't see over the plank. I drive off standing up.

I'm repeating the directions aloud. "Straight on, then follow the road round and take second left." I go to turn left but there's a sign blocking the way. It says 'Road Closed.' I'm beginning to crack up. I race round several buildings but there's no-one around to ask. I pass a stack of Calor gas bottles then take another left and then a right, then I take a left fork and I'm passing them again ! Then at last I turn a corner and I can see a helicopter ! It's not a yellow one from 22-Squadron – but it's a helicopter. "Thank goodness ," I say out loud "They haven't gone without me."

I jump out of the car and walk across to a nearby hut with an open door. Here two men in flying suits are drinking from mugs. "Want a cuppa ?" one says and I accept gladly as I collapse onto a bench. "I thought I wasn't going to make it in time," I gasp, and they laugh. "Plenty of time mate," the other says, and I peer down the corridor. It's very quiet. "Where are the others ?" I ask. "What others ?" they say. "The others" I say again, as a little knot tightens in my stomach. They shake their heads and one says "There's just us three this week.." I've now broken out in a cold sweat and I say "But where are the others ?" and again they say "What others ?" I'm on my feet now. "The others! we're going to the Skerries!" I shout, and they laugh. "Well we're not," they say, "You want 22 Squadron."

As I run out of the hut they're trying to tell me how to find 22-Squadron. I hurl the dog and the plank into the back and tear across the airfield as fast as I can go. I know how to find 22-Squadron, I've been there dozens of times. I'm so mad I'm shouting my head off, "I know where 22-Squadron is !" I get there, swerve round the corner and there's the yellow helicopter still on the tarmac !! The rotors are turning but it's still there !! I grab the tape recorder and run to it as fast as I can. I can see everyone on board waving. Great. As I run I wave back. Then with a surge of extra noise it soars majestically into the air. They were waving goodbye.

It took a couple of hours but I waited for them to come back. I had a big argument with the pilot and did it there. With the rotor blades of another helicopter whirring in the background I recorded a minute with the RAF Liaison Officer who told me why this trip had to be the last, and as we spoke, I said we were picking our way over the rock pools having just landed on the Skerries. That completed the first part, and then – inside the lighthouse (a building by the runway where the guests were having tea and cakes) I spoke to the Trinity House Lighthouse representative who told me how wonderful the RAF was, and then with an imaginary hamper being opened to the accompaniment of Christmas greetings and everyone cheering, I wrapped up the report by saying, "Well, that's it, the RAF has delivered its last hamper to the Skerries light house. So from the Skerries - Happy Christmas."

Pure theatre. And yes, I'll say it again. You don't go back to the studio without your story.

I don't know what it is about the RAF. They never seem to be quite 'with it'. I remember on my very first visit to RAF Valley I was visiting 22-Squadron on that occasion too, and at the gate I was told to drive straight across the airfield. Later you drove round the perimeter, but in those days you were told to drive straight across the runways and you have to understand that this was always an extremely busy place. They always used to say they handled more landings every day than Heathrow, and I'll never forget that first visit. I drove off down this runway and came to a junction, a crossroad, where another runway crossed my path, and here I noticed a small red light sitting in the grass. Fortunately I thought perhaps I'd better stop to see if it meant anything, even though it was very small. I'd no sooner stopped when a jet fighter hit the tarmac only feet away and flashed past my bonnet.

It has to be said, the RAF has done

some wonderful work in the mountains, plucking injured people to safety, and from the sea too of course. I've seen those yellow rescue helicopters come in to some very awkward situations, especially in bad weather. But the most amazing rescue operation I ever came across happened at a small caravan park near St. Asaph. Out of the blue, with no warning whatsoever, a convoy of rescue vehicles raced up the drive of Eryl Hall. There were fire engines, ambulances and police cars, even a coastguard vehicle, all with their sirens going full blast and with their blue lights flashing. The owners of the park said it was pandemonium !

When at last the sirens and the flashing lights were switched off, it was revealed that a Russian satellite passing overhead had picked up a distress signal from that very spot – from that very small spot on the earth's surface. It seemed incredible, but a search was made of the park and no-one in distress was found. The whole thing appeared to be ludicrous, but the only thing that anyone could think of was that it was down to the mouse scarer. This was a small electric gadget they had in the office which apparently was sending out scary squawks too highly pitched for humans to hear, but audible to mice and sputnicks. Needless to say, it was switched off.

With so many vehicles racing up the drive the emergency services were certainly putting on a good show, but why the coastguard bothered to turn up was anyone's guess, seeing as the place is nearly five miles from the sea. You would have thought it might have occurred to them while they were on their way really, but fortunately many rescues do end happily, and one happy ending involved a dog – another one down a hole.

The dog belonged to Maldwyn Jones of Capelulo. They'd been up on Tal-y-Fan and she'd chased something, a rabbit or a fox perhaps, down into a crevice. It was a deep one and it was very narrow , too narrow for anyone to climb down into. Maldwyn called her several times but although he could hear her barking she didn't emerge, and it became obvious that she couldn't climb up again. When I got up there half a dozen men were wielding crow bars in an effort to get down to her, and they were even bringing over a JCB. There's no road up there, the terrain is rough to walk over let alone drive any vehicle over, but such was their determination.

As you know I'd seen this situation before. The dog was a long way down and it appeared a hopeless task. I always carried a microphone extension lead and using this I managed to lower the mic deep enough to record the poor thing barking, but it was a long way off. However, this was one 'dog in a hole' story that ended happily. The following day the rescuers lowered a rope down through the hole. On the end of it they'd tied a sack with some food in it. The line suddenly felt heavier and they hauled it up. Wonderful. On the end was the dog, but she wasn't in the sack. She was hanging onto it by her teeth. I was told afterwards that she licked their faces, drank a flask of tea, and then enjoyed a good roll in the grass.

Maybe I should have kept that story until last in this chapter, but I'll close on red tape. A reporter will see a lot of this stuff, and it's always very satisfying to catch hold of it and hold it aloft for everyone to see. This can be good for a laugh but at the same time, for someone bound up in it, red tape can be very distressing, and I think one red tape story will be quite enough.

The story concerned our local road sweeper in Trefriw. Nefydd was a very big, heavy built, jolly, red-faced young man with a mop of black curly hair. Everyone liked him. He was without a doubt one of the nicest and most courteous and inoffensive people you could ever wish to meet, and many of us had a cuppa ready for him as he brushed and shovelled his way around our village. He was one of those people it was always a joy to have a chat with, but one day Nefydd's steady, unhindered way of life came to an end. He now had a code book to work to. Everything he did had to be entered into a book, and everything he swept and shovelled had to be written down in accordance with a

code. Everything from leaves to gravel were represented by a code.
I saw him studying this book one day. Leaning on his broom he was looking far from happy. He showed me what he was having to contend with and I got the tape recorder.

BBWB 169

Barham	"What are leaves ?"
Road Sweeper	"They're V8."
Barham	"V8 ?"
Road Sweeper	"Yes V8 for leaves, and different things for the litter and different things."
Barham	"What's the litter ?"
Road Sweeper	(Consulting list) "Er …. V11 on the pavement, yes. We've got different codes for the road and the pavement."
Barham	"And what about in ditches and things ?"
Road Sweeper	"Oh yes that's er ….. a different code for ditches, and it depends if you've got a different ditch. Maybe it's more a country ditch than a village ditch."

I left Nefydd scratching his head again and went to the Council depot and asked to see the full list. It was incredible. Wet and dry things warranted different coding, as did wet and dry places, and I remember wondering what SMV meant. It turned out to mean 'Standard Minute Value' and furthermore there was a different SMV for each operation. This related to stretches of road needing to be swept within a certain time-limit, and this in turn meant the road sweeper having to measure certain stretches of road. In particular I remember seeing that he was required to sweep one section of road in 0.9 of a minute.

In trying to work to these demands the poor man was, as some of you might have guessed, contributing to his own demise. It wasn't long before he was out of a job and they introduced their new toy, a huge road sweeping vehicle - which didn't negotiate all our steep and twisting village roads.

Nefydd took it all very badly and for one reason or another died not long after. A few months before he died he was taken ill and I was told that it took two ambulances to get him to hospital. The first one got to his cottage in the forest only for the crew to find that they couldn't lift him, and so a second crew had to be summoned. Apparently, when they eventually got him to hospital in Llandudno, the sight of this huge and hairy mountain man caused quite a sensation. Those of us who knew him can well imagine the scene.

CHAPTER S.
Snowdonia, Singers, Spies, and Scientists.

Although my patch covered the whole top half of Wales, a focal point of course was Snowdonia, eight hundred square miles of mountains, forests, lakes, rivers, waterfalls, and vast areas of moorland, indeed some of the most refreshing scenery in Great Britain.

There are many mountains in Wales. According to the findings of Ken and Norah Mills of Ledbury, two good friends and life-time explorers of the Welsh hills, there are two hundred and thirteen over two thousand feet, with the highest being in the north . Snowdon itself (Yr Wyddfa) is three and a half thousand feet, and thanks to the extremely varied weather conditions the elements here sometimes combine to give you a special treat.

I remember one very special occasion with my teenage son when we were overlooking the Nant Ffrancon pass one night, not far from Ffynnon Lligwy lake. We were walking from Betws-Y-Coed to Aber on the north coast, and as we sat by the tent, scoffing our supper in the blue glow of our camping stove, we realised the blanket of cloud that had enveloped us all day had disappeared, and instead of sitting in the mist we could see the stars and a big bright moon.

We went then to the edge of the cliff and saw the cloud had sunk deep into the valley below. We now had a vast silvery gleaming white ocean at our feet, and right opposite us towered the great rocky peaks of Tryfan, Glyder Fawr and so on, each one standing alone in the moonlight like uncharted islands. It was a marvelous sight, and above it all, scattered across the deepest of blue velvet skies, were the most enormous stars, literally glittering like diamonds.

You can often climb above the clouds in Wales, but to see it at night like that was something special, and it was specially good for a youngster to see it too. That experience eventually became a programme called 'Two days in a cloud', and I remember it was accompanied by some beautiful music.

To try and name all the memorable people of Snowdonia would be impossible so I will mention only a few. There was Ifan Roberts of Capel Curig, the old Quarryman who took to climbing mountains to study the wild plants of Snowdonia. His love of Snowdonia and its alpine plants was boundless, but tragically his sight began to fail, and those beautiful little flowers surviving high among the misty crags he used to climb became nothing more than a memory, and when you think of Snowdonia, you have to think of the National Park Wardens who risk their lives rescuing sheep from ledges as well as people. Furthermore, I can't zip through Snowdonia without mentioning two others who were once famously husband and wife.

Together they owned a rugged rain-drenched hill farm in the 1930's overlooking the twin lakes between Capel Curig and Pen y Gwryd , and whilst he was there he wrote a best seller called 'I Bought A Mountain', a book that spelt out to the comfortable masses the cold reality of sheep farming on a bleak raw mountain. His name was Thomas Firbank and she was Esme, the beautiful little shrew who was as hard as the rocks they stood upon and who, after he'd moved away, carried on alone and stamped her wilful foot on the whole of Snowdonia.

Eventually, having married Peter (the Great - the ever toiling cheerful giant who also ran Caernarvon Castle's Splendid Royal Welsh Fusiliers Museum) Esme became Esme Kirby, and we all got to know the remarkable Esme. Using any means, fair or otherwise, she dominated every aspect of conservation here for decades. Having formed her 'Snowdonia National Park Society' she attacked friend and foe alike, until her uncompromising attitude eventually got her thrown out of her own society. This would have finished anyone else, especially someone of her advanced years, but not Esme. She simply formed another conservation society and worked in opposition.

Thinking I might be useful, she took me onto the committee of her original outfit, telling the members at an AGM at Pale Hall, that I was a member, which I never had been. Then, having found myself co-opted her scheme became apparent. On the eve of the next month's meeting, she rang to tell me which way to vote on every item on the agenda. This I refused to do, being for instance very much in favour of widening the A470. This infuriated her. Poor Esme, one more cunning plan down the drain. But I do look back on those few months that I stuck it out with a measure of affection. We used to meet at Ty Hyll, that ancient stone cottage by the road near Betws y Coed known as 'The Ugly House.' The meetings were so acrimonious you had to carry a knife.

Her first husband, the very tall and gently spoken Thomas Firbank left for service at the start of world war two and finished up living in Japan. There he married a Japanese lady, but many years later came back to Snowdonia to be with his daughter in Dolwyddelan, and died not longer afterwards.

His book had made him a legend in Snowdonia and his return, after so long, came as a big surprise and on his return I made a request. I asked if I could drive him to Plas y Brenin and that bend in the road where, all those many years before, he'd first set eyes on the twin lakes of Mymbyr and up on the hill the mountain farm he was to buy. I wanted him to read aloud the first few lines of his book. Those memorable lines in which he describes the scene, his first glimpse as the wind tore back the hood of his car. But sadly he shook his head. He agreed to the interview and he read those lines for me, but he wouldn't go back to that spot.

Up at the other end of that great valley, and close to Snowdon itself, there was another man who made a good name for himself. Chris Briggs owned the Pen y Gwryd Hotel which became famous for accommodating the 1953 Everest Team as they prepared for their trek to the Himalayas. These were the climbers who were first to conquer Everest, and over the years there were several reunions there which I was pleased to attend. Here I met both Sherpa Tensing and Sir Edmund Hillary, the two men who first got to the top, (as I think I might already have mentioned) but Chris Briggs was more than a genial host, he was very much involved with mountain rescue and did much to organise the way in which rescues were carried out here. He was good to reporters, and even under pressure (whether coping with casualties or even guests) he always found time to talk to us.

The next man, short and tough, was just as much a part of the Snowdonia scenery. I met him often I'm glad to say, and I always refer to him as 'Slate Man'. He lived in Blaenau Ffestiniog where he was a slate miner, and for me at least he will always represent it, that little town which called itself 'The Town That Roofed The World'.

Here the slate lies deep, and until a few years ago there were dozens of slate mines in this area, and once upon a time millions of roofing slates were carried every year by the little steam trains of the narrow gauge Ffestiniog railway all the way down to Porthmadoc, where they were loaded onto schooners and such like to be shipped around the world. And before the days of steam they free wheeled with their cargo a dozen miles down the line, with men heaving on brakes and carrying horses in wagons to pull the trucks back up again.

During my 32 years I watched this industry shrivel to a shadow of its former self in spite of the indomitable spirit of men like Slate Man. His name was Meurig Evans. He was old and grey, just like the slate he'd worked on for a lifetime, hauling it to the surface in great chunks and cutting it and splitting it into shape, amidst all the dust and the wet and cold of a life-time.

Like the other main slate towns of Bethesda and Penygroes, this is how Blaenau Ffestiniog won its reputation, but the vast majority of all the slate brought to the surface over the years was destined for the tips. Only the best pieces were usable, and consequently these little communities became engulfed and over shadowed by gigantic slate tips - mountainous things, and incredible though it may seem, some of them have now been removed with much of their content going to constructive land fill etc. But when the first was to be removed Meurig didn't like it at all To his way of thinking these tips were monuments, testimonials to the sweat and toil that produced them.

Blaenau was a lovely place to visit. It was far from pretty, but here you always conducted your interviews with cups of tea or coffee and home-made cake. This extract featuring Meurig is from an interview I recorded with him about the slate tips for the World Service in the early 1970's

BWB 12

Mr. Evans   "They're like the pyramids you know. They're like
big monuments. It took years and years to get these,
but still they're beautiful to me, these slate tips,
because like the Pharaohs, they built their pyramids.
I think we've got prettier pyramids in this town than
they've got in Egypt. If I had the money I'd buy them
and keep them just as they are."

Wales is a fascinating place, colourful and diverse, and compared to many other places life here is good, but unlike Pop Larkin's Provence, it's not 'perfic'. Here the problems are still mainly related to inadequate incomes, and as with all other beautiful areas of Gt .Britain, the aggravation of second homes is a constant source of hostility.

For the un-informed it's worth mentioning that people from more affluent regions, who can afford to come to a poorer but beautiful region like this and buy a 'holiday home', inadvertently, but inevitably, encourage house prices to rise above the local norm. Very nice for local people who have a house to sell, but disastrous for local people seeking to buy, in particular the young. Then as the housing stock in a particular area tips out of balance, with a high proportion of houses occupied only for short holiday periods, the inevitable happens. Shops close down, bus services are withdrawn, and even schools close down.

Also holiday home owners, like incoming full time residents, are occasionally accused of watering down that unique element of life in Wales which is the Welsh language. Harming someones language is not something they're accused of in many places around the UK, and saving it isn't a priority with us all, but you can see that if a language goes then it goes forever, taking with it vast reservoirs of culture and possibly vast volumes of wit and wisdom too, as well as the basic choice of a preferred way of life.

This problem has been debated for many years, and has led to far too many initiatives to be mentioned here, but between 1979 and 92 we saw the clumsiest of them all. During that period one hundred and three holiday homes became victims of an arson campaign.

Singers come next on my list, and for some reason that I've never understood, classical singers are often a bit nutty, and probably a good many musicians are too. I think they probably need to blow off steam more than most, but it was always enjoyable to watch somebody singing something terribly serious one moment, and then fall back into the habit of being human the next. They're usually very amiable too. I found Bryn Terfel, in spite of his huge global fame, (I nearly said frame) to be very easy to meet and talk to, whereas pop singer Tom Jones was more difficult to reach than Prince Charles. The security around Tom Jones was beyond belief, it took hours for me to get through the various layers, even though it was all arranged in advance.

I mentioned Bryn Terfel just now and he would only have been a schoolboy when I met his father on their farm at Pant Glas. His dad was being attacked every morning by a buzzard. As soon as he left the house this very large and menacing bird of prey swooped down with talons outstretched and knocked his hat off.

The one thing that separates the wheat from the chaff amongst singers is the ability to warble a few notes at perfect pitch at the drop of a hat, and with no accompaniment. Pop singers will probably go to the bottom of this class, but here I must point to one pop singer who was the outstanding exception – Lulu. She was appearing in Rhyl and during the interview in her hotel room she belted out the number I requested without batting an eyelid.

We sat facing each other in a couple of armchairs and she sang into my very inadequate microphone without a care in the world. For that I thought she was first class. I remember too that she told me the strength of her voice was all down to the Glasgow trams. When she was a kid she used to sit aboard with her mother and sing away to her heart's content, much to her poor mother's embarrassment.

If you were around in the 1950s you will remember the name Ruby Murray. Here was a superstar, as big a star as any of the world's top names of today, and with songs like 'Softly Softly Turn the Key' this gentle soft voiced Irish girl took the popular music world by storm, but on a cold January night in 1974 I found her singing in a motel and transport café. It was on Anglesey, and it was one of the saddest things I've ever seen. There was no stage, no footlights, no spotlights, just a pianist, and every now and then he'd nod to her sitting in the corner and she'd get up and sing a song. She was still singing her old ballads but there was nothing about her to suggest the global fame she had once enjoyed. She sang very nicely too, but even in the interview there was no hint of 'I was once a big star.' She was so nice to talk to, and so very humble. She was only there for one night I think, and it couldn't have been much of a fee. The poor girl must have needed it badly though, and didn't live much longer.

Another 'sad' story. When my daughter was still at primary school I took her to meet Cliff Richard (Sir Cliff now). He was appearing in Llandudno and it just happened to be his fortieth birthday. It was something of a surprise to see him in North Wales. I think he was going through a bit of a lean period (by his standards) with competition coming from so many new singers, and although he did his best to impress this one little member of the up-and-coming generation, it was to no avail. After the interview we shook hands and he said "Bye-bye Julia," and turning to me my daughter asked "Was that John Travolta ?" It was a shame. He looked so disappointed.

I wouldn't say Llandudno was an entertainers graveyard but we saw a few on their last laps, if not their last legs. I met old-age pensioners Frankie Lane and Guy Mitchell here and one time super star Peggy Lee amazingly flopped in the ramshackle Arcadia Theatre. After performing to a half-empty auditorium she said "That's it. Last tour. I'm finished."

You do have to admire singers though. Professional or amateur they just love singing, and I'd like you to meet some of the amateurs now. Singers who were often in the news, like this one with a shaven head, a guitar hanging round his neck, and wearing the brown robe and sandals of a monk.

This was Father Francis who was a

friar at the Pantasaph Priory. He was brought to our notice because he'd been allowed to perform at a charity concert, and it was said that he'd bought the house down with a take off of Gary Glitter doing his 'Want to be in my gang'. It was long before Mr.Glitter's fall from stardom but it didn't sound as if it could possibly be true and so I was sent to Pantasaph to find out, and sure enough in a bare and austere reception hall, in that big old stone cold, and echoey priory, he took hold of his guitar and let rip. I've still got that recording, and if I could I would play it for you. He was cavorting around as he sang with such abandonment that I kept looking over my shoulder expecting a gang of monks to come and throw us out.

He was a nice fellow. He raised thousands for charity but I lost count of the times he was singing for the last time. I was sent to Warrington once to see him singing in the street. That was yet another last time. Every now and then an edict would silence him for a while and then, hey presto he'd be back in the news again, singing away on street corners and in theatres too, but on one occasion I went to Pantasaph because he'd written a book and had got a sensational foreword to it. It was written by the American actress Linda Carter who played the part of Wonder Woman in the TV series. He thought Wonder Woman was fabulous, and the cheeky so-and-so had written and told her.

I don't know if it's all the deep breathing they do but by and large singers seem to enjoy disgustingly rude health. Take Stan Ryder's dad. Stan was an organist and his father was the vocalist and they were doing gigs along the North Wales coast. When I saw them perform last Stan was 63 and his dad was 93! He was another who knew how to keep going, and in Aberdovey Stan Hugill was knocking on a bit too.

This big old fish-out-of-water, with a grey beard, pony tail and a big voice, was a seafarer from stem to stern. He'd worked for many years at the outward bound centre there, teaching kids to sail, but he'd also become famous in the folk singing world as a genuine singer of sea shanties. In his early days he'd been a shanty man aboard a sailing ship. This apparently was a proper job, singing those 'Hey Hoe' numbers to get the less fortunate members of the crew, who had to flex their muscles, to work together rhythmically pulling up anchors and topsails etc. and Stan reckoned he'd been the very last one in the trade. (They'd probably thrown the others overboard.)

If you wanted to know anything about the days of sail, or a comment on anything old and nautical, you went to see Stan. He lived with his lovely cheerful wife in a little house in Aberdovey, full of wonderful seafaring pictures and things. It was gorgeous, but among Stan's stories was an intriguing mystery.

He told me that just before the Japanese came into the Second World War he was in the Indian Ocean serving on the merchant ship 'Automedon'. The ship was fresh out of Birkenhead sailing alone for the outposts of our empire when she was stopped by a German warship. The Automedon was hit by several shells killing many including the captain. The story is mentioned in at least two books, 'Blue Funnel Line' by Duncan Haus and S. W. Roskill's 'A Merchant Fleet at War' so I will say little else than this – among the cargo of crated aircraft and motorcars, various pieces of machinery and uniforms etc. there was a suite of furniture, secret documents in a 'strong box', and a mysterious woman. If you wish to pursue this story I wish you luck with your research.

From what has come to light since, it's been said that the Germans discovered much to interest them when they came aboard, especially in the 'strong-box' , which is said to have contained documents addressed to the British Far East Command, outlining a defence strategy for British strongholds in that part of the world. Whether or not these documents contained genuine information or purposely 'misleading' information I can't tell you, but as Stan said, it was strange that documents like these should be aboard a merchant ship, and furthermore, a merchant ship sailing alone in such dangerous waters. With a nod and a wink he told me that his previous ship had almost suffered a similar fate out there in that very same area, so the admiralty would have been well aware of the risk, and his account of the episode lacked no element of drama.

"That woman," he said, "Claimed she was setting up home in Malaya and when the Germans were preparing to scuttle the Automedan she arrogantly told the officer in charge that she expected him to transfer her furniture to the German ship for safekeeping, and she insisted that they came below with her to see it. Stan suspected the woman was on board to make sure the documents were found, but in reality the Germans were obviously keen to search the ship anyway, and as well as transferring the strong-box and its secrets, they also transferred to their own ship the Automdan's survivors, large quantities of food and drink, cigarettes and whisky, and also the lady, and her furniture.

Just as intriguing was a situation I stumbled across once, right there where Stan worked at the outward bound centre, or to be precise, at a house the centre owned, a little to the north of Aberdovey.

First though perhaps I should explain that the outward bound school had been set up during the second world war to toughen up young Merchant Navy men. It had been found that survivors, those found on life rafts or in lifeboats, tended to be the older men. Most youngsters just weren't tough enough to live through such an ordeal, so in order to drag them up to the fitness level of the Royal Navy they took them to Aberdovey and chased them over the mountains and chucked them in the sea. Then after the war the facilities there were used to toughen up school kids, and these unhappy souls were also chased over the mountains and chucked in the sea. In time these 'services' were extended to adults and in particular to groups of business people like managers and teams of salesmen, who (by being chased over the mountains and chucked in the sea) were expected to become better managers and salesmen. Although why, I have absolutely no idea.

At the time of this particular incident these courses for business people were springing up all over the country, and when my producer wanted a feature on a typical group of wet and muddy salesmen I chose to visit Aberdovey where it had all started, but he certainly didn't get a typical group. What I found was something the BBC discreetly decided not to put on the air.

As with most features it was arranged on the day with a single telephone call, and the manager – pleased no doubt to have some publicity, confirmed that they had a businessmen's group there that week and he'd be delighted to see me, adding "Do come for lunch".

As we ate he told me that this group was a bit different to the ones they usually had because they'd brought their own instructors, and they'd booked the centre's other house up the road. This they'd done to be completely independent and self-contained. However, we soon found that he didn't realise just how different this group was. These people had little interest in being chased over the mountains and chucked in the sea.

The house up the road was called Rhowniar. It stood nicely secluded in its own grounds and had once been a girls school. During my early days with the BBC it was unsuccessfully bidding to educate Princess Anne. I don't think they stood much chance but it was good for publicity. However when the manager and I got there that day the door was locked. I'll never forget his face.

Although we rang the bell several times and we could hear noises inside, it remained locked for quite a while. The manager was puzzled, even embarrassed, and more than a little agitated, and none of these irritations were alleviated when at last the door was opened and someone showed us into a room and left us there. He'd asked for the course director and although we were told that he'd be down in a moment, we were kept waiting for another twenty minutes. During that time the manager spotted one of his own staff through the window and called him in.

He'd been loaned to them as a driver for the morning and when asked what was going on the driver came up with some interesting observations. Observations coupled together with those of one or two observant people in neighbouring Towyn. It was said that some on the course had spent a good time in the local library reading local papers and asking questions about local people, while others appeared to be following people through the town, even to the railway station and onto trains. Then, as if that wasn't sufficiently intriguing, he told us that he'd seen some of them carrying small radio sets into the house. Once again my companion's face was a picture, and perhaps mine was too, and I just said out loud, "It's like a spy school." An extravagant guess perhaps, but it certainly made us wonder.

When at last the man who claimed to be the course director came down the stairs we both wanted to know what was going on, but we didn't get much out of him. I have never heard a smoother tongue than his. He was without doubt, the smoothest purveyor of waffle I have ever had the misfortune to listen to. Very quietly he spoke at great length of the 'Unique value of having people working together on tasks where the reason for completing them wasn't initially identifiable.' It was that bad, and eventually I asked if he was running a school for spies. This at least prompted a smile and an amused denial, and so I asked him about the library, the enquiries about local people, and following people onto trains, but all this did was to produce more waffle about 'tasks being imprecise and unrelated and the value of group focussing.'

We listened to this sort of drivel for several minutes until I asked about the radio sets. This at last brought a hesitation. It was only a brief pause but here was the breakthrough. I asked what they were doing with them but all I got was more nonsense about 'the value of learning to deal with new challenges, and how this was essential for these people who were strangers to each other and coming together from different firms with no idea of each other's capabilities.' It was very tiresome, and

I asked if I could meet some of these people, especially those with the radio sets. After another pause he went upstairs to see if this might be convenient.

To our surprise he returned with consent, but upon one condition. He said that as no-one had permission from their firms to speak publicly he couldn't allow any interviews. I accepted this and it got me upstairs. Up there I found half-a-dozen young men assembling radio sets. Parts were scattered on a table. My informant was at it again, but now becoming repetitive, telling me again it was 'a way of building team work, and that it was character building having to cope with unexpected tasks.'

I prepared my feature and said what I thought. I said it appeared to a spy school, and like I said – it never went on the air, and furthermore, the tape disappeared.

Actually, when we came to think about it, it sounded like a very good idea. We were still in the throes of the cold war and we began to realise that if you needed to train people for espionage duties it would make sense to hold classes on the hoof, perhaps never in the same place twice, and there were some intriguing questions too. If those on the course were genuinely from UK firms did they know they were volunteering for undercover work ? Or did they really think they were on a management bonding course, while all the time - they were actually being 'assessed' for their potential usefulness ? Might the day come when some of them might be asked to do a little favour whilst abroad somewhere ? It wasn't unheard of in that period for British businessmen to be arrested in certain countries on charges of espionage. It was always denied, but no doubt they were spying. But on the other hand, if these people did know why they were at Aberdovey that week, whose side were they on ?

We will never know about that gathering, but if it was a spy school, I can imagine with a great deal of satisfaction that smooth-talking front man getting back on the Friday night to Whitehall (or the Kremlin) and at last being able to blow his top. "You'll never guess!" he's shouting, "You'll never guess! Some buffoon from the BBC turned up and did a feature on us !!"

It was a funny sort of war – the 'cold war'. Annihilation was coming at any moment, maybe even in the well publicised next six minutes, but then, on the other hand possibly not. Nobody knew, but to be on the safe side the government, county councils, and at least one milkman, dug themselves underground atomic bomb proof shelters. The milkman showed me his. He had a milk round in the Betws yn Rhos area. I can't recall where exactly, but I do remember he was good at geography. He reckoned the Russians would definitely drop an atomic bomb on Liverpool and if it was a windy day he didn't want to get caught in the fall-out. I remember going home and wondering if our cellar might do.

Now for some of my favourite people. I love enthusiasts and theres no-one more enthusiastic than a scientist who's after public funding. Blinkered and tunnel-visioned they might be, but they positively vibrate enthusiasm, especially when someone stands in their way, and such conflicts often end up in public enquiries.

I reported on some big ones. There was one at the old Town Hall in Welshpool involving Sir Bernard Lovell who wanted to build another enormous radio telescope on a beautiful hill above Meifod. It was going to be another Jodrell Bank giant but that plan got no further than the drawing board, whereas the Shell Oil company was able to go ahead and build their offshore oil terminal at Amlwch. Not that it was in operation long, but in all such cases you have scientists and engineers displaying wondrous vision, seeing everything so clearly, in their view. That's when the battle starts, when the smart fast bowlers of industry pitch into the stolid village stonewall Jacksons, and it's good to watch. Especially when a little local knowledge hits the city slickers for six.

For a considerably more balanced

view of scientific endeavour, go to the Centre for Alternative Technology near Machynlleth. Here they combine technical achievement with conservation. They generate energy with wind and water, they build houses needing very little power, and they grow food in a garden that was once a quarry. They've really done wonders there, and I remember having to find them when the first disciples arrived to set it up in the seventies. It took some finding too as I'd only been told that an old quarry in the area had been taken over by a 'strange' bunch of people. But that was a long time ago now, long before wind farms, solar panels and compost toilets, way back BC (before conservation) whereas today you could hardly miss the place. It's a great green theme park now.

I mustn't give the impression that mixing with scientists always makes for a nice day out. Occasionally it can be extremely uncomfortable, and on one occasion it was both uncomfortable and extremely smelly. This was when I was invited into a disused sulphur mine that smelled like rotten eggs.

My hosts were Ian Kelso and Barry Johnson both bacteriologists from Bangor University, and on their advice I won't say where this chamber of horrors can be found because it's becoming very dangerous. (If you're in the area just follow your nose.) The stench was awful but in we went, into what appeared at first to be a natural cave opening, but then down and down into a most unpleasant labyrinth. As we slipped and slithered down the muddy slope they were telling me that the mine was rich in iron and pyrites which was being eaten by a form of bacteria. This they said was a 'phenomenon' and I believed them. Apparently this weird activity has been known of since the 1940s, but forty years later it was realised that here in North Wales we probably had the most awesome example of it in the world.

After a while the yellow beam of Ian's torch lit up a horrible slimy mess. We'd arrived at the feast. It was everywhere, and hanging from the roof were some very strange things. They were horrible, all 'oozy' and 'slimy'.

BWB 1C

Johnson   "Look at these stalactites. Now you won't have seen stalactites like these before. Look at this, look at this, see they wobble."

Barham   "Yes, they're made of jelly aren't they ?"

Johnson   "They are. Strictly speaking they're stalactites because they hang down from the roof of the cavern, but they are in fact made of bacteria. They're alive."

They were gruesome indeed, wobbly and horrible, and as we went on things only got worse. After a few more yards we came to what appeared to be a long pool of blood.

Johnson   "Well, not exactly blood. This is a very deep red colour as you can see, and the red colour is caused by the fact that here we have a very acidic pond in which iron has been dissolved. Normally iron is not dissolved in water because the p.h. as we know it is too high, but here we have a very acidic solution and iron goes into the solution and gives you a red colour."

Barham   "What would happen if I put my hand in there ?"

Johnson   "It would depend if you had any cuts. It would sting like mad if you did."

Barham   "Oh, come on then, press on."

Kelso   "And if you didn't have any cuts to begin with, if you had your hand in there for ten minutes or so, you would have open cuts by then I think. The skin would start to come off."

Leaving this ghastly pool behind us, we went deeper into this stinking pit of despair and were soon

291

confronted by a whole gang of the   stuff. It looked like clotted cream lying in wait for us in a line thirty yards long and eighteen inches deep. Very bravely Ian scooped up a handful for closer inspection.

Barham	"Is it going to cause the destruction of this mine ?"
Johnson	"Yes eventually because the rocks are being destroyed."
Kelso	"The bacteria will eat away the pillars."
Barham	That are holding up the roof ?"
Kelso	"Holding up the roof and then the whole thing will collapse."
Barham	"Right well, time to go."
Kelso	"Yes I think so, it's a dangerous place to stay."

Of course science isn't only the preserve of the professionals. Ordinary folk get embroiled in scientific theories and just like some of their professional counterparts, their claims can astound. One person I have in mind right now was an old boy in the Lleyn peninsula who assured me he could solve a particular construction problem 'scientifically'.

He wanted me to see the old red telephone box outside his little garage and filling station because it was leaning over to one side like the Leaning Tower of Pisa. Infact it leant over to one side so much he'd written to the Mayor of Pisa with an offer. He reckoned that he'd thought of a very clever way of stopping the Mayor's tower from falling over. Unfortunately he wouldn't part with the knowledge in advance, and in advance the Mayor of Pisa wouldn't part with the fare.

You might think, from the way I've described it, that broadcast with him alongside the leaning phone box was a complete waste of time, but because of his engaging personality it wasn't. It made a little radio 'gem' typical of its type, just three-and-a-half minutes long. Both amusing and intriguing.

Did he have the solution or didn't he ? If he did, what was it ?

I like mysteries, and I met a few people who'd had incredible encounters with 'ball lightening' or 'St.Elmo's Fire' as it's sometimes known. One floated into a housing estate on the outskirts of Conway once. It blew a branch off a tree and then attacked a house, Pam Wignall's house.

BWB 16T

Pam Wignall "Yes I'd just sat down and had a cup of tea and the phone rang and I went to answer it, and I heard this great big bang, like it sounded like a cannon actually and then I saw a blue flash and then it went down my arm and hit my chest and threw me across."

Barham "And it didn't break any windows or doors in your house ?"

Pam Wignall "No it just set fire to the cable at the side by the door, and that's all I can remember".

Three houses were hit. Pat Stafford next door actually saw it coming. She saw it coming up the road and then she saw it making its first impression on the neighbourhood.

Pat Stafford "When it hit the tree it exploded the bark, and the bark went three houses away onto the road at the end of our road here."

Barham "What do you actually remember seeing ?"

Pat Stafford "Just a ball of very bright neon-type white light. That's all I can describe it, in a ball with like a flickering edge, flickering blue edge going round it."

Barham "And how big was this ball ?"

Pat Stafford "Well, I took it from the window to be about the size of a football, but you know it's hard to tell, but that's what I thought, about the size of a football hit the tree."

Another person who received a visit from one of these things lived in Barmouth. He told me that as he opened he front door one evening he saw a ball of 'fizzy fire' slowly floating down to the garden path. When it touched the ground it blew up! The blast knocked him backwards into the hall. On another occasion Mrs. Gladys Hughes of Trefriw was driving along the B5106 when she realised she had company. One was travelling right beside her. "If I'd wound down the window I could have touched it," she said, and when a particularly big one came 'floating' up the river Mawddach towards a couple of men fishing close to the Llanelltyd bridge, they did what anyone else might have done in the circumstances, they ran for their lives.

Scientists are often accused of being blinkered, which is only being single-minded I suppose, but engineers can qualify for this criticism too, therefore please let me include them in this chapter because I'm sure they belong here.

I usually enjoyed my visits to the Ffestiniog railway, but on one occasion it was just a bit boring. Their engineers had won a prestigious award and before the presentation we were all standing around in the cafeteria drinking coffee. The earnest chatter all around was about valves and steam pressure, and after a while I turned to look out of the windows. The view from there is a particularly fine one, and on that day the tide was right up to the cob, and what I saw made me shout out loud.

"Look !" I shouted. Everyone turned to see what I was pointing at and gradually the place fell silent. Six enormous dorsal fins had risen from the depths. They were gigantic and they were very slowly drifting along like a flotilla of yachts. It was a wonderful sight. Where they were was a couple of miles from the open sea but I can only guess they were Basking sharks, those giants of the deep that are more like whales than sharks and grow bigger than buses. It was a wonderful sight and it lasted no more than a couple of minutes, but long before they sank from view faces were turning from the windows and the chatter was back again onto valves and steam pressure. In the end I think there were just two or three of us watching them go, gradually sinking beneath the surface.

CHAPTER T.
Terror, Tourism, Trains, and Treasure.

They're difficult to quantify, but of all the worst moments I went through I think nearly falling out of a helicopter was perhaps the most terrifying, and once again I was a pawn in that game of chance known as the RAF.

For some reason they'd taken it into their heads to combine the issue of a new postage stamp saluting the RAF with an exercise on the summit of Snowdon, and wanting some publicity for it they offered us a helicopter lift. Unfortunately though they'd chosen an extremely windy day, and when the pilot landed at Llanberis he wasn't at all keen to take us up. He'd flown there at a very low altitude and with the wind howling over the summit he was planning to make us walk.

There were three of us, myself and my old colleagues – television reporter Elfyn Thomas, and cameraman David Sutcliffe, who of course wanted a 'view' for his camera, and he managed to change the pilot's mind.

With the rotors spinning again the three of us sat side by side, attached to harnesses and leads hitched up somewhere behind us, happily looking out of the big open doorway, but within a few minutes of take-off we were being thrown all over the place as the wind took charge and violently we lurched from side to side. One minute we were squashed – piled back on top of each other against the fuselage with the big open doorway above us, and then gaping below us the next, leaving us hanging from our leads. I was struggling to hold on to my tape recorder of course, and with my free hand I was hanging on to my lead close to where it was tethered somewhere behind my head. It seemed the natural thing to do, but suddenly …. it came off in my hand !! At that very moment we plunged over again and I was on my way out. That gaping door was below us and I was sliding down towards it. I really thought my end had come. Desperately I flung out a hand and somehow managed to grab hold of someones leg, but by that time my legs were out the door. Whose leg it was I can't remember but I hung on to it, literally for dear life, until I was aware that we were hovering. It was too windy to touch down and the others were jumping out.

You can imagine what a relief it was to see all the grass and rocks of mother earth close below us, and every bit as enthusiastically as the others, I too jumped. The only difference was - they landed and I didn't. Instead I found myself dangling like a puppet and I realised that I was still hooked up afterall. By the time I'd climbed back on board I found the lead I'd been hanging on to was a spare one. Mine, which I think must have been longer than the others, was still attached to the fuselage.

As I said, it's difficult to quantify these experiences and actually this next one might qualify as the worst. It's difficult to say, but it happened soon after I joined the BBC. My producer had heard from the Army Press Office that a bunch of madmen known as the South Wales Borderers had been issued with new mortars, and for a laugh they were going to bring them to Snowdon and attack the Summit Café (I've told you about the types Snowdon attracts) and he wanted me to accompany them. It might have been a pleasant stroll, sauntering up the Llanberis Path, pausing only to fire off a few rounds, but there was a drawback, they were going via Grib Goch and the whole of Snowdonia was buried under a blanket of snow.

Grib Goch, or as some call it – the Knife Edge, is one of Britain's sharpest ridges and their two very young officers thought it would be fun to approach the summit that way. One had done it in the summer, but now it was winter and altogether a very different place. Unfortunately it was to be my first time on Grib Goch, otherwise in those conditions I might have been able to tell them it wasn't such a good idea.

To your left you have a drop of a few hundred feet that's nearly vertical, and on your right you have a similar drop that is vertical. It's more like a 'razor's edge, and these starry-eyed optimists had brought no mountaineering equipment with them except one short rope. They carried six-foot long mortars and walkie-talkie radios, but that was all. Except for the rope they had nothing to actually climb with.

Even where we met in the Pen y Pass car park the snow was almost knee-deep, and up a little higher we were obviously going to be on ice, and yet they were wearing ordinary soft-soled Army boots. They were completely unprepared and ill-equipped. They had no ice axes and no crampons, and worse still – neither did I. At that early stage of my career I too was completely unequipped for climbing and Grib Goch is where people plunge to their extinction even in summer.

Some years earlier during my time in the Army they'd engaged me on active service in Cyprus in conflict with the Eoka without managing to kill me, and as we trudged off through the snow I couldn't help thinking it was a bit unfair that they were being given another go. And as we started to climb in glorious sun-shine up from the Pen y Gwryd track, the snow immediately turned to ice. Hard smooth wet glassy ice.

It was madness, but up we went with steps being hacked into the ice with anything that came to hand, like penknives and even the aerials taken from the radio sets, and at this stage the rope was uncoiled. Unusually for the Army it was all quite democratic, you could choose to be on the rope or choose not to be. These lads had never seen Snowdon before let alone climbed it, so the decision for me was easy. I stayed off it.

We got up to Grib Goch. It took a long time but by mid-afternoon we were basking in glorious sunshine, lying on the ice, We were on a huge cornice, a massive frozen wave of ice, and we were lying down because we didn't dare stand up. We lay there in silence, too scared to speak, clinging on to any little lump or crack in the ice with a sickly slide to oblivion on either side. It wasn't nice, and I remember a couple of real ice climbers arrived on the scene. We heard them below us a good ten minutes before they arrived, crunching into the ice with their crampons and stabbing home their ice axes with every slow and methodical step, and when they came over the rim and saw us they stared in disbelief. At first they thought we'd been dropped there from a helicopter and when someone said, "No mate, we walked," they said it was madness, and shaking their heads they went on their way, putting as much distance between us as they could.

By then our leaders were getting worried about the time so we had to move on. This no-one actually wanted to do, but going down the way we'd come up wasn't an attractive option. Just looking down made you feel ill and carrying on seemed the only way, but it was dreadful.

Because the ice was overhanging the ridge you never knew if you were on it or off it so to speak. No-one said a word for a very long time as we crawled along, even when I pulled the microphone out of my rucksack, the comments I got either side of me were short and tense, but the lads carrying the mortar barrels on their backs had the worst of it. These barrels were long and ungainly things, lurching first forwards and then backwards. By any standards the whole thing was a nightmare, and about half-way across it was decided to abandon it. But how could we ? I thought we were going to be stuck there for good, but after a short discussion it was decided to try and abseil down. This sounded fine, everyone wanted to get off, but where to ? That was the first question, and after that, the next question was – what does abseil mean ?

To abseil we were told you need the rope and those of us who'd never done it before (all but three) put our minds to learning very quickly. One of the officers went over the edge first, which was nice of him, and he was soon shouting from somewhere below that he'd found a ledge. That in itself didn't sound all that promising, but it was enough for the rope to be pulled up and the first man to step forward.

In the years that followed I came to enjoy abseiling, but as many will know it's usually done in a safety harness, but not that time. They didn't have a harness or any sort of tackle, instead we had to step backwards off the cliff in the normal manner, but then lower ourselves by letting the rope out from around our shoulders by hand. It was primitive to say the least and it was terrifying.

Abseiling for the very first time, in its most primitive form, on ice, and from Grib Goch of all places, was quite an experience. One who didn't lean back far enough (which is exactly what you don't really want to do) very nearly fell, but eventually, with the last man having secured the rope in a crevice we all made the descent and found ourselves squeezed into a rift in the ice which provided us with a sort of ditch to make our way along.

It was such a relief to be off that ice cap, and before long we reached a spot where we were looking down a long steep snowfield that glistened in the sun and stretched as smooth as a wedding cake all the way down to lake Glaslyn. We were no longer on ice but the snow was crisp, and someone said, "Don't slip or you'll never stop." They were words of good advice, but suddenly one of them did slip and slid off like an up-turned turtle, yelling "Yippee." Everyone then followed suit, me too. It was crazy but it was exhilarating. We hurtled down that mountainside on our backs at a tremendous speed and only stopped at the lakeside because we landed in a soft snowdrift. We were down and we were safe, soaked and frozen, but safe.

We were all very pleased with ourselves of course, but as we waded through the snow, freezing cold and following the Miners Track home as best we could, I began to realise how lucky we'd been. That area we'd tobogganed down is covered with boulders and it was a bit sobering to realise that some of the largest might have been lurking only a few inches below the surface. Hitting one at that speed might not have been pleasant.

On another snow-bound occasion I got into trouble all on my own. By then, some years later, I was properly equipped, but not on that day I'm afraid. I was on a fox hunt and I didn't think it was necessary to take my crampons and ice axe on a fox hunt, but I should have done. I'd been sent to Nant Gwynant to go hunting with a pack of dogs kept by a local farmer. He called them hounds but they looked more like wolves to me. This was a farmers hunt, on foot with dogs that would have scared off any of the Baskervilles.

I've told you there are lots of mountains to choose from, but once again this little mis-adventure took place on Snowdon itself. We were covering an area up and beyond the Watkin Path, and as well as thick snow we were also having to contend with a damp mist. We were well up into the cloud with the dogs ranging higher still, and you could tell they were on the scent of something . They were making a wonderful noise. You could hear them in the distance 'howling' – eager for a kill. The atmosphere was fabulous - wonderfully eerie in that dark snowy gloom, and breaking away from the hunters I set off into the mist to climb up closer to the dogs.

I wanted to get nearer that wonderful sound, and soon I was happily kicking steps into the snow, (remember what I said about mountains leading you on ?) and with the howling coming now from my left I was soon crossing a steep slope, edging along sideways like a crab. The howling was getting louder, the dogs were definitely over there somewhere, so I carried on, kicking steps and leaning with my right elbow against the snowy slope.

After a while I began to wonder how far down it was through the mist beneath my feet, and eventually I also wondered if I should stop and go back. I didn't seem to be getting any nearer to the dogs, and it was now getting very cold, but when I stopped I found that I couldn't turn round.. I can't explain why, but for some reason I felt 'locked' into the way I was facing. My balance had gone, and for a long time I just could not turn round. I managed it eventually, but it was a nasty experience. I was freezing and I just felt all the time that if I moved I'd fall.

For anyone with a leaning towards 'Vertigo' roofs are a good source of terror. There's always someone doing something stupid on a roof. It can be someone holding aloft a banner claiming that he's the real Prince of Wales, or it can be someone in a seaside town hitting seagulls eggs with a stick with a nail poking through it. With seagulls as urbanised as foxes, people get very annoyed with their feathered friends taking a fancy to the lead around their skylights and the base of their chimneys, hence the nail on the end of the stick.

It's a sad fact of life that seagulls are very destructive and they like nesting on roofs, but if you smash or remove the eggs they just lay some more, but if you puncture them the birds continue to sit on them, thinking they'll hatch but of course they don't. That's why a radio reporter will sometimes be heard up on the roof of some blessed hotel or somewhere describing how an 'egg-pricker' is pricking eggs.

Builders and roofers in particular are very good at roof walking. In my experience, reporters are not. Actually I remember someone inventing 'roof' shoes in the shape of wedges. They had soles that were extremely thick on one side to accommodate the slope of the roof. Excellent for walking in one direction, but, strange to say, somewhat lethal if you turned round.

Birds can be very aggressive. remember what was happening to Bryn Terfel's father, and once I had to talk to a paper boy who was forced to do his round with a cardboard box over his head. He sounded like he was inside a parcel, and when it comes to terror, show-off rally drivers can be a pain. Prior to an event there is always some clever dick who wants to show you the route. This invariably means a suicidal drive through a forest with either very solid looking trees on your side of the car, or a sheer drop of several hundred feet - also on your side of the car.

On one occasion I was given such a ride by a resentful individual who'd just been dropped from his team. He, more than any of the others, was particularly keen to show how wonderful he was. It was hell. So was horse jumping. I understand some people do this for enjoyment, but then they don't have a microphone in one hand and a tape recorder hung round their neck. This girl who reckoned anyone could jump a horse said there was nothing to it, but to me it was the Horse of the Year Show.

Actually I think the female of the species probably is the deadliest. There was the girl for instance who wanted to carry a man down a flight of stairs. She wanted some practise because she was hoping to be a Fire 'Person', and so naturally my female producer just - gave me to her. It was like - "Yes of course, take Barham."

Without giving you too much of a surprise this too was hell. Maybe you can imagine what it's like to be up there on the landing lying over the shoulder of a 'wobbling' woman. She's going to come down backwards and while she's trying to find her balance, you're looking straight down the stairs. From up there, believe me, it looks an awfully long way down.

Don't let anyone tell you that in time you acquire a good head for heights, you don't. You're stuck with the head you've got, and it doesn't make it any easier to hang onto it just because it's gone dark. I'm talking about Snowdon again here. Although it looks solid enough, Snowdon is riddled with holes, and inside them it's very dark indeed.

The holes I refer too are tunnels, tunnelled a long time ago to extract stuff like copper, and for a while they provided a certain schoolteacher with the perfect location for inflicting an interesting form of discipline. The lucky recipients were the cocky young residents at a special 'naughty boys school' in Deganwy, and one of their masters was a short but tough middle-aged rugby referee by the name of Dennis Hoare. He used to take them to explore these old workings. They were of course death traps, but Dennis had a good use for them.

I went with him once to his favourite spot so I could see what he did with his young villains, and it was amazing. "Come on boys it's quite safe," he announced, cheerfully leading us on all fours into what appeared to be a small cave. "Come on," he kept saying, and shepherded us down a steep slope until we could at last stand up in a typically dark and damp mine tunnel. "Where are we going Mr. Hoare ?" they were asking, with more than a hint of trepidation. "You'll see," he said, and we didn't have to wait long. The beam from his torch was soon showing that we were approaching an old wooden bridge perched across a gaping black chasm .

"Look," he said with relish, as he shone his torch down the hole, "Look, you can't see the bottom," and he was right, but the boys had gone very quiet. Then he said, "Come on, onto the bridge, it's perfectly safe." This alarmed me as much as the boys. It was obviously ancient and it was covered in green slime, and frankly it looked anything but safe, but with further assurances that he'd often walked over it, we all followed him and when we were half-way across he suddenly shouted, "Right, now hang on !!"

To our horror he started to jump up and down !! He was leaping up and down and the old bridge was literally bouncing beneath us. The boys were screaming "Stop it Mr.Hoare stop it !!" but there was no mercy. The bridge was bouncing and creaking, and even twisting now from side to side, and Dennis was laughing and shouting, "Jump ! Jump up and down ! come on !" but it was all we could do to hang on. We were bouncing up and down so violently we couldn't run for it, and I thought at any moment we were going to go crashing down into that abyss.

When at last our laughing tormentor relented and we scrambled off the thing, the boys were in tears, but then according to Dennis that was all to the good. He reckoned that once in a while their over-developed young egos needed to be given a set back, and perhaps he was right. All I know is that once they'd got over it and we were on our way home, you could see they'd developed a huge respect for Dennis.

Respect seems to be in short supply these days, and few years after he'd retired I met him again and reminded him how he used to take the boys exploring the old mines.

BWB 157

Mr. Hoare	"Yes we did indeed."
Barham	"And scared the life out of them."
Mr. Hoare	"We explored those very much."
Barham	"I don't know that one would be able to do that these days, because kids are handled so delicately these days."
Mr. Hoare	"Well yes, a lot of what I did with youngsters I probably wouldn't be able to do today."

He was an extraordinary fellow, and of course I reminded him of the bridge and the way he made them bounce up and down on it.

Mr. Hoare	"We did, that was the box shoot, it goes through all those levels actually (he laughs) it must drop about 300 feet."
Barham	"It did them a lot of good though ?"

| Mr.Hoare | "Oh yes, yes, yes, got a lot of fun out of it, and they got a lot of fun out of your visit too." |

I saw to it that my daughter got the chance of a 'young achievement' with a taste of Snowdon in bad weather. She was twelve when she came with me and Dennis one day and got to the summit in a gale and driving rain, and it was good to see how she got to grips with it. Like her brother she loves the outdoors and I'm sure that was a lesson in respect for mountains.

Just how to progress from terror to tourism might have been a problem if it hadn't been for fairgrounds. At the start of almost every tourist season I had to try out all the latest bare knuckle rides. This went on until my children were old enough to press buttons on a tape recorder and I sent them up to do the screaming.

AB1SG

Barham	(Meeting his children.) "Here they are. How did you get on ?"
Gareth	"Fantastic, you should have come dad."
Barham	"No thank you, and Julia ?"
Julia	"Great, made you feel funny."
Barham	"Did it ? You've recovered have you ?"
Julia	"Yep."
Barham	"Good. How did the recording go ?"
Gareth	"Fine I hope."
Barham	"Okay give me the tape recorder, let's see how it went."

(They stand and listen to the recording)

Gareth	(On the ride) "We're being pulled up the ramp here and we can see way across the fun-fair across the marine lake to the surfers."
Julia	"That surfer's going fast."
Gareth	"Yes and we've come to the top. Oh dear. It's quite

windy up here too, oh we've stopped ...... Oh no we haven't. Oh,.down we go ! Oh this is it !!....... Ooooooooowwwww !! Aaaaarrrrrhhhhhh !! Ooowwww !! – we're upside down !! Aaaaarrrrrhhhhhh !! Aaaaarrrrrhhhhhh !!" (etc.)

At places where I often made return visits I made a lot of good friends, places like Bob and Pat Brown's marvellous Museum of Childhood at Beaumaris, and the Welsh Mountain Zoo at Colwyn Bay for instance, and being sent to see new sights and new ideas meant seeing some very novel ideas put into practice. Hiring out lamas to carry people's rucksacks up Snowdon was a pretty novel idea, but the people operating that service were very dependent on the weather. Not many people want to walk in the rain and be spat at by a llama, but I suppose the Punch and Judy men were amongst the most vulnerable in a wet spell, and without doubt one of my favourite entertainers on the promenade scene was one by the name of Professor Codman of Llandudno.

He wasn't a real professor, it's just that by tradition all Punch and Judy men qualify for the title professor by common consent, and Professor John Codman's father and grandfather had been 'squawking' away in his booth before him. In fact his grandfather had made it, and the dolls, out of driftwood he collected from the beach. That was back in the 1800s.

This that follows is an extract from something I broadcast with him just before he died, and I found it very moving. He looked so very tired that day.

BWB 3
(Punch and Judy actuality)

Policeman   "Get up those stairs with you."
Mr. Punch   "Oh dear."
Policeman   "You know where they are, I hold a warrant for your arrest."

Mr. Punch	"What for ?"
Policeman	"What for ? For the murder of your wife and children."
Mr. Punch	"Ooh, ooh, oh." (Fade out.)

(Extract from interview after the show)

Mr. Codman "Do you know I enjoy it as much as the kids. If not more than most. I do, and I'm the one behind it, I'm the one looking at their faces and what's better ? To watch the expressions on a child's face. To watch a different fleeting expression of this and the other. The enjoyment or the anxiety and the actions and everything. It's all there on a kid's face, and I'm the one who is responsible for it, so I'm enjoying that, knowing that I'm doing it, I'm enjoying it myself. It makes me want to put more effort in. More and more. In fact, today I'm feeling tired, but once I get going I forget all about my age. I forget all about anything else because of what I'm doing you see. Oh they enjoy it, and so do I."

Rhyl had a Punch and Judy man too. He was Professor Green and he too was excellent, but while some lose out in wet weather others flourish. Not many it's true, but there are always some who find that silver lining in the rain clouds. The manager of the Lake Vyrnwy hotel was one such genius. He introduced 'brolly' breaks and as far as I know they may still be available. The hotel commands a wonderful view over this long forest lake but it gets an awful lot of rain, so this was the deal – choose this hotel for a winter weekend and if it doesn't rain you get a bottle of champagne. Worth a gamble ? Lots of people thought so, but I can tell you it was very very rare for a bottle to change hands.

I featured these weekends more than once and this invariably brings up the question of advertising.

307

Whether or not the BBC should advertise is a huge question, but long before you get into the deep debate on commercialising the service with all the likely benefits and all the likely drawbacks, the immediate question is – does the BBC advertise already ? The answer is no, but it does 'publicise'. The reporter mustn't say 'You really must try one of these brolly breaks. It's a truly great hotel and those bottles of champagne are just bursting their corks to make your weekend a truly memorable one.' That would not be allowed, but there are times when the path between advertising and publicising isn't quite so clear, especially if, for example you're featuring a new go-cart track, and you're whizzing around the track, enjoying yourself.

On the other side of the coin we also featured commercial ventures when they closed down, often throwing large numbers of people out of work. There was always a ghoulish appetite amongst news producers for these gloomy stories whether they involved large concerns, or at the other end of the spectrum, the closure of a village shop. They loved stories like these and of course these stories sometimes provided enormous dollops of nostalgia. You know the sort of thing. - 'When my mother, poor old soul, opened this shop it was Christmas Eve and that night she gave everything away to the poor and needy. They were queuing up at the door. Happy days. You could buy a box of candles and pills for your rickets for less than what you youngsters pay now for a packet of crisps.'

Thinking of old shops closing down reminds me of an old fishing tackle shop in Llangollen and the old lady who owned it. It had belonged to her grandfather and in the 1890s the historian A. G. Bradley dropped in with a young lady artist he'd picked up along the way. (Yes even in those days). She was an American tourist (yes even in those days), and no doubt being bowled over by anything old (yes even in those days) she wanted to paint the old man in the shop who was busy tying fishing flies. However, our informant Mr. Bradley told us in his book

'Highways and Byways of North Wales' that she was rebuffed ! The old man said he was far too busy to be bothered.

Ninety years later, or thereabouts, I had cause to visit that shop. I had a new series - travelling in the wake of Mr. Bradley, and when preparing for the Llangollen instalment I discovered the shop was still owned by a member of the same family. I was told that if I went there I'd find the grand daughter of the old man who'd sent the American artist packing. (You'll love this). "She's getting on a bit now," I was told, "But she's there in the shop every day." So I rang and asked her if I could record a little interview with her. "Oh goodness me," she said, "I'm far too busy to be bothered with that," and rang off. Isn't that wonderful. A little crustiness was obviously still in the genes, but a few weeks later she relented and I fondly remember sitting with her while she reminisced about the old days. (The salmon were much larger then.)

I used to love hearing about times gone by and in Llandudno Jim Williams was always good to listen to. He was a long-standing public servant, a councillor for many years (when they gave up their time to manage your town without being paid) and a hotelier of long-standing too. When he started in the tourist trade people not only came by train, but they also provided their own food, and another elder of the catering trade told me once about his research into cheese on toast.

Like most people I was brought up to snootily call it Welsh 'rare-bit'. But he'd discovered that it's actually plain old Welsh rabbit. This was because the ancient drovers of livestock had to provide their own food on reaching their destination, and whereas drovers from around England snared rabbits, those from Wales usually carried great blocks of cheese. On arriving at the markets, like London's Smithfield, the town cooks simply melted it on bread and called it 'Welsh Rabbit'. (Cockney humour)

The old railways of Wales are always

good for a bit of nostalgia. Most of these lovingly restored antique lines are narrow gauge to help them twist round the tight mountain bends, and most of the engines are still steam engines puffing real sooty smoke up through the forests. They're a great sight to see, and with their paintwork always bright and shiny and the brass-ware always gleaming, they're a credit to the companies and the volunteers who run them.

They all go through spectacular scenery and if I had to choose a favourite I suppose I would have to choose the Ffestiniog line. This is mainly because of the struggle I saw they had re-routing it back to its origin among the slate tips of Blaenau Ffestiniog. On the other hand, could anything be more spectacular than the Swiss built rack and pinion railway that climbs to the top of Snowdon ? Even here the old steam engines are still in use, well over a hundred years old, and holding their own with the diesels every day.

I sometimes found myself shovelling coal working as a fireman on those old trains, and although it's true the Snowdon railway does run up the gentler side of the mountain, it's still a strange place to find a railway, climbing right up to the top of the highest mountain in England and Wales. I've known people climb up there from the other side in a thick mist, and not knowing of the railway, be startled out of their fog-bound wits by suddenly hearing a platform announcement. It must be like finding yourself transported into a science fiction story

One of my favourite recordings was made on that railway when I was crammed into one of those little carriages with the entire Llanrug Silver Band. They were celebrating their success in a big competition and although they only came from down the road, they thought they'd have a day out playing on a train, and what a day it was.

The engines only push one small carriage at a time up that five mile track, and so it was a very tight squeeze in there. Their engine was a steam engine and as soon as it puffed out of the station, the band struck up with the rousing march 'Blaze Away', and the engine joined in ! Puffing away the old engine provided the beat, and with their rosy red cheeks swollen fit to bust, those eager bandsmen blew their hearts out all the way to the summit. It was fabulous, and the only way I could tell the listeners what was going on was by hanging out the window. It was such a crush in there, and the noise was so deafening, hanging out of the window was the only thing I could do.

After a while the engine stopped to pick up water at one of the halts, and after a few interviews on the train, they started off again, but I jumped off, letting the tape run on as the sound of the band and the strenuous puff –puffs of the engine gradually faded away up into the clouds. I love that tape. If I could I'd share it with you.

You can get some really wonderful noises from steam trains. If you ask the driver nicely he'll pull away with the brake on which causes the engine to work extra hard and produce some extra big 'puff-puff' noises, and of course it's a good idea to ask the driver for a blast on the hooter when he's gone about fifty yards, but you have to be careful with trains, they stop for no-one, and for that reason it doesn't pay to be too clever.

Naturally there were many occasions when I had to interview important visitors to Wales, and there was one occasion in particular when I didn't do too well. It was on the Ffestiniog line and it was arranged for me to meet this important fellow and travel up the line with him from Portmadoc. I think he was a foreign government representative from somewhere or other, but somewhat unwisely I chose this occasion to over-do it a bit.

They sat him in a carriage a long way back from the engine, and from there I knew I couldn't pick up the sound of it getting under way. It was a windy day so I couldn't hold the microphone out of the window, and I therefore decided to leave him aboard for a couple of minutes and introduce the identity of this important guest whilst standing next to the engine.

To the background noise of the engine gently steaming I said into the mic - "I'm about to board this train to join Mr. (Whatever his name was) who is making his first visit to our part of the world, and as we travel up to Blaenau Ffestiniog he'll be telling me of the importance of his visit." At this point the guard blew his whistle and the train started to pull away with huge great puffs and lots of hissing steam. "So," I concluded, "It's time now for me to step aboard."

It was going so nicely, very nicely. Except that I'd forgotten one thing. One quite important thing really. I'd forgotten they lock the carriage doors. As the carriages went by I was desperately trying as many doors as I could, but I couldn't open any of them, and before long I was left standing on the end of platform watching the train and my interviewee disappearing down the line.

Chasing after the train in the car was extremely embarrassing, but among our volunteer railways the Llangollen railway is another special one to mention. It's an old standard gauge line. Here you'll find the big boys, and riding through the Berwyn tunnel on the footplate was an eye-opener, or perhaps I should say an eye closer. It was the first train through after they'd re-opened that tunnel, and it certainly showed what a dirty job it is driving a steam engine. They left the fire box open to provide some light but the smoke completely blocked it out, and it was a very rough and rocky ride too. You had to hang on, it was like riding a bucking bronco.

It was on this line that I learned to drive steam engines, and the first one was the Flying Scotsman. It was incredible to start with the world's most famous locomotive, and I can only say it was like having driving lessons in a Bentley. My instructor was Bob Maxwell, the Scotsman's real driver, and I'm glad to say that I also had a fireman alongside to keep me going.

BBWB 18

Barham	"What do I do again ?"
Mr. Maxwell	"Well you sit on the driver's seat for a start. (Barham sits). Now the lever on your left is for the vacuum brake. Now, we don't move till we've created 21 inches of vacuum. You lift the lever into the 'up' position."
Barham	(Lifting lever) "Okay." (Engine hisses).
Mr. Maxwell	"The next thing you do is to put it into gear so wind this handle here. (Barham winds handle). And the next thing you do is pull this lever which is the regulator, which allows steam into the cylinders, and then you pull the whistle …. Pull on this wire. (Barham blows whistle). That's it."
Barham	"Oh! I've got it moving." (He laughs). "We're moving, okay, but wait a minute ! I've forgotten something. I've forgotten to look at the signal ! Is it safe to go ?"
Mr. Maxwell	"Well, we've already checked those, you're okay."
Barham	"Oh thank goodness. I'd hate to go down in history as the man who wrecked the Flying Scotsman."
Mr. Maxwell	(Laughing) "So would we !"

Some months later I was back for another programme to take some more lessons, this time on another monster – the Union of South Africa. The enormous power of these things gives you a tremendous thrill. You sit there holding all that power in your hands, and then you gently unleash it. Wonderful. By the end of the day I was able to take it packed with people out from the station at Llangollen and up into the beautiful Dee Valley. That was quite a responsibility but such a pleasurable task.

You're sitting with your heart in your mouth, knowing that whatever happens you mustn't jerk all those people off their seats. You check the signals to see that it's still clear to go. You look back down the platform. All the doors have been shut and you see the Station Master put the whistle to his lips. He blows it, and everyone then is waiting for you to do something.

As carefully as handling an unexploded bomb, you very, very gradually release the beast and your ears are filled then by the sound of a monstrous 'chug', followed after a few seconds by another great 'chug', and as you gain speed the 'chugs' come more quickly and you're on your way. On your way with your enormously powerful pet monster straining at the leash.

That was in the nineties and the Flying Scotsman was over eighty years old then, but the oldest engine I ever came across was the Fire Queen. She'd worked in the Dinorwic slate Quarry at Llanberis, and I was there when they pushed her out from her hiding place. That might have been in 1968. She'd worked there until 1886 and was put into a little stone building for safe-keeping. Then, when the world wars arrived in the first half of the twentieth century, someone, fearing she'd be taken for scrap iron, built a wall round her hiding place.

When she emerged, covered in cobwebs of course, we couldn't believe our eyes. I was among a dozen or more reporters and we all thought we were looking at another Stevenson's rocket. It had a long tall chimney standing high above a green wooden clad boiler, and it had no cab, the driver and fireman had stood in the open, and its buffers incidentally were made of leather. Someone was telling us the wheel formation was 040 and it ran on a 4-foot track, but it was hard to take it all in because it was like a dream. It was real enough though, and you should see it now. It's on display at Penrhyn Castle. All the brass pipes, wheels and knobs are beautifully polished and the green and black paintwork shines like new, just like it must have done when it was built in 1848.

If you go to see the old Fire Queen to-day and marvel at her primitive construction, it's worth remembering why she's there. The slate quarry was closing down.

Hundreds of workers were being thrown onto the scrap heap, as they were at other mines and quarries through-out that period. Their labour intensive product was losing more and more ground to cheaper products like man-made tiles, and just like farmers, quarry owners had to try and diversify .

Some of them managed to, but always with a reduced labour force, and at the Llechwedd slate mine at Blaenau Ffestiniog they led the way into tourism, running little electric trains through one of the tunnels, explaining how the slate is extracted, and winning several awards in the process. Later they introduced a spectacular ride down a steep incline as others in the industry followed on.

Other mines too were reopened, like the copper mine near Beddgelert, but I'm afraid hopes of turning the huge Dorathea slate quarry at Nantlle into various things including a vineyard withered on the vine. Instead, this enormous hole, five hundred feet deep, gradually filled with water like other quarries that pock mark the area. The Dorathea then attracted divers, and became a death trap.

In spite of several brave efforts, they were hard times for many across Wales, and it was sad to report on so many people being thrown out of work. We saw redundancies in all manner of industries. I remember the Bersham and Gresford Collieries closing, and Point of Ayr too, and thousands of steel workers lost their livelihoods at Shotton. Every job lost produced a family in crisis, and we had many a tragic tale to tell.

If the Fire Queen is a treasure, and surely it is, it must be said that in the Welsh hills we have a more basic form of treasure in the shape of real gold. I saw numerous attempts to re-open old gold mines. I've followed lots of eager beavers into dripping wet long forgotten tunnels, hardly bigger than rabbit burrows, listening patiently to their dreams of striking it rich, but in my time there were actually two working gold mines here. Now they too are closed.

The first one I got to know was the Cloggau St. David's mine. This is hidden away in a wooded ravine above the village of Bont Ddu. It had gone through a chequered history and opened and closed a few times during my days even, nevertheless this is where the gold came from for the Royal Family's wedding rings. That was in its hey-day, and all the more surprising when you see how small it is. I loved going there. The boss was a huge old man by the name of Jack Williams, a soft spoken giant with a world-weary voice, deep and slow and very Welsh. He used to draw diagrams in the dust with a stick to show me how he was going to find the next seam of gold.

I don't think he got much out of it and most of the time there only seemed to be old Jack and his son there. When you think of gold mines in places like South Africa, with all that fierce security, with gun-carrying guards patrolling with dogs, and floodlights and sirens, and electric fences and all that sort of thing, the Cloggau St. David's mine can only be described as 'rustic'. As you approached, ducking under the trees by the stream, you did come to a gate it's true, but it was just an ordinary farm gate, and on it was a sign that read - 'Gold Mine. Keep Out'. Having climbed over the gate, you came to the tunnel, closed off by an old door and secured with a padlock. If you'd seen the Seven Dwarfs coming out you wouldn't have been a bit surprised.

I've still got old Jack Williams on tape, but as you can't really appreciate his wonderful slow, dark voice on a page, I'll play his son Jerry instead, because this was one of the tapes recorded inside the mine and he's explaining how you find the gold.

BBWT 703
(Underground in the Cloggau St. David's Gold Mine. Dripping water. Echoey.)
Barham   "I haven't seen any sign of the gold yet Jerry. How do you find it ?"

316

Mr. Williams   "Well, you see that white reef in front of you ?
Barham   "That sort of milk-stone stuff ?"
Mr. Williams   "Yes."
Barham   "The quartz ?"
Mr. Williams   "The quartz. Sometimes it's say – about a foot thick, then it can go up to thirty foot wide, but it's never been proved there's anything in the white quartz itself, but you see that little reef coming in from the side there, well that is a sure sign of gold every time."
Barham   "What's it like when you find it ?"
Mr. Williams   "Well the feeling is, you feel you're going to have a heart attack (laughing) it starts pounding like mad you know, it's very exciting."
Barham   "And what does the gold actually look like – is it nice and yellowy and goldy as we might imagine ?"
Mr. Williams   "Yes it is. You find little nodules sticking out of the rock, and if you look at the top of it you'll find the gold on the top, you turn it upside down and it's still there, all the way through, like little fingers going all the way through it you know. It's very exciting."

As I said it's only a little place but during the 1800's three hundred men worked there, and the biggest lump of gold they ever found came to light when they widened the doorway. So much for drawing diagrams in the dust.

When it was open the Gwynfynydd mine was quite a bit busier, and one of my visits there was when they'd had a particularly good 'strike' as they call it. Looking at the rock they'd cut into, it was like looking into a golden 'milky way', a cloud of tiny golden specks that sparkled in the torchlight. It was a beautiful sight, but they'd only found that by accident when they blasted a shortcut from one tunnel to another.

Most of the gold mines were in that

area not far from Dolgellau, and you can sometimes find gold panners at work around there. These prospectors can be a bit shy sometimes, and I was always on the lookout for one in particular.

This chap was rumoured to spend weeks hiding in the forests panning and writing a book on the subject. When in the area, and working on a feature that wasn't needed straight away, I often used to delve into those deep forests looking for him along the banks of the various rivers, and after a couple of years I found him. I found his van first hidden well off the track, and further up a river I found him knee-deep in the water sifting through the gravel. He was a bit taken aback when I appeared, but it wasn't long before he was showing me how it's done.

This is a short extract from that tape and I'll call him only by his first name in case he's still hiding, and as promised at the time, I won't say in which river I found him.

BBWB 96

Barham	"Right here we are then. Doug is now busy panning and we're down to the last dregs of sand and gravel, and as yet I can't see anything."
Doug	"The gold will be under the far bottom corner. Oh, there's a nice flake there. I saw a quick flash in the pan."
Barham	"Really ? Is that where the expression came from ?"
Doug	"Yes, yes."
Barham	"You're using a blue plastic pan I see with ridges down one side."
Doug	"Yes, it's very easy ...."
Barham	"Oh, wait a minute, I can see something gleaming there."
Doug	"Yes."
Barham	"In fact one or two bits of gold dust, yes ?"
Doug	"No, no, ha, that's Fool's Gold."

Barham	"What are all these other little things ?"
Doug	"Well, we've got a couple of pieces of gold flake, quite a few little gold nuts or dots. The silvery stuff is arsenic and pyrites."
Barham	"Were you trained as a geologist ?"
Doug	"No I was a radio engineer in the Royal Navy, mending radars and radios."

Very occasionally I'd seen others gold panning but this chap was a dab-hand, swirling the fine gravel round and round with such rhythmic ease, giving the heavy gold plenty of time to sink to the bottom.

I can't imagine a more risky business than gold mining, and things must have reached a pretty low ebb at the Gwynfynydd by the nineties because they too were suddenly going into the tourist trade. An earlier attempt to do exactly that at the Cloggau mine had failed to clear the planning hurdles, but thousands of tourists had been welcomed into the slate mines at Blaenau Ffestiniog, so why not a gold mine ?

I remember my last visit to the old Gwynfynydd mine. It was a bright fresh day and there was such a bright fresh optimistic feeling to the place.

AB17G
(At gold mine entrance alongside river, with manager Nick Worrel.)

Barham	(Speaking over sound of torrent.) "We're in the midst of the vast Coed - Y- Brenin forest high on a bank overlooking the browny-gold waters of the River Mawddach before they plunge down those creamy-white waterfalls, and just along the track here there are some of your men. What are they doing here ?"
Mr. Worral	"Just finishing the new entrance to the mine."
Barham	"Let's have a look …. Oh yes it's got a nice timber frontage to it. It looks very 'Klondike' doesn't it ?"

| Mr. Worral | (Laughing) "Yes it does." |

As we walked in through a brightly lit tunnel and into a wide cavern, he told me (as he always did) about the history of the place, and how they'd produced over two thousands ounces in the last nine years. As it always does when working with a real enthusiast, it was going well. We even had an electric train with several trucks rumble by, adding nicely to the slightly echoey atmosphere, and soon I was asking if tourists would be able to see some gold.

Mr. Worral	"Yes they will. They'll see gold-bearing strata certainly and they'll be able to mine for their own gold as well."
Barham	(Surprised) "Really ?"
Mr. Worral	"Yes, yes."
Barham	"To take away some samples ?"
Mr. Worral	"Well anything they find they're entitled to."
Barham	(Very surprised) "Really ?"
Mr. Worral	"And that includes the gold panning outside."
Barham	"Gosh, can I have a go ?"
Mr. Worral	(Laughing) "You can have a go any time you like."
Barham	"Well where is this gold ? I'm looking around me now and all I can see is common or garden rock."
Mr. Worral	"Common or garden rock it may be, but I assure you it's got gold in it. Come on let's go."
Barham	"Alright then. (They set off). I'll follow you. I don't know where we're going now. Crumbs, oh down another tunnel. (Barham sings) Hi ho, hi ho, off to work we go (they laugh) with a hi and a ho and a hi hi ho"(etc. Fade on singing).

(Further into mine).
| Mr. Worral | "Here we are Allan, you can see the glistening sulphides on the face of this area. Here, deep in the |

heart of a very productive and rich ore body, which is a massive quartz formation full of sulphides. Anywhere round here there could be a small or large pocket of gold."

Barham   (Peering close at rock) "Well I can see little golden specks in this quartz can't I ?"

Mr. Worral   "You can indeed, yes."

Barham   "Is that real gold ?"

Mr. Worral   "No that's Fool's Gold, that's iron pyrites."

Barham   (Laughing) "Just my luck."

Mr. Worral   (Laughing) "Yes."

Barham   "What will people do, have a little pick at it ? (He digs at it with fingernail) It's quite soft and crumbly really."

Mr. Worral   "In that there will be a few grains I'm sure of real gold."

It was a good idea, but it never really got going and soon the mine closed down. As I write a decade or more later it's still closed, boarded up and abandoned. So many hopes left in the mud.

As far as I know the Welsh treasure chest never contained any gems of great worth, but if you run out of gold there's always the family silver, and to me that means the York family and Erddig Hall, a mansion on the outskirts of Wrexham.

Here was a family of aristocrats that died out soon after the last of the line handed his crumbling home and its estate over to the National Trust in the 1970s. The last squire of Erddig was a nice old boy who did much to maintain his family's reputation for eccentricity by riding a penny-farthing bicycle. His name was Philip, but that was hardly surprising. The family abided by a very strange and self-inflicted rule. All the boys were named alternately Philip or Simon, which must have led to terrible confusion in the days of large families. But here was a family that ignored convention, and could well have been scorned for it by others of their standing.

For instance, for the times in which they lived, they were actually good to their servants. So considerate were they, they had their portraits painted and hung in the house, and when someone invented the camera the following generations were treated to this new form of immortality. However, although famed for their kindness, the family couldn't resist scribbling a descriptive verse or two at the foot of each picture, and not all were entirely complimentary. No wonder the poor devils looked worried, having to sit there having their pictures taken and wondering what their masters and mistresses were going to say about them.

The Trust has done a magnificent job restoring the house, seeing as it had been practically broken in half by a coal mine running beneath it, and because of the York's famous attitude to their 'extended' family, the house is shown primarily from the servants perspective. Visitors enter through the farmyard and stables, and come into the house through the great kitchen instead of the front door, but on my first visit I came through the front door.

It was very late one night during March 1973. This was the night before Philip, the last of the line, handed it all over to the Trust. We wanted to talk to him but as he wasn't on the phone I simply had to go and knock on the door. Seeing as it was going to be late by the time I got there, this was obviously going to be a gamble. He might have been in bed, but we thought it was worth trying.

I found the house exactly as I expected it to be, enormous and in total darkness. We knew there was no electricity there and when I got out of the car I was struck by the silence of the place too. It was as still and silent as a massive mausoleum, but with a pale moon filtering through the clouds I found my way up the impressive steps and banged on the door. I might even have tugged on a bell pull and after a while the door was opened by an old gentleman with a cheerful face illuminated by the

322

glow of a lantern. I said I was from the BBC and he replied with a big smile "Come in, come in," and I walked into something quite amazing.

We've all seen beautiful mansions restored to former glory but here was one in absolute decay. It smelt of mildew, pieces of wallpaper were hanging from the walls, and damp-stained dust sheets lay sprawled across the furniture, and yet everywhere, shining through the cobwebs, there was silverware. There was so much silver that afterwards I was told by the Trust's press officer that the first thing they did next morning was to seek assistance from the police to get it to safety into a bank vault.

For the next hour or more that night my genial host took me on a conducted tour, taking me all over that old house, going in and out of every room with grotesque shadows crowding around us with every swing of the lantern. He showed me the dining room and the sitting rooms, the kitchens, the bedrooms, and even the family's chapel built into the house, and in one big room there was suddenly a weird scratching noise coming from behind the long tattered curtains. "Nothing to worry about," he said, and drawing back the curtain I saw it was the branch of a tree. "Years ago there were no trees quite so close, " he said, "Out there it used to be nice parkland, all lawns you know."

He so willingly told me everything, the family's background, his life there and why he decided to give it all away, but we cannot find any part of that tape. Parts of it were taken into several other programmes and I never saw any of them again.

The Erddig jungle has now been cleared away and everything inside and outside reinstated, and the wonderful thing about Erddig is that the York's threw nothing away. From tin openers, to horse-drawn carriages, and bed-warmers, to Penny Farthings, everything was still there, just like the old squire who involved himself with much of the restoration work, living on there until his death not long after it opened. He loved it. He used to lure people away from the guides and give them his own guided tours, as he did with my mother. I took her there to see the place and they hit it off straight away. I nearly had to leave her there.

The Manod Slate Mine at Blaenau Ffestiniog held a lot of treasure. During the Second World War the bulk of Britain's art treasures were stored there, safe from Hitler's bombs, and although they were taken back to the National Galleries when the war ended, the Crown held on to the place. This gave rise to some pretty weird rumours, and a lot of people believed the caverns were being held ready to accommodate the Royal Family in the event of an atomic war. These stories used to appear like a recurring rash, with reports coming in of new furniture being delivered there, and even a lawnmower once, though what use a lawnmower would be in a slate mine I've no idea.

Eventually it all came to an end in the eighties when Whitehall released its holding so that it could be returned to its original purpose. As you might expect, reporters from far and wide wanted to see inside, and early one morning the big steel doors were pulled open and we walked into a very large and brightly lit tunnel.

It was so well appointed it was like walking into a James Bond movie. The first thing we saw were enormous great fuel tanks. These we were told were for the central heating, and a little further on we came to a huge cavern large enough to house several rows of neat single-storey brick buildings. If I remember rightly they were flat-roofed and it was in these neatly built air-conditioned buildings that the pictures had been housed. We went inside them (any of our choice) and we found rows and rows of wooden frames from which they'd been hung, each one of them bearing the familiar name of a famous artist, old masters like Rembrandt, Constable and so on.

It was a strange sort of place, and it was weird also to think that all those wonderful paintings had hung there for years with just a handful of attendants having them all to themselves. I hope they enjoyed them, but beauty is in the eye of the beholder and 'treasure' comes in many forms. Joe Watkins was a lonely man. He was an old farmer in very poor health, living alone on the outskirts of Newtown, and all his life he'd dreamt of flying - jumping off his tractor and wheeling around the sky in a dog-fighting Spitfire, so he bought one. He bought a real old RAF Spitfire and parked it outside his kitchen window. He had his Spitfire at last, and he was ready 'scramble'.

There have been so many treasures. Ancient coins and jewellery dug up and washed up on remote beaches, and heirlooms bought for pennies in markets and car boot sales, but one day I too discovered treasure, treasure that some people might kill for.

I found it in Marianglas, a small village on the Island of Anglesey. This little backwater had been the childhood home of Hugh Griffiths, that crusty old hook-nosed Holywood Oscar winning actor who revelled in playing lecherous old drunks, as in the 'Titfield Thunderbolt.'

I'd met him in the 70's. With an eye to publicity the proprietor of Cobden's hotel in Capel Curig had phoned to say that she had a big star in for lunch, but within the hour I'm afraid she was getting more than she bargained for. Emerging from the dining room, and squinting at me through a well sozzled haze, he agreed to an interview, but turning away from his escorts, two very sober looking middle aged ladies, he insisted on having his host, the proprietor, at his side. She was more than willing to oblige, but her smile quickly disappeared to be replaced by a look of horror. He slurred his way through the entire interview with one hand very firmly clamped to her left breast, while she stood petrified like a startled rabbit.

His greatest success came in the Hollywood epic – 'Ben Hur'. He played the sheik, and at the time it was the most expensive film ever made. It cost over12 million dollars, which was an absolute fortune in 1955, and it was for his part in this epic that Hugh Griffiths won his 'Oscar'. In the glittering world of entertainment nothing, but nothing, has ever compared with a Hollywood Oscar, but now he was dead. That's why I was in Marianglas. To mark his passing his sister had pinned up a few of his photographs in the village hall, which I believe had been the village school when he was a boy.

When I got there little Marianglas was as sleepy as ever. There was no-one in sight and when I opened the door of the village hall I found the photos pinned up in a corner over by a window, but there was no-one there. The place was empty - empty except for those photos and.... a Hollywood Oscar ! It was unbelievable. Standing right there on a trestle table and completely unattended, was his golden Oscar, absolutely gleaming there in a ray of sunlight.

I took a photograph of it, and for a few minutes I just stood there thinking of all that priceless Holywood glitz and glamour. I could see it all. All the world's film-makers, all the world's film stars, and I could see the awards being presented, I could hear the wild applause and the screams of delight, and I could see the world's press surging forward, and the flashbulbs flashing as the Oscar is held aloft .... and there it was .... a Holywood Oscar, left standing on a table in an empty village hall, and I just said it out loud - "Wales I love you."

CHAPTER U.
U.F.O.s and Other Unsolved Mysteries.

I covered a lot of UFO stories and most I didn't believe. On the other hand there were one or two that quite honestly were difficult not to believe After all how could you accuse a whole class of little primary school children and their teacher of being bare faced liars.

The news broke out at lunchtime

when the kids ran home to tell their mums. A whole class in Llandudno Junction had seen a flying saucer fly over the roof of their school Ysgol Maelgwn. It was 11th February 1977 and I got there by mid-afternoon to find they were housed in a pre-fab classroom at the bottom end of the playground. From there they had a full and uninterrupted view of the main building.

BWB 4A

Barham	"What did it look like ?"
Child	"A flying saucer really."
Barham	"Did it have any colours, or ..?"
Children	"Silvery, silvery. Orange, bright, yeah."
Barham	"Was it circular ?"
Children	"Yes, yeah."
Barham	"Was it dome-shaped ?"
Children	"Yes, yeah, there was a dome on the top and a dome on the bottom."
Teacher	"Yes, that's exactly what I saw, what the children just said. That's what I saw, just skimming the roof of the building."
Barham	"You weren't all dreaming were you ?"
All	(Amid laughter) "No, no, no."
Teacher	"No and we weren't drunk either were we ?"
All	"No, no."

Later that same afternoon a group of girls playing netball at a school on Anglesey also claimed that they saw a flying saucer.

Of course there were cheats, people having fun, like the gang in Llanerch-y-Medd who, I'm told, knotted ropes together to form a large ring, and hanging onto it one night they ran round and round holding torches to simulate a flying saucer in a distant field. When I got there everyone was talking about it, especially about the 'men from the ministry' in white overalls that someone had seen inspecting the area at dawn.

I always liked Llanerch-y-Medd, it was a good example of a quiet village having things going on under the surface. For instance, walking down the high street late at night it would be quite normal for the deep slumbering peace to be shattered by blood-curdling yells and villainous chants. This would only be a meeting of the local Vikings and nothing to worry about. They'd just be sitting around in their horned helmets having a chat and a few beers after hammering out a few more swords on the forge. Making swords out of motor car leaf springs seemed to be their speciality, but I'm sliding off the subject. UFO reports were actually quite tricky things to cover.

My attention was drawn on one occasion to the letters page of a Caernarvon paper in which there was a claim by a woman that a large ball was making a tiresome habit of flying over her house. She lived near Trefor on the north coast of the Lleyn peninsula, and she said it was coming in from the sea, changing colour, zooming over her house, hovering on a mountain top, and then shooting off at supersonic speed.

I was lucky in those days. We didn't have Sat Nav and Mobile Phones, but every village had its village shop combined with a little post office counter tucked away in a corner, and if you couldn't find someone in the phone book you rang the village post office instead because they knew everybody. They would tell you where they lived, how to find them, when they went to the doctor, when they went to do Auntie Molly's washing, what time they'd get back – everything. They'd even tell you if you needed to go round to the back door, and once I was told "The door's always open, let yourself in she won't be long." And in those days few rural doors were locked, so although the lady claiming to see strange things fly over her house wasn't on the phone I soon had an address for her. Also, as usual, I'd been given a brief description. "She's okay." I was told "But she's German."

The fairly isolated house was about a mile outside the village and it had a good view over that part of the coast, and I remember very clearly standing there knocking on her door. This is because when she opened it she was holding a meat cleaver. Furthermore this meat cleaver was raised above her head ready to split me in half. Fortunately those wonderfully soothing words, "I'm from the BBC" steadied her hand, and when she knew I'd come to ask her about her 'ball' she invited me in. But she never let go of the meat cleaver, not once. She told me people in the village were plotting to kill her, and with polite diplomacy I said how sorry I was to hear it, and would she be so kind as to describe her ball ? "Come," she said "I will show you what I see," and she led me upstairs, still clutching the meat cleaver.

We went first into a front bedroom and pointing out to sea she described how this huge ball often floated into the shore, changing colour as it approached, and then she strode into a back bedroom, and pointing up to the top of a mountain, she told me how it flew up there, hovered for a bit, and then shot off into the distance at a fantastic speed. I switched off the tape recorder, refused a cup of tea, thanked her very much for a nice interview and left her at the door, pleasantly waving goodbye with her meat cleaver.

It went on the air the next morning, and except for those occasions when I drove past the house, I forgot all about her. The house was sold soon after, but before long I was once again in that area talking to a British Rail union man living in a house with the same view. Parcel deliveries from Pwllheli had ground to a halt following a dispute, and he was telling me (as union leaders always did) that the strike would go on for as long as it took to address the injustices of it all, and when I'd finished the interview his wife brought in cups of coffee.

We sat chatting about this and that, and I started to tell them of this incredible woman up the road who reckoned she used to see a big coloured ball come in from the sea and fly over her house etc. As you might guess, I was enjoying myself telling this story, I was laughing about it, but suddenly I realised they weren't laughing, "We saw that," they said, very solemnly, "we saw that," and they went on to describe it just as the woman up the road had described it.

I don't know if that sends a little shiver up your spine, but this next one might, especially as it happened on a 'dark and stormy night', and the evidence was indisputable - they were lying dead in the road.

It was on that most mystical of islands again, Anglesey, and as I said - on a dark and stormy night a man who was driving along a lonely country lane found his way blocked by a pile of dead birds. They were starlings and it gave rise to a multitude of wild and scary theories, especially as (upon dissection) it appeared that their livers had been cooked.

The Wylfa atomic power station was only a few miles down the road and questions were being asked from all quarters. Were they victims of radiation ? Did they fly into a poisonous gas cloud ? The smoke from the aluminium smelter is said to be lethal and that wasn't far away, or were they hit by an aircraft ? And yes, did they have a close encounter with a UFO ?

This is an extract from an interview conducted on the spot with the man who found them, Jim Clark. He'd come across them on his way home from work at Lake Alaw.

BWB14

Barham	"This was the spot then, was it Jim ?"
Mr. Clark	"It was indeed."
Barham	"Hmm, just in the road here ? How far did they stretch, all these bodies ?"
Mr. Clark	"Well about 25 metres, in a block from this gate here up towards Bodedern. It's about 25, 30 metres."
Barham	"And how many would you say there were ?"
Mr. Clark	"Well, I picked about 90 up. There was at least double that left I would say. I picked 90 up to be taken for examination."

Barham	"They were just lying on top of one another were they ?"
Mr. Clark	"Well yes, spread out on the road, it just looked like somebody had tipped them there."
Barham	"Were they all starlings ?"
Mr. Clark	"Yes, every one was a starling."
Barham	"Yes, you came across them while driving along the road here, you must have wondered what had happened."
Mr. Clark	"Yes, I didn't realise they were birds at first, I thought they were either bits from the side of the road or muck from a lorry or something. No I didn't realise, it was only after driving over them initially that I realised, when I saw a couple flapping about, that I realised they were birds."

As for their livers being cooked, this especially raised alarm, but a word of caution suggests that effect might have been caused by heat generated when the bodies were piled into plastic bags.

Who would have thought that Jack the Ripper might have lived on Anglesey. He's said to have lived in Aberfraw, a village that lies on the west coast of the island on the edge of the sea and all those wonderful sand dunes. Some people there believed their suspect had received medical training and that he would have had anatomical knowledge, and I was told that he'd travelled to London each time the murders were committed. Not exactly enough evidence to convict him, except that each time he returned he was said to be sorely depressed and after killing himself, the gruesome murders ceased.

That tale is pure gossip, and as we all know there's no stopping gossip. Take King Arthur for instance. No-one's sure if he ever lived, but I've been on so many King Arthur stories I qualify for a seat at the round table as his publicity officer.

News and photo editors please note –
King Arthur will be at Barclays Bank, Aberystwyth at 10.30 am.
tuesday to take possession of the Holy Grail. Interviews and
excellent photo opportunities.

Perhaps I've become a little biased,
but from what I've seen it definitely looks as if old Arthur belonged
with us in North Wales. Although of course I should have asked
him where he lived when I met him. That was in a field near Dinas
Mawddwy where he was unveiling a plaque on a memorial stone to
mark the site of his last battle.

AS105

Barham	(Horse whinnies) "I'm talking now to Arthur – Arthur Pendragon, dressed in sack cloth and white Druid robes, and he's carrying a long shiny silver sword and a shield."
King Arthur	"My name is actually Arthur Utha Pendragon, my signature is Arthur X, and I'm generally known as King Arthur."
Barham	"Presumably you were born with a different name but you changed your name by deed poll ?"
King Arthur	"Eight years ago I changed it to Arthur Utha Pendragon."
Barham	"Right."
King Arthur	"I believe I am the re-incarnation of the Celtic Chieftain known now as King Arthur.

He said this is how he earns his living
and added very quickly that he doesn't draw any state benefit, and
after the unveiling I asked one of the organisers of the event, local
Arthurian author Laurence Main, for some evidence to suggest that
this was a battlefield at all, let alone King Arthur's last battlefield.

Mr. Main	"Place name evidence for a start. The field is

actually called Maes Camlan – the 'field of the fierce battle'. Overlooking it on our left we have Bryn Cleifion – the 'hillside of the bruised', in the sense – the 'wounded', and the Afon Cleifion flowing towards it, and if you go five miles up the valley of the Afon Cleifion you come to Nant Saeson – 'Saxon valley' where the locals will tell you the Saxon mercenaries of Medrawt camped the night before the battle."

Barham	"And who was Arthur fighting ?"
Mr. Main	"Medrawt his nephew who hoped to succeed to the throne."
Barham	"Everyone lays claim to Arthur, where did he go from here and was he in good shape ?"
Mr. Main	"No he was grievously wounded. He had to be tended by the Lady of the Lake didn't he ?"
Barham	"Is there a lake here ?"
Mr. Main	"There was, this is called Minllyn – 'the edge of the lake', and I think people haven't known about it because the history was written in Welsh."

I didn't see a lake. If it ever existed it's dried up, but back now to nature and a mystery as good as anything I ever came across. Maurice Giffin was a keen hill walker, and one summer's day in the mid-nineties he was making his way down towards his home in Tal y Bont. That's the Meirionydd Tal y Bont near Harlech, and he was on a route that he'd often taken in the past. Everything seemed perfectly normal, until suddenly he realised something was actually wrong.

He was on a completely bare part of the mountainside where he'd often heard 'bees' humming in the past and they were humming again now, but this time he realised there were no bees to be seen. It sounded like a whole swarm but there wasn't a single bee in sight. This intrigued him so much he went back several times and although he could always hear them he never saw them. The only thing he discovered was that the noise started in the afternoon and ceased around 4 o'clock.

When he invited me to come over I also heard the noise. It was loud enough to record, but there was nothing there.

BWB 137C
(Bee-like humming noise is heard).

Barham — "I can certainly hear it Maurice, even though the birds are making quite a noise."

Mr. Giffin — "Skylarks over there."

Barham — "But you'd really think we were surrounded by bees."

Mr. Giffin — "Yes, that's the impression isn't it. I was just walking along the path one day, having been up in the hills, I heard the humming noise, presumed it was the bees among the gorse blossom, then I realised there was no gorse blossom. I stopped and thought about that for a bit and realised it was a very localised sound and there weren't any bees about, and so that was the first indication I had that there was something odd going on here".

To quote Alice, this story now gets curiouser and curiouser. As the news spread, people began to tell Maurice that they too had heard this noise in four other places. So he got out the map and found that these 'humming spots' lay in a dead straight line running north to south. Back home he showed me the map.

Barham — "Yes, I see you've drawn a line straight on the map."

Mr. Giffin — "Yes that's it, right through to Portmeirion the most northerly site to be identified."

Barham — "How high are we above sea level here ?"

Mr. Giffin — "We're about eight hundred feet."

Barham	"The other sites, are they about the same height?"
Mr. Giffin	"Yes, most of them are the same heights, the one at Portmeirion is somewhat lower."
Barham	"Are they similar in other ways ?"
Mr. Giffin	"Basically yes. Yes, yes, they're bits of hills, more or less, with a lot of stones lying about."
Barham	"Well the question is, what do you think it is ?"
Mr. Giffin	"Well I have thought long and hard about this and I've absolutely no idea. I think it may be associated with some geological feature of the area, but there's no evidence to show that, but the fact that all the sites occur on the same line, it must be something to do with the underlying rocks I believe. If you go away from that sort of theory you are into the realms of magic and mystery, and I'm not wandering into that territory."
Barham	"Yes, because we are on a 'lay line' here ?"
Mr. Giffin	"A so called lay line, yes. That runs very much along the line of pre-historic sites, ancient burial chambers along the way here. There are mysterious cairns along this way, and when you get above Harlech there are all sorts of curious earthworks which are at least Iron Age and possibly older."
Barham	"Strange isn't it ?"
Mr. Giffin	"Very odd."

We checked that story very carefully. There were no underground cables there, no culverts, no gas mains, and no overhead cables of course, and the next day I went to Dai Hughes. He lived up in the remote Cwm Croesor at the foot of the Cnicht, the Welsh Matterhorn, and he was a man you went to see about lay lines and he confirmed it. The line on Maurice Giffin's map was held to be a lay line, one of those so called ancient and mystic routes of energy as some people see them, though few are willing or able to explain them.

Dai was an interesting fellow. For one reason he carved totem poles. They were huge and magnificent, and as he said – "If the spiritual Americans can have them why not the Welsh." And talking about poles, I once came across a girl who'd been tied to one.

She'd been left standing tied to a sign post outside a ladder factory at Johnstown. I stopped the car and she said, "It's always happening," and inside a bunch of women just shrugged their shoulders and said they did it to any girl who got engaged to show her what it was going to be like.

I love these old customs, and on the subject of damsels in distress a coach load of Australians pulled up one day in the village of St. George near Abergele. They all got out and tied a girl to the war memorial. She wasn't there long though. They all took photographs of her, quickly untied her, got back on the coach and drove off. This I heard from the vicar. He couldn't understand it, and a year later he rang to say that it had happened again. This time he sounded really worried.

When a gigantic bang sent shock waves around the Corwen and Bala area we didn't expect that extraordinary event to be repeated either, but it was, twice more. It was January 1974 when the first bang echoed around the Berwyn Hills. It was enormous, and as conjecture rapidly built up as to what might have caused it, and just where it might have occurred, the whole area filled up with teams of personnel wearing every conceivable military and civilian uniform. It was a complete mystery and still is, and as time passed the rumours multiplied. There were reports coming in of men in white coats carrying away earth samples, and several offerings of the extra-terrestrial. One rumour was of the army taking away the body of an alien, but on the Lleyn peninsular there was no such speculation.

This second unexplained 'wallop' reverberated across the peninsula a week later. I was there within the hour and found people in the area still reeling from the blast. The coastguards at Morfa Nefyn were checking their shipping lists to see if a ship had blown up, but again there was no solution, and neither was there five-and-a-half months later when another unheralded bang one night smashed light bulbs around the Conway Valley.

I can't really say there was a solution here either, but I did find one family of new comers living high above the valley near Trefriw who told me that it had been caused by a space ship. They said it had come down to earth in a cloud burst of torrential rain to unload a bolt of surplus power. This they claimed to have seen and fully understood, and furthermore had witnessed it colliding with a tree as it took off again. Fortunately reporters on such assignments don't have to say if they believe or disbelieve, but I must admit the tree was interesting. Large branches had been literally torn from it, but no part of it was burnt or scorched as you might expect had it been hit by lightening.

Eventually, ten years later North Wales was hit by something we could understand. We had an earthquake. Apparently we have lots in the UK every year but they're usually too small to notice, however this one was a big one. It measured well over 5 on the Richter scale, but it did little damage for its size because it happened very deep down. Nevertheless it provided an interesting experience, and although I said it was something we could understand, I'm told that as the crockery jumped around the breakfast table and our eardrums were assailed by a deafening 'roar' I asked three times if it was the washing machine. Although I think I was only asking that because I couldn't believe it was a helicopter on the roof, but that's what it sounded like.

I went to the door and outside the forest all around us was making an amazing noise as millions of densely packed fir trees jostled for space. Then, everything simmered down .... and it was suddenly very quiet.

No doubt you will have realised by now, I like the challenge of a mystery, and one of the best was over and done with in less than a minute, just like that earthquake, but I still can't imagine how that conjurer did it. He'd invited the BBC to see a table float across the road and they sent me - carrying the BBC's reputation for completely un-biased reporting firmly lodged upon my shoulders. Therefore I should have remained stoically sceptical but no, I failed dismally. I applauded as loudly as the rest.

He was appearing in a summer show and I met him at the top end of Rhyl's High Street where it meets the prom. There he stood with his table, an average sized kitchen table, and within a couple of minutes he had half-a-dozen volunteers, myself among them, placing their hands on its top. Then, with very little warning, it rose suddenly and careered across to the other side of the road. It was so sudden people were screaming, and we had difficulty in keeping up with it until it crashed down onto the opposite kerb. It was astounding. No-one had their hands under it, but it just took off - and flew !

His triumph was cut short however. The road wasn't pedestrianised in those days and within seconds a traffic warden arrived to start an argument about parking it there, which made a nice tail end to fade out on. Incidentally, that's a good tip. Never switch off too soon, you might miss something.

Tom Munson who turned up in Llandudno provided us with a nice mystery. Just imagine driving a car on water. By that I mean running it on water not floating on it, although seeing as he claimed to be the Motorists Saviour perhaps he could have done that as well, and to show that he could provide us all with incredibly cheap motoring at no cost to the environment, he filled his car (under supervision) with his 'Munson's Mixture ' and drove it round the Great Orme.

We became fascinated with this painter and decorator. He claimed he'd been given the formula during the war by a German officer. He told me it was basically water with some soap thrown in, and because his informant thought he was going to be shot and had nothing to live for, he unloaded his great scientific revelation on young Tom. Why is anyone's guess, but as he appeared to be somewhat down at heel and living in a dingy back street flat, we wondered why he'd waited thirty years to make his fortune. His reply was that he'd been perfecting it, and now he was ready to show that it worked at last.

He certainly had faith in it. Keeping his job as a decorator was of no importance to him. I was with a crowd of reporters outside a house he was working on one day. The boss came out eventually and told him to either get on with the painting or be sacked. He decided to go on talking to us instead and when he was sacked on the spot he still went on talking to us. He definitely wanted the publicity, and went on for weeks making the news with his demonstrations. Suddenly however he vanished.

Several months elapsed and then out of the blue I had a call from one of my contacts who lived in Blaenau Ffestiniog to say that Tom had turned up there and was lodging with an elderly lady. I found the address and she took me upstairs, telling me that he was recovering from the flu. Actually, sitting up in bed he looked very well because he had a tremendous suntan, and inviting me to sit on the edge of the bed he told me an incredible story. He told me he'd been living in the Mediterranean on a palatial motor cruiser as the guest of an oil sheik. He told me he'd been offered £250 million for his formula, and he was back now to think it over.

Being careful not to smile, and trying to maintain the reporter's open mind, I asked him what he was going to do. "They'll destroy it to protect their oil revenue," he said "Which will be a shame, so I've got a lot to think about." I shook hands with him, wished him well, and came downstairs. On my way out I thanked the old lady. "That's alright, he's had a lot of visitors." she said. " Oh, who ?" I asked, thinking she meant reporters. "Arabs," she said, and closed the door.

I never saw any further sign of Tom Munson, and his tapes too are among those that disappeared.

Another great disappearing act happened some years later in Llandudno Junction. Shirley Priestley lost one of her garden gnomes. It absconded from her garden and embarked on a world tour. She was heartbroken, but the little fellow obviously missed her because he kept sending her postcards. Just how he managed to travel the world and write postcards is another mystery, but I was glad to report that he got back safely. He arrived home one night with a baby and a stick of rock.

BB19

Barham   "You're obviously pleased to see your gnome back".

Mrs. Priestley "Oh yes, and the others are."

Barham   "Are they ?"

Mrs. Priestley "They're chuffed."

Barham   "They must have been very worried about it."

Mrs. Priestley "They were yes. They were very worried, yes. I'm frightened of them all going (laughing) because he's bragging about it now."

Barham   (Laughs) "He went to several countries around the world for a whole year ?"

Mrs. Priestley "Yes he went …. where did he go ? America, France, Euro-Disneyland, York, he went to Guildford as well."

Barham   "Oh well that's a nice place."

Mrs. Priestley "Beautiful."

Barham   "And you have postcards from all these places ?"

Mrs. Priestley "Yes."

Barham   "And they're all properly stamped ?"

Mrs. Priestley "Yes. All had stamps, original stamps, yes."

Barham   "And his handwriting was legible ?"

Mrs. Priestley "No, it was funny. It was different. Well he was excited wasn't he ?"

Barham	"Well I suppose so, yes. Anyway he's back now".
Mrs. Priestley	"He's back, yes."
Barham	"So he came home with a baby."
Mrs. Priestley	"Yes."
Barham	"And a stick of rock.."
Mrs. Priestley	"A stick of rock from Malta."
Barham	"Yes. Funny combination isn't."
Mrs. Priestley	"Oh it was, yes, and he said he'd had a good time with his Uncle Charlie. So, who this Uncle Charlie is I don't know."
Barham	"Well you know why he came home don't you ?"
Mrs. Priestley	"Oh yes, he was missing me wasn't he. "
Barham	"Yes, he was gnome-sick."
Mrs. Priestley	"Oh !" (more laughter).

CHAPTER V.
Very Queer Ideas, including Vicars

I think it was sometime during the eighties that breweries had the sudden urge to introduce bookshelves into our pubs. I like a good read myself, but for the life of me I couldn't understand it. They'd already started to turn our pubs into restaurants and now they were becoming libraries. I thought pubs were places where most people went to have a drink and mix with other people, not isolate themselves by sticking their noses in a book.

In one particular pub in Llandudno however, presently known as the Washington Wine-bar, reading the books was out of the question. Someone had managed to cut the shelves too narrow for books to sit on. A remarkable lack of foresight in itself, but the solution they came up with was unbelievable. They took all the books to a saw -mill and had them sawn in half. They do sit on the shelves now, and you can read the titles along their spines but being only half books, full of half pages, they're completely useless.

The extract that follows is taken from my interview with the manager. He wasn't very forthcoming on who had decided to saw the books in half, but to his credit he was very patient with my sarcasm. Stoical even.

AB15 G

Barham	(Looking at the bookshelves) "Have you got – One and a half men in a Boat ?".
Manager	"No sir."
Barham	"Oh, shame. What about - Around the world in forty days ?"
Manager	"I'm afraid not sir."
Barham	"Anything on the - Three and a half wonders of the world ?"
Manager	"No sir."
Barham	(Suddenly pleased) "Oh look - Very Little Women."
Manager	"Yes sir."

They hold books in far greater esteem in Holyhead if one event is anything to go by. To raise money for some cause or other, dozens of people spent hours sitting in the town's excellent Ucheldre arts centre reading aloud from a whole set of encyclopaedias. They all began chattering away with the word aardvark. "Aardvark - a mammal usually placed in the order edentata ….. etc. etc." Having recorded the start of this marathon I then caught up with the organiser who was reading aloud from his dictionary whilst walking around the town backwards. Others were coming in loud and clear on radio links. Someone was reading aloud out at sea. "Brick - block of baked clay, or stone, used in .... etc etc," and flying overhead even a pilot joined in, dictionary in one hand, controls in the other. "Crash – to lose control, to impact, to suffer catastrophe !"

I like Holyhead. They do things there.

A town with an amateur dramatics company and a concert party's got to have a good heart, and the 'Great Pub Race' of 1968 was pretty good too. You had to have at least one drink in every pub and then rush off to another. It was probably letting them race round the town, to get to any pub in any order, that knocked so many heads together on street corners. But it was interesting. Very tactical, and it gave everyone something to think about. Especially those sitting on the pavement.

More on books. I love them, probably due to being brought up in a house for so long without them, and I find it very difficult to pass a bookshop without an urge to venture inside, but there was one in Llandudno that had the opposite effect. All the books were new but there was a bad feeling about the place. It was the way they were sold. Book shops usually have a certain 'something' about them.. There's the mystique of what lies hidden between the covers, and perhaps a good book shop gives you an uplifting experience, there's that feeling that books are special, but not when they're sold by the pound like potatoes.

BBWB 14C
(Inside the book shop)

Barham	"What do you think of this idea ?"
Man	"Yeah it's a good idea."
Woman	"Well they do it with material, they sell that by weight."

Overcoming my preference for all things traditional, I thought I'd better give it a try and I approached the Manageress.

| Barham | "I wonder if you could help me. I'm looking for something on medieval Welsh history. How about a couple of pounds of Welsh history, and say half a pound of ghost stories ?" |
| Manageress | "I'll see what I can do." |

343

Barham	"And two or three ounces of poetry perhaps."
Manageress	"Okay. Well we'll start with this little book of verse, and when you put it on the scales its.. ….. 19p."
Barham	"How many ounces is that ?"
Manageress	(Studying scales) "Two ounces."
Barham	"Right, so how much a pound do you charge for your books ?"
Manageress	"They're £1.49 per pound."

Some things do have to change I suppose. Take medicine. (If you have to.) Some of the home-spun remedies used by our rural forebears were really queer, and enough in themselves to kill the faint-hearted outright. Many years ago I came across a whole list of them. They'd been collected for the WI up in the hills above Dogellau by a Mrs. Megan Evans of Llanfrothen. (I remember finding a couple living in a tee-pee by a lake up there once.)

Mrs. Evans was very nice, and I have very fond memories of this tape. I called to see her on my way to Cardiff one day in the very early 70's. I was presenting 'Good Morning Wales' the next morning and it was going to be my first experience of presenting a live programme. She wondered if I might need something to calm my nerves, so would I like to try something ? I very politely refused and said I didn't suffer from nerves, but she said I might wake up with a headache, and again I politely refused. It was awkward really. It wasn't that I didn't appreciate her concern, it's just that I'd seen a list of her ingredients.

BWB 19T

Mrs. Evans	"I think you'd have to be very brave to try any of them. For whooping cough – soot sandwiches ?"
Barham	(Laughs).
Mrs. Evans	"Which I couldn't think of giving anybody. And mare's milk, they specially recommended that. And I

was given a remedy when my son had whooping cough which was five black slugs to be carefully skinned, sprinkled over with brown sugar, leave overnight, and given with syrup. I prepared it but I couldn't use them in the end."

Barham "No. Dear, dear, well what sort of people would offer these remedies? Were they peculiar people in any way ?"

Mrs. Evans "Oh dear me, no."

Barham "Old witches up in the woods here ?"

Mrs. Evans "No indeed. You just had to try these things or perhaps somebody might die."

Barham "Have you tried any yourself ?"

Mrs. Evans "Yes, I've er, even last week I ate a dish of nettles. That's very good for purifying the blood. Just boil them slightly in salted water just like spinach."

Barham "Hmm."

Mrs. Evans "And a few years back I suffered from neuritis, very, very badly. My arm went numb, and I was advised by the doctor to fill my apron with nettles and have my arm in it for half-an-hour, so many times a day. Well, gradually the feeling started to come back, and then worse was to come. He advised me to let bees sting me in my arm. Well I was a bit of a coward in the beginning but it was worth it. The feeling really did come back into my arm."

Barham "So what else have you tried ?"

Mrs. Evans "Well I would try this anyway if I was a long way from a doctor. Onions boiled and mashed up and a big black spider ground into it."

Barham (Laughs).

Mrs. Evans "This is made into a poultice."

Barham "Erm, what would you use it for ?"

Mrs. Evans "Would you believe it, for pneumonia. The poultice to be changed every ten minutes and the patient would be out of danger within a few hours."

They say eggs are good for you, and there was a man in Caernarvon who used to swallow vast quantities of raw eggs as a party trick. Fortunately he worked in a hospital.

Then there was the man who showed us how he could survive in the wild terrain of Snowdonia by eating worms. He hasn't been seen for a long time now, and I always thought it was a shame more women didn't manage to throw off the chains of conformity more often, although I did meet a lady Father Christmas once. She had the right spirit, and her eyes twinkled nicely through her whiskers, but she was a bit weak on the "Ho, ho, ho's," and of course queer ideas can actually pay if you can find someone to buy them from you.

I'm thinking now of the man who made walking sticks with cupboards attached to them, just large enough for a sandwich or two I suppose, and I mustn't forget the lady not far from Criccieth who made butter in a washing machine. It was very nice butter too, and there was the woman who must have come close to drowning several competitors in a cardboard canoe slalom. But if you volunteer to paddle a boat you've made out of cardboard and attempt a course on the Chain Bridge rapids, what else can you expect ? I must say though it was great fun. Several of these brave souls were in command of very impressive craft which included warships and ocean-going liners. But alas, in the best traditions of the cardboard navy, most went down with their ships, and roller skating on grass didn't work out too well either.

This was being attempted down a very steep slope on the Gt. Orme by people wearing boots fixed onto caterpillar tracks, and after consoling the casualties at the bottom of the hill the lady promoting it said it was a craze that would soon be sweeping the country. Thankfully it didn't, but I'm not sure whether this next activity deserves to be labelled very queer, because it required considerable skill.

When the North Wales slate quarries were teeming with thousands of quarrymen, they would sometimes spend what little leisure time they had turning large boulders into musical instruments. This they did by drilling holes into the rock to varying depths, and then connecting them with a network of chiselled-out grooves. They would then ram some sort of dynamite they called black powder into the holes, and then run some along the grooves as well. This meant that when the powder was lit, the holes would explode in turn, with a varied pitch to the 'bangs' depending on the depth of the holes– some high and some low, thereby producing a tune. No doubt these boulders would have been in great demand by families who couldn't afford a piano.

I came across a few of these things, and Mr. Robert Hughes of Half-Way House Bethesda, explained the first one for me. A lot of them are covered in moss now, forgotten and lost, but he showed me one close to his home probably dating back to Queen Victoria's reign and with the holes still visible.

BWB 9.

Mr. Hughes	"They had black powder and they used to pour the black powder into the grooves and also the holes. This one may have played God Save the Queen or something for any big occasion. The deeper holes made the deeper sounding bangs. The shallow holes made the lighter higher-pitched bangs, it depended on the depth of the holes."
Barham	"Could this one be used today ?"
Mr. Hughes	"Well I don't know. It was tried some years ago. Some quarrymen came and tried to fire it but it all went up in smoke and was no success at all."

These boulders were known as Cannon Stones, and I was told that some played Happy Birthday and were used to celebrate the birthdays of important people. In that neck of the woods the most important man in those days was Lord Penrhyn, and although I have no personal grudge against the aristocracy, this one does appear to have been a little over indulgent. He owned the slate quarries thereabouts, and although long since dead he's hated to this day for the way he dealt with his quarrymen. Many locals won't go and visit his castle even though it's now owned by the National trust, but in spite of this sour relationship, it's said that some of these cannon stones were situated where his lordship could view their 'salute' from his extremely large and palatial castle.

Seeing as the firing of a cannon stone was far from foolproof, it's not difficult to imagine the scene. His lordship is seated with his family on the castle balcony to celebrate his birthday. They have their opera glasses focussed on the distant serfs.

(Serfs miserably call) "Happy Birthday Lord Penrhyn."
(They light fuse)........ Fizzz .... Plop ...... lots of smoke ..... it
                        fizzles out.
(Gleeful serfs)   "Sorry Lord Penrhyn !"

Among the 'Time Lords' (and there are several) there's a cheerful fiddle-playing restaurateur of Talybont near Barmouth, who celebrates Christmas twice a year. He does this with a second helping in August. It was tried in a couple of other places but here it became a not to be missed regular occasion. The larger than life Tony Wadsworth makes a splendid Father Christmas and every August his place is fitted out with Christmas decorations and they serve up piping hot turkey and Christmas pudding to happy revellers exchanging Christmas presents and kisses under the mistletoe. This all started one nasty cold August day when a customer, who'd been looking forward to sitting on the beach, said "Crumbs Tony, it might as well be December," and from then on people were booking up a year in advance.

Queer ideas, and even very queer ideas, often spring from the minds of that race apart that call themselves experts. In fact there have been times when it looked as if they were cornering the market, and it's a credit to the ordinary people of Gt.Britain who have fought back to keep eccentricity open to us all, but this very queer idea does come from an expert, a horticultural expert. He reckoned that if you dug up the weeds in your garden after dark, your garden would remain free of weeds for longer than if you'd dug them up in daylight. This valuable advice appeared in some journal or other, and it had to be very dark apparently, infact the darker the better

To mull over this theory I went to talk to John Dennis, the Marquess of Anglesey's head gardener at his Lordship's mansion Plas Newydd. John was puzzled but agreed that in the name of scientific research we should give it a try. Late that night we stumbled into the gardens of Plas Newydd armed with forks, spades, and a bucket.

BWB 7

Barham	(Digging) "I'm sorry about this John, you must feel as silly as I do at this moment, digging in the dark."
Mr. Dennis	(Digging) "Yes."
Barham	"Something you've never done before, I bet."
Mr. Dennis	"Mind your foot because I'm not sure where you're standing."
Barham	"Well come to that, where are you ?"
Mr. Dennis	"Yes, erm."
Barham	"Whoops, oh dear. I've just bumped into him. If I go to the left a bit ....."
Mr. Dennis	"If I can try and dig this weed out here".
Barham	"You reckon there's one down there ?"
Mr. Dennis	"Yes I think so."
Barham	(Sounding lost) "Oh I don't know."

Mr. Dennis	"It's got big roots."
Barham	"The only light we've got here is the light of the moon, and that's pretty pale to put it mildly. But there's a weed down here."
Mr. Dennis	"If you can knock the soil off …."
Barham	"Yes."
Mr. Dennis	"Like that …."
Barham	"Right."
Mr. Dennis	"You get the weeds out by …."
Barham	"Let me get out of your way a bit ….(clatter !) Oh, Oh. (Hopping around. Clatter ! Clatter !) Ahgh"
Mr. Dennis	"I could use that bucket to put the weeds in."
Barham	(Clatter) "I've got my foot stuck in it (clatter) John, wait a minute …Oh. (Clatter). There we are."
Mr. Dennis	"I think the main thing is whatever you're doing, you've got to get all the root out of the weed. There's no point …."
Barham	"But that's impossible isn't it, in the dark. I've been told that you mustn't even do this by the light of the street lamps because that would diminish the effect apparently. It's got to be done in the dark you see."
Mr. Dennis	"I suppose the main thing is that you actually do it. I mean does it really matter if you can see what you're doing ?"
Barham	"Well perhaps not."
Mr. Dennis	"I can feel the soil here."
Barham	"Yes, okay."
Mr. Dennis	"Soil's cold and wet."
Barham	"Yes, well I've certainly got something here …."
Mr. Dennis	"Here's a root, I can tell this is a root by the feel."
Barham	"And I've got something, oh this is rather a nice leafy thing, John, John just feel my spade here. What have I got here ? What have I dug up here ?"
Mr. Dennis	"Let's just, erm, oh dear that's an aquilegia, we want

350

	to keep that."
Barham	(Apologetically) "Oh crumbs."
Mr. Dennis	"This herbaceous border has got quite a few in this corner."
Barham	"Oh, sorry John."
Mr. Dennis	"Well."
Barham	"Shall I leave it on one side for you to stick back in?"
Mr. Dennis	"Yes, if we leave that there, and let's get this bucket out of the way."
Barham	"Oh crumbs. Sorry John."
Mr. Dennis	"And then we can …."
Barham	(Again apologetic) "John, John, sorry John I think I've just trodden on it. Sorry about that."
Mr. Dennis	"Aah."
Barham	"Have you got plenty more ?"
Mr. Dennis	"Yeah, well there's lots over that side. I'm just worried now that you'll trip on the fork and hurt yourself. They're dangerous things you know."
Barham	"Yes, yes, I suppose I could even put it through your foot, couldn't I ?"
Mr. Dennis	"Well yes, that's it."

There's a postscript to this story. Some of the inmates of a women's prison heard that broadcast and asked the Governor if they could be let out at night to do some weeding. As you might guess, she refused.

Also you might guess a few queer ideas came from vicars, such is their reputation. There was one in Glan Conway who made a habit of photographing peoples fireplaces. These happy snaps he compiled into a 'Who's Who' of local fireplaces. It was supposed to bring people together, but rather more conventional was the one in Llanberis who organised an egg race with parishioners rolling their eggs down the hill, and then there was the Vicar of Gwernymynydd who got rid of his moles by sticking plastic windmills in their molehills. He believed the vibration from these things would drive them away, and from the way their little hills were heading for the fence he could well have been right.

Surprisingly, vicars and their like can be very noisy. The one in Holyhead could be heard a mile away. Every Sunday he was 'yelling' out a wailing African chant whilst sitting cross-legged on the altar steps, and he did this I might add, whilst banging on his bongos. I suppose to be fair, it made a change from hymns ancient and modern, but more surprising was the fact that the congregation, like him all white and mainly middle-aged, took to joining in. (I told you, there's something about Holyhead.)

I met a few irritable vicars who fined brides for being late, and those who withheld deposits of those who dared to throw confetti (lazy vicars who didn't want to sweep it up) and another noisy one was the Reverend Ray Pentland at the little church alongside the RAF station near Holyhead, (Yes it's Holyhead again) who kept a trombone by his pulpit. Woe betide anyone who nodded off during one of his sermons. As soon as someone's head slumped forward he'd wake the sinner up with an ear-splitting blast fit to wake the dead. Even I failed to sleep.

Now that women are becoming vicars and such like, I do so hope they don't start giving the clergy a good name. They seem to be taking the job far too seriously.

CHAPTER W
World Service, Writers, and the Weird.

At the same time as working for the BBC in Wales I was also co-habiting with the World Service for ten years, telling the world about the fluctuating fortunes of Wales. I enjoyed this and as well as working on a number of their general programmes, I also presented a weekly programme that went around the world called 'Wales Today', although sometimes it was called 'Wales this Week' and if I remember correctly also 'This week in Wales' and so on. There are always people (upstairs) who want to keep changing things. The maxim seemed to be – if you've got a good format at least change the name. This sleight of hand gives the appearance of progress. Essential for the upwardly mobile.

You always get a thrill when you sit in the hushed plush carpeted claustrophobia of a BBC studio and prepare to start speaking. You're watching for the green light intently, and when working from a script, the worry is that you will trip over your tongue, and that concern is a little greater when you're working for the World Service and you know there are millions of people listening out for you all over the world. When that little green light came on I always got a special thrill when I heard myself say - "This is the BBC World Service. My name is Allan Barham, and this week I'm looking into... ." (etc etc)

I worked for some excellent producers on the World Service. In turn Gareth Bowen (who took over Good Morning Wales) followed by Gerry Monte and Alan Stennett, and we certainly did our best for Wales. There were times when we had to show it 'warts and all' as they say, but mostly I think we managed to show Wales with a brave face, and indeed put a brave face on the map. We told of a proud region struggling with unemployment and all it brings, welcoming new industries, new ideas, and of course tourists. Goodness knows how many times I told the world that Wales is a land of mountains, forests, lakes and waterfalls, and of course the Tourist Board loved us. They invited us to some very grand dinners at places like Portmeirion to meet foreign dignitaries and foreign travel writers who came to see if it was true !

Naturally we were speaking in English, but not only to the English speaking countries of the world. We were also broadcasting to people in other lands who were keen to learn English, often gathered with interpreters. Also reporters like myself were often called upon to serve the 'language sections' of

Bush House, the London home of the BBC's World Service, and from here each section broadcasts news and current affairs to a particular country in its own language.

Very often they'd hear of someone interesting from their country visiting Britain and if they couldn't get him or her to a studio, they would send a radio reporter to 'do' them on the spot. This might be in a hotel, at a conference centre, or wherever you could catch up with them with a tape recorder. This required a special technique because they were to speak on these occasions in their own language, and you the reporter (not being a linguist) spoke in English. So you finished up with questions in English and answers in another language. If the interviewee could at least speak a little English it was okay, he or she would understand what you were asking, but if they didn't understand English then you had a problem. If you couldn't find an interpreter you had a major problem.

One thing you positively had to avoid was speaking at the same time as your interviewee. It was most important that you didn't chip in with the next question before he'd finished speaking, and it was equally important that he shouldn't start to answer your question before you'd finished asking it. This was because of the technique employed. When the tape arrived at Bush House they cut you out and replaced you with a recording of someone else asking your same questions in the required language. Because of constant difficulties in this respect, I devised a series of hand signals, although devised is a bit of an overstatement. I simply raised my hand when I'd finished asking a question and they raised a hand when they'd finished answering it.

This usually worked very well but it agitated a few eyebrows when in the presence of others sometimes. I was recording a piece with a foreign gentleman in a restaurant once, and understanding the problem exactly, he complied with my request most willingly. It was going very well, until I saw that we were attracting some funny looks from around the room. Realising that our fellow diners had come to an unfortunate conclusion, I attempted to keep my hand signals at a lower level, but not my companion. Not only was he speaking in German, and very loudly too, but he was shooting up his hand in what I can only describe as a once familiar salute.

Before leaving you always needed to record some background noise. In the location I've just described it was simply the sound of people in a very quiet restaurant, but this practice enabled them in Bush House to play the correct background noise behind the newly-recorded questions in the studio, keeping the whole interview 'background co-ordinated'.

We covered all the big events of course including a few anniversaries too, and it must have been around 1980 that people were celebrating the fiftieth anniversary of the Youth Hostel Association. We were particularly interested in this because the movement had started in Wales, and after going down to London to meet the association's president I met some of the founder members. There were some in Cheshire and a couple living near Ruthin, but originally they'd all lived and worked in the Liverpool area and had been on a walking holiday together in Germany during the late 1920s.

On that trip, while walking through the Black Forest, they'd met a local schoolteacher with a group of children, and they learned that he was walking them from village to village, sleeping each night in village schools. It was that meeting that started the Youth Hostel Association. They came home thinking it was a wonderful idea and set about its formation, except that instead of commandeering school rooms, they planned to acquire houses, and the first one they acquired was called Pennant near Eglwysbach, south of Colwyn Bay.

My four main interviewees were very elderly, but in no time the memories came flooding back. They were memories of a Christmas eve so very long ago, and how times had changed. They told me how they'd been working in Liverpool all day (as usual) on Christmas eve, and how they'd hurried excitedly straight from work to catch the train to North Wales. They told me how they'd got off at this tiny little station called Tal y Cafn, which was only lit by oil lamps, and they told me how wonderfully the moon was reflected in that broad sweep of the River Conway. Then, as the old train steamed off into the night, they set off to walk the five miles up through the village of Eglwysbach where carols were being sung, and on to Pennant. When at last they arrived they were welcomed by the local lady they'd engaged to look after the house, and once inside, they found she had a roaring fire and a piping hot dinner ready for them.

How I'd love to have a Christmas like that, but as it turned out they didn't keep Pennant long. I think there were a few problems with the house, and there were definitely problems with the water supply. It came from a tank set into a stream and when a dead sheep was found in it – that was the end. They must have acquired new members very quickly though, because before long they were building a brand new hostel near Mold, designed by an up and coming young architect by the name of Clough Williams- Ellis. (He of Port Meirion).

Thinking of building has made me stop to ponder for a while on some of the enormous building projects I 've reported on. I watched the giant Wylfa atomic power station being built, with progress reports on every stage, (eventually with sound effects from our washing machine) and then there was the aluminium smelter also on Anglesey, and the pumped storage power station built deep inside a mountain under the slate tips of Llanberis.

I honestly lost count of how many times I saw the docks of Holyhead being re-modelled and re-built, and the Mostyn docks grew a bit too, and I've already mentioned the Shell oil pipeline, with its off-shore terminal at Amlwch. Here they had a floating funnel into which the tankers poured their oil, spilling it only occasionally. We also witnessed enormous road building projects, mainly in the building of the A55 expressway, a second-class motorway with roundabouts and tunnels, including one under the river at Conway.

Up river we also watched the salmon being provided with their very own tunnel of easily-jumped steps by-passing the previously impassable Conway Falls, and leading up to brand new spawning grounds towards Ysbyty Ifan.

Being involved with all that building work was always interesting and full of great radio noises, whereas another day featuring the work of a writer would provide a complete contrast. Life as a radio reporter was certainly varied, and whenever a publisher sent me a book to review I always made a point of visiting the author, if he or she was available, and out of all those people a handful stand out in my memory just a little more prominently than the others.

Alexander Cordell came unexpectedly into my patch to live out his life, and he was an interesting fellow. He was the author of The Long March, the story of the Chinese long march into communism, and I can't forget BBC colleague Ian Skidmore who was uniquely entertaining. He could have brought cheer to a statue. We all remember his wonderful weekly spoof on 'local radio' broadcasting called Radio Brynsiencyn complete with wind-up gramophone. He was a columnist on the Daily Post, as was Ivor Wynne Jones, and as a thoroughly out-spoken and thought-provoking journalist Ivor was second to none.

There was also another that I regarded as special. He was completely different from the others. He wasn't a historian, a novelist or a journalist, but he did write for a newspaper. His work had appeared in the Daily Express for over thirty years and his name was Alfred Bestal. If the name means nothing to you I can only tell you that he produced the Rupert Bear cartoon strip. He not only drew all the pictures but he also made up all the stories. He was an extremely polite old gentleman who even lapsed into speaking in little 'Rupert like' verses, and one felt that he really was Rupert Bear.

I was sent to meet him on several occasions after he'd retired to his holiday cottage in Beddgelert. On my first visit I sawed some logs for him. The saw was dreadfully blunt, and at the door he said, "Oh dear, oh deary me, I bought it in 1953. Do come in now and have a cup of tea."

I wish I could say he was wearing a red jumper and yellow checked trousers, but on one occasion an old envelope was lying on the table and on it he'd drawn Rupert. I wanted to ask if I could have it but I just couldn't bring myself to ask, and I expect it got screwed up and thrown in the bin.

BWB56T.

Mr. Bestal	"I had a ball-point and I wanted to see what sort of point it was and one instinctively starts to draw Rupert. So any envelope that happens to be there gets Rupert all over it."
Barham	"Supposing people ask you to sketch Rupert perhaps when they meet you or ask for your autograph, do you sketch it for them then?"
Mr. Bestal	"No, I refuse."
Barham	"Why is that?"
Mr. Bestal	"Well, because the curious thing is, people won't believe it, but although I was drawing Rupert for over thirty years and after I'd retired, I haven't ever drawn Rupert in either a story or a painting or anything, have I ever drawn Rupert with anybody else in the room. I have to be alone, and I always have been alone you see. People think I'm putting them off with some excuse, but it is perfectly true, the presence of anybody else prevents the complete concentration, and I have to have concentration because drawing Rupert isn't a slick thing that you can turn into a musical act, it has to be thought of."

Barham	"When we think of children writing to you, do any letters in particular stand out in your mind, or are there any recurring questions they ask you ?"
Mr. Bestal	"Well, I think what stands out in the mind is if these children happen to be writing from a hospital. If they're ill it puts a lot more pressure on you to answer them and as I said, some of them are asking for drawings but a great many more of them simply want my signature."
Barham	"Do they ask you to sign yourself Alfred Bestal or Rupert Bear ?"
Mr. Bestal	"Oh not Rupert Bear. I think they want a real signature. Some of them of course, send their own drawings of Rupert hoping I shall say something nice about them which I generally try to do."
Barham	"Do the children here in Beddgelert realise who you are?"
Mr. Bestal	"Oh yes, oh everybody knows who I am here.
Hardly	anybody calls me by my proper name."
Barham	"What do they call you ?"
Mr. Bestal	"Rupert."

Showel Styles of Borth-y-Gest was another favourite old-timer. He was the author of the 'Mr. Fitton' sea stories in the Hornblower mould. He always seemed to be too gentle to be writing about such a tough existence, but then he was an old navy man himself, and when he wasn't writing about the sea he was writing about the Welsh mountains, still tramping over them at a ripe old age, and sleeping out in a tent he'd used for fifty years. They don't make them like that any more. The men or the tents.

It's not commonly known that Beatrix Potter started her career in North Wales. She wrote her first 'Flopsy-Wopsy Bunny' stories at her uncle's grand house – Gwaenynog near Denbigh. That accident of birth makes Peter

Rabbit a Welsh rabbit (not a Welsh rarebit) a fact already shown among the pages of her first editions with her sketches of the house and other notable things like Mr. McGregor's Potting Shed. Nevertheless, it has always been the Lake District that has taken the tourists money. It's true she did go to live there, and she continued her work there, but it's another case of Wales being too slow to seek the benefit.

After three coach loads of Beatrix Potter fans from all over the world had travelled up from Heath Row to stay at Windermere so as to feast themselves on the atmosphere of Beatrix Potter's Lakeland, I was at Gwaenynog a week later to see them explore the Welsh connection. Only one coach arrived. None of the others could be bothered with Wales.

So what's weird ? According to my dictionary, it's something that's odd, uncanny, and unreal, and some of the weird things I came across were all of those things. We once heard a rumour that a weird gang of hooded men had moved into a remote farmhouse in a wood with no road to it, and of course I was sent to find out what they were up to.

It was near Betws Gwerfil Goch, and it was true. A padlocked gate barred the way to nothing more than a cart track. (Oh how I miss this sort of assignment) So I climbed over the gate and walked, and after a while I came to the old house. It looked empty and no-one came to the door, but every now and then I thought I could hear something like a low moaning noise, and gradually I realised it might be coming from a big stone barn.

I walked quietly across the yard towards it and the noise became more distinct. I looked for a door and when I found one I put my ear to it. The weird noise was certainly coming from in there, and it sounded somehow like men murmuring. Then it went quiet, so I knocked on the door. I waited for a moment but no-one came so I opened it, and what a sight. I found a crowd of men with bald heads kneeling before a gigantic Buddha.

It was quite a surprise for them as well as for me. They got to their feet and told me they were establishing a Buddhist Study Centre. I enjoyed my visit. They were fortunately very friendly.

One of the most weird experiences occurred one evening when I went to meet a lady who was living alone in an old mansion, a decrepit historic relic standing between Mold and Wrexham. It's called Brynteg and it might have been done up now, but nevertheless to my mind it must be the ugliest and most morbid looking house in the country. It's gruesome, yet this lady, who remained on her knees and never looked up at me once, was intending to restore it.

One of our researchers had made contact with her on the phone. I was told that I would find a door open at the back, and that I would find her upstairs, but it was nearly dark as I drove into the courtyard. When I found the door it was ajar. I either knocked or rang a bell I don't remember which, but there was no reply, so I stepped into a dingy musty-smelling hallway and called out "Anyone there ?" This time there was a reply, but from nothing human.

From upstairs there came a raucous squawk. It was a bird. I called again, but again only the bird answered. When it fell silent I slowly climbed the creaking stairs, and as I came up into the gloom of the first-floor landing, I saw that I was being watched by two of them, two enormous pitch-black birds in cages. They were silent now but their bright little eyes were watching my every step. Beyond them, a little way along the landing, there was a strip of yellow light seeping from under a door. Passing the birds I approached the door and knocked on it. From within a woman's voice softly invited me to enter.

I opened the door and found that I was in a sitting room, and kneeling in front of the fire with her back to me, a woman was slowly sewing a piece of fabric that might have been a curtain. I introduced myself, but there was little response and she didn't look up. Her head remained bowed and she just slowly went on sewing. I asked if I may sit down and turned on the tape-recorder. I told her I'd like to record a few questions with her and I asked why she'd bought the house and what she was having to do to re-furbish it. Quietly she answered all my questions, and in the same quiet voice she took it upon herself to tell me about the people who'd killed themselves there. Still she didn't once look up, but then I was asked if I'd like to look around. I accepted, and leaving her to continue her sewing I went and looked into pretty well every room.

They were damp and depressing, and going down a narrow back staircase, I found myself in a filthy old kitchen. This was home to another big ugly bird in a cage. It stared at me intensely, and when it started to flex a scrawny talon towards me I went back upstairs and thanked her for the interview. She was still sewing. She nodded, but still she didn't look up, and I left.

Another weird place was an outdoor activity centre in Meirionydd. It was close to Bryn Crug in an old farmhouse, and whereas people running other centres took great care of their customers, here they seemed to concentrate on losing them. They weren't specialising in children's activities it's true, but for a start they liked to have people dressed in drab coloured anoraks so they'd be more difficult to find if they got lost. Everyone infact was made to understand that they were at risk as soon as they arrived.

Actually they were quite nice people running the establishment. They just felt that guests would appreciate being led across bogs in the dead of night at the end of a rope, walking chest-deep along rivers, and sleeping on beds made of sheep netting, and actually I found very few complaints among the survivors. Perhaps it was fortunate though that I didn't have time to stay for supper.

It's not often that one gets invited to have lunch in a nunnery. This was at Hawarden and I sat alone, confined in a small rather bare room. A Sister served me with each course, but she appeared to be the only one on the loose. Even the Mother Superior was safely locked away behind bars when I spoke with her, but she had an excellent story for me.

They'd just buried one of the Sisters in the garden She'd always liked gardening but for many years she'd struggled unsuccessfully to grow mushrooms. She just couldn't do it, but then up came the mushrooms – all over her grave. They'd never appeared in the garden before, but there they were, growing all over her.

I was at that nunnery three times I think. They were often up to something, but the first one I visited was near Dolgellau where they were making biscuits for the Pope's visit to Ireland.

Here's another weird story, courtesy of a British Telecom gremlin. When a middle-aged couple got married it was because this little gremlin had been playing Cupid. Elsie Clutton was sitting alone one evening in Llandudno Junction when her phone rang. On the line was Henry Glanville, a complete and utter stranger phoning from the South of England. He'd got the wrong number, and every time he re-dialled he got this woman in North Wales again, but I'll let them tell their own story.

BWB 32F

Elsie   "He dialled the wrong number five times, then Thursday night he dialled twice and same again next week, the same again next week, the week after he said, "I'll have to stop phoning you like this, your husband will get suspicious." I don't know why but I said I'm a widow, and I don't normally tell people that, so we got talking and he said "I'll phone you later on" or next week or something, and when he rang next week he said " I haven't made a wrong number this time, I want to speak to you". So we started to talk and I told him I was going down south for a holiday, Bournemouth. "Oh" he said, "I live down South" but he didn't say where. I hadn't a clue. I went to Bournemouth and he came to see me on the Saturday night.

Barham	"You must have liked the sound of her, Henry."
Henry	"Oh I don't know because she used to keep saying 'Yeah' all the time."
Elsie	"My Lancashire kept coming out."
Barham	"Well how was it that you were dialling the wrong number and getting this number all the time ?"
Henry	"Don't ask me, it was just one of those things."
Barham	"Who were you trying to dial ? Another girlfriend ?"
Henry	"No, it was actually one of the chaps I play snooker with at the club."

He said the problem was with the code number. He wanted 04892 and he was getting 0492. So who's hand was dialling the number ? They are certain it was fate, and soon he told her he was going to marry her.

Henry	"I think so. Yes definitely. I told her that."
Barham	"Well, it must have been one of the most extraordinary engagements."
Henry	"Well it was. but you know I don't think I'll meet anyone like her again."
Elsie	(Sounding alarmed)"I hope you're not going to look?"
Barham	"I shouldn't let him use the phone too much."
Elsie	"No, I take it out of his hand now as he's picking it up !"

This is another strange story that I remember. One that involves a factory and an oil painting. The painting is of a girl named Emma Dolben who married into the

Stanley family of Holyhead in the 16th century. The factory is the aluminium smelter, built in the 1970s and at the start at least beset with problems.

The factory had been built on part of the Stanley family's run-down estate at Penrhos, (later Ken William's nature reserve) and when things started to go wrong, locals among the work force shook their heads. "Since Emma went from here this place has been cursed," they said.

Apparently it had always been said that Emma had never wanted to leave Penrhos. She'd obviously enjoyed a happy life there, but one fateful day, many years after her death, her portrait was taken to another branch of the family in Switzerland, and when the smelter's production schedule lay in tatters, the current Lord Stanley came to their rescue. He brought Emma back from Switzerland and she was hung in the boardroom. "It was like magic," one of the managers said, "Once she was here we picked up straight away, and we've never looked back."

CHAPTER X.
X – Rated.

Working for the BBC in the twentieth century (even the second half of the twentieth century) gave little scope for anything X-rated on the radio. On television yes, but strange to say not on the radio. I don't really think anything X-rated went on the air before people started to grunt at Wimbledon.

However, I did have to interview some nudists once on the beach south of Shell island, and it's true you don't know where to look, and I suppose I should mention the sea horses at the Rhyl Sea Centre. Every one around the world thought they mated for life, but that bunch were holding out their tails to anyone who came strolling through the coral, and back in the human world it's true there were bathing beauty competitions to report on, but not even I would have dared to describe those swivelling hips and provocative glances as they strolled round the pool, and therefore those particular events will have raised no more interest among the listeners than a conjurer in a railway tunnel.

Without doubt, the closest I got to exciting radio audiences with a genuine 'X' rated broadcast was recording a couple of water snails doing what all water snails do at the bottom of a pond

This pond belonged to Tim Davies. He was a great old boy with a wonderful sense of fun, a high-pitched voice, an infectious high-pitched laugh, and a devilish twinkle in his eyes. He lived on the High Street in Llangefni, and he was a technician at the University's Electronics Department in Bangor when I first met him. That was in 1968 when he showed me his electronic fish barrier on the Cefni Reservoir. He was a genuine genius. Later he retired and made a name for himself by recording everything he could get a microphone to, even into, and that even meant the inside of a tree.

I trampled through quite a few bogs and ditches with Tim in his search for new sounds, and for each new challenge he invented special microphones to fit all occasions behind a curtain in the front room. This was his workshop, and it was here that I heard many of his recordings.

BWB918
(Scraping noise)

Mr. Davies	"This was an octopus and it's caught a crab, and it's scraping the shell of the crab with its parrot-like beak so as to get a hole at the back of the crab, but the most memorable and most interesting one was the leaf-cutting ants. They're very clever."
Barham	"How on earth do you think of these things ?" (Mr. Davies laughs). I mean, who else but you would have thought of recording the inside of a tree ?"

Mr. Davies	(He laughs) "We're just touching the fringes of that and these noises."
Barham	"Have you any plans for anything else coming up ?"
Mr. Davies	"Yes I have. I've got plans to catch the sound of flies being caught by plants, the meat-eating plants."
Barham	"Ah, like the Venus Fly-Trap, that sort of thing."
Mr. Davies	"Yes."
Barham	"Gosh, bit of a horror story really."
Mr. Davies	(Laughing) "That's what everybody says, like the one with the spider, you know the one I did with the spider and the spider catches a bluebottle and the bluebottle screams ! And they say, "Ooh horrible blood-thirsty thing." (He laughs.)

The tape in which one heard snails mating is another that disappeared. The BBC obviously wiped it.

CHAPTER Y
Yet More Blunders and Disasters.

There is no distinction in the BBC's rule book between blunders and disasters. Blunders are entirely of your own making, no-one else is involved - so it's your fault. With disasters, other people are involved - and it's still your fault. Someone might be there to lead the way, but if it goes wrong you will get the blame. There's no-one to hide behind, not even if you're the back end of a pantomime horse.

I had that job once, fitted up with a microphone at the Prince of Wales Theatre in Colwyn Bay. I was there to tell the listeners what it was like in there and I can tell you it was awful. I was being dragged all over the place, I had no idea which way we were going, and when the front end decided to break into a gallop, the back end tripped over Widow Twankie's carpet and got left behind. At the inquest the front end insisted that breaking into a gallop was in the script, and I have to admit well trained pantomime horses can go very fast.

They've even had pantomime horse races at the Towyn race track near Rhyl, which I thought were more exciting than the trotting horse races they have there, but the season of pantomimes is always a dodgy time. Christmas is when a reporter often falls victim to a disaster. This is the time of year when even the most ghastly children have their play pens unlocked and there is always the producer who wants to know what it's like to be Father Christmas in his grotto. This means only one thing – having kids pee all over your lap. Not that any producer is going to see for himself what it's like. Of course not. They always send a reporter and it's not an assignment to fight over.

This reporter wore waterproof trousers under his robes, but still you get to the studio stinking like a cesspit. Your shoes look as if they've been soaked in acid, and your face is stained with half-sucked jelly babies and chocolate buttons. That's why Santas always wear whiskers. With the wisest you can hardly see their faces at all, but then they get poked in the eyes.

It's true, all Bank holidays can be difficult. There's often a shortage of real stories during these periods, and at times like these you need to call upon your initiative. These are ideal times to produce a feature on someone or something unimportant, and always remember - cobbling together a perfectly unnecessary report on a done-to-death issue is always a good way of filling a programme at any time of the year, and with a minimum of research too. To start with you will already have the contacts.

This of course is terribly boring for reporters and listeners alike, but safe. You're not breaking new ground and you're not stretching things too far. However, there's a lot of truth in that old saying – 'necessity is the mother of invention', and I would have to say that some of my best efforts might have occurred when I was stretching my initiative to the limit. Although,

I must admit there might also have been a few mistakes made during these periods. Going to the 'Hard of Hearing Club' didn't go down too well. It certainly wasn't the place to hold a quiz, but everyone makes a mistake once in a while. After all, when all is said and done, that old saying is very true – 'He who makes no mistakes makes nothing'.

I'm thinking now of a big mistake and a marvellously embarrassing moment a certain mayor had when visiting Conway (Conwy in Welsh) and actually it involved a wonderful old custom in that little old castle town.

Once in a while, Conway's mayor has to play host to an English aristocrat. In a less tolerant society this might cause a revolt, but it boils down to the fact that whenever the Marquess of Harford leaves his stately pile in Warwickshire and journeys through Conway, the Mayor has to present him with a dish of fish. Even as strange customs go, this takes a lot of beating but it's true. I was there in the castle once when it happened.

BWB 79

Lady Mayor	"May I present you with your dish of fish ?"
The Marquess	"Well Madam Mayor, thank you very much indeed. That is simply magnificent. (Onlookers applaud). It's not obviously a very serious custom. One doesn't claim it every week, we might be running a fish shop mightn't we ?"
Lady Mayor	(Laughing) "Yes."
The Marquess	"But I think it has a certain charm and I hope we'll be able to go on claiming it from time to time."
Barham	"Your Lordship, you have collected your dish of fish once before I believe ?"
The Marquess	"Just once, thirty-four years ago."
Barham	"Tell me about this custom ?"
The Marquess	"Well, I didn't know very much about it, but I'm told that it began when one of my ancestors, who had

been paying six shillings and eight pence to the Crown for the rent of Conway Castle, which he had for several centuries, since King Charles Ist infact agreed to surrender Conway Castle to the Mayor of Conway in exchange for a dish of fish, which has to be presented to the Marquess of Harford whenever he comes to Conway. So perhaps it is just as well that we live in Warwickshire and don't come every day."

Barham "The Mayor of Conway is Millie Wildig, looking very smart in her red gown today, chain and three-cornered hat. I believe there was a very amusing incident concerning this old custom some years ago."

Lady Mayor "Oh yes, yes there certainly was in 1894. The mayor of Hereford passed through Conwy and he heard about the dish of fish and he came to claim it. The mayor at the time said "I'm very sorry but it's the Marquess of Harford that has the fish." Anyway, they took him to lunch. Fish I suppose."

Barham "Mustn't he have been embarrassed ?"

Lady Mayor "Oh yes, yes! (laughter).

Swans gave me one of my silliest blunders. Several hundred of them glided down one day and landed like a blizzard on a farmer's field. This was near Llanfrothen. They looked fabulous but within minutes they were scoffing every blade of grass in sight, and of course it was precious grazing land ready for livestock to feed on. It was a serious problem, and after I'd recorded a few words with the exasperated farmer I went in among them.

I wanted to describe the incredible scene but, strange to say, they weren't making any noise. They were absolutely silent. There was no atmosphere whatsoever. There wasn't a squawk or a honk, not even a quack. Time was running short too. I was going to be terribly late. Apart from the farmer explaining why it was a disaster, all I had on the tape was me, a distraught reporter saying "I'm absolutely surrounded by these swans. There are hundreds and hundreds of them here. You can hardly walk between them ! Just listen to them !...... ....just listen to them !.......................... just listen to them !....................... Just listen – oh for goodness sake !"

When at last I got to the studio, late again, hot, raving, bothered and jet-lagged, a nice lady sat me down quietly, held my hand, and gently explained that those really quite nice swans could never have made a noise for me because they were ..... 'Mute' swans.

I loved visiting farms, and one of my favourite jobs was to visit farms up in the bleak northern most part of Anglesey when the mighty squadrons of wild geese arrived. A few hundred geese can strip a field of its grass in no time, so these occasions were not actually celebrated. Nevertheless, the sight and sound of wild flocks of geese flying in on a grey winter's day to that wonderfully wild part of the island, is very special.

There's a mystique about Anglesey. Here among the prehistoric Standing Stones and the wild terrain that sweeps down to the sea, the past is never far away. It's not lost. It's there, tugging at your sleeve at every turn.

There are days when a reporter does have time to stop and stare, even wander round a little, and that's really nice, but usually it's a rush, and I can't stress enough the 'stress' of getting to a studio on time. There's so much that can delay you. Naturally it's prudent to be well organised, and when going out to record an interview it's important to try and clear two hurdles before you leave. Will they talk, and where will they be found ? This isn't always possible to assess however. Sometimes you just have to go and search for people, but a big problem occurs when you arrive at the scene and find you're being told of another angle to the story, and you have to go in search of someone else as well.

The afternoon programmes always caused the greatest race against the clock, but even when a recorded piece was for the morning you still needed to be in the studio by 5pm or you would miss your turn to unload your piece and have to wait a couple of hours and miss your dinner. This happened a lot, and if I haven't made it clear I should explain that my reports and features were usually transmitted to the listening public from Cardiff or London, therefore I had to get my tape 'down the line' to either Cardiff or London.

This 'line' was actually a very special studio phone line that preserved perfect quality of sound, and as I played the tapes and read the scripts in, say – Bangor, someone in London or Cardiff would be listening in and re-recording them at the other end. This of course was standard practice, except for non urgent material which went by the 'internal mail'.

Reaching a studio to 'unload' your piece comes as a great relief. Out on the road there's the potential for a delay at every turn. I stopped in Trefnant once to ask about the whereabouts of someone and chose the wrong door.

It was opened by an old lady, and immediately a little terrier shot out through her legs and disappeared round the corner. "Look what you've done !" she screeched, and at that precise moment a gust of wind slammed the door and shut her out. "Now look what you've done !" she yelled, which was strange really, because from what I could remember I hadn't done anything yet, but she was really furious. "You'll have to climb in the bedroom window," she shouted and sent me to bring a ladder from a barn.

This I found quickly enough. It was hanging on a wall but it was being guarded by two horses. Normally I like horses but these were like elephants, and they made it absolutely clear that they didn't want me to have their ladder. When they saw me coming they immediately went and leant against it. It must have taken me at least ten minutes to prise it away from them, and I eventually left them stamping around and snorting angrily at each other for letting it go.

With their precious ladder now leaning against the old lady's bedroom window sill, and ignoring her constant warnings not to break anything, I climbed into the house, ran down the stairs and opened the front door. This at last quelled her ranting and without a moment's pause to say thank you, she pushed passed me, went inside and slammed the door.

There was never a shortage of daily snags, and as you've seen it was a life of extreme variation, and I'm sure I haven't provided you with enough of the sad stories, or the down-right tiresome stories, to show you exactly what it was like. Neither have I attempted to tell you what it's like to be struggling late at night, or in the pouring rain for hours on end, to get something finished, or even to just get something right ! And of course people sometimes wonder why you've gone to so much trouble. Take the cycle ride to Cardiff. I mentioned it earlier but I didn't tell you about the two old ladies.

I got soaked on that first day and booked in for the night at the Royal Oak, the hotel in the centre of Welshpool. I had a shower, put on some dry clothes and went down for dinner. On the way I looked into the lounge. I knew they were giving my bike ride a mention on the television just after the news, and being curious to see what was being said, I watched it. It was just a still picture of me and the bike, and the voice of an announcer telling viewers that my journey and my encounters would be on the air each day on Good Morning Wales. It was just a brief advert really for Good Morning Wales, but I was standing behind a settee on which two old ladies were sitting. There was no-one else in the room, they had no idea that someone was standing behind them, and they had no way of knowing that I was standing behind them, but as the television fell silent and the rain continued to beat at the windows, the one on the right leant over to the one on the left and said "He must be mad."

I very nearly said, "I must be." But I thought I might give them a bit of a fright, so I slipped out quietly.

CHAPTER Z.
Zoos, zeniths, and Zeros.

There's not much you can do with the letter 'Z' unless you go for Zany ?Yes but there have been plenty of those already.... Zeal ?Yes the enthusiasts had plenty of zeal.... Zealot ? No, none of those thank you..... Zeniths ?I didn't notice many.... Zeros ?I'm afraid so.... Zip ?Just occasionally.... Zoom ? Probably that too.... Zoos ?Yes definitely. Colwyn Bay's Welsh Mountain Zoo and Chester Zoo had some good stories. At Chester they once felt obliged to take in a deadly puff- adder that had been confiscated from some misguided soul. They managed to find a spare cubicle for her thank goodness because she immediately gave birth to forty six more, and a zoo labelled the worst in Britain could be found once on Anglesey, but today the island is known for its Sea Zoo. It's a real 'hands-on' place where, as well as singing to them, you can also stroke fish on their noses. They love it. But Colwyn Bay's Welsh Mountain Zoo is special too.

As with all good zoos they're involved in a lot of conservation projects with endangered species, and as with Chester, even the tigers at Colwyn Bay wander around in the open-air, and the bears too. It's run by the Jackson family, and I should have put their mother into my woefully inadequate list of heroes. She lost her husband when the place was in its infancy, and although her three boys were still at school she managed somehow to carry on, and the boys run it now for the Zoological Society of Wales.

I spent some very happy hours in that zoo, and if I did have an occasional zenith perhaps I can recall one in particular. It was there, and it's a visit I will always remember. It was a Red Nose Day and the children of Mochdre's Cystennin Primary School were holding a very unusual sponsored event. They were off to the zoo to tell jokes to the animals. I'm not sure now how that raised money but it was a great idea and they invited me to go with them. It was a lovely morning, and incidentally this was recorded before the monkeys also moved to an open air world of their own.

BWB 612G

Barham	"Well unfortunately we haven't been able to find a hyena in this zoo. That would have been a good thing to find because hyenas are things that laugh all the time. They can't stop laughing – hyenas you know.
Children	"Mmm".
Barham	"We've come to the Monkey Enclosure, we've just arrived, where there are two monkeys in this particular cage, and the children have got their jokes ready. These are really very funny indeed. I've been having a good laugh at these jokes. Are you ready ?"
Children	"Yes."
Barham	"There's a little boy on my right here, what's your name ?"
First Boy	"Gareth Coleman."
Barham	"Gareth ? Alright (shouting) Now come along you monkeys, gather round, we've got a joke here for you. Alright Gareth, let them have it."
First Boy (Silence)	"What has got a bottom at the top ?"
Barham	(Shouting to monkeys) "Did you hear that, what has got a bottom at the top ? (Silence) Go on, tell them."
First Boy (Silence).	(Shouting) "Your leg."
Barham	"Well I thought that was funny."
Girls	(Giggle).

Barham	"No reaction. That monkey's just sitting up there on that branch sucking his thumb. Alright try them with another one. (Asking another boy) Have you got a joke ready ?"
Second Boy	"Yes".
Barham	"Yes ?"
Second Boy	"Why did the monkey fall off a tree ?"
Barham	"Oh yes, this is a good one isn't it ?" Go on tell him."
Second Boy (Silence)	"Cos he's dead."
Barham	(Shouting) "Did you hear that ? (Silence). Look I don't think he heard that, tell him again, but a bit louder. Go on shout."
Second Boy	(Shouting) "Why did the monkey fall out of a tree ?"
Barham	(Shouting) "Did you hear that ? (To boy) And again."
Second Boy	(Shouting) "Because he's dead."
Barham	"Wait a minute, wait a minute! You've got to deliver the punch line with a bit of timing you see. Once again, once again."
Second Boy	(Shouting)"Why did the monkey fall out of the tree?"
Barham	(Shouting) "Did you hear that monkey ? Why did the monkey fall out of the tree ? (To boy) Right, let him have it."
Second Boy (Silence).	(Shouting) "Cos he's dead !"
Barham	"Louder, I don't think he heard you."
Second Boy (Silence)	(Shouting) "Cos he's dead !!"
Barham	"Oh dear, he's just picked something up to chew."
Girl	(Laughs).
Barham	"They don't look at all interested these monkeys do they, oh wait, here comes a black one. Ah now this one looks as if he's got a sense of humour, look at the way he's climbing up the wire there ! (Turning to

	another boy) Right have you got a joke ?"
Third Boy	(Shouting)"Why did the two monkeys fall out of a tree ?"
Barham	"Go on, tell him."
Third Boy	(Shouting) "Because the first one was holding the other one's hand." (Silence)
Barham	"Oh dear. They're still not laughing though. None of them are." (Distant loud cry).
Boys	"It's the elephant !"
Barham	"What's that noise ? (Loud cry) Is that the elephant?"
Boys	"Yes."
Barham	"It sounds as if the elephant is having a good time. (They all start running). Perhaps the elephant has got a sense of humour. Let's go and find the elephant, never mind the monkeys."

(They continue to run).

Children	"Where is it ?"
Barham	"It's the elephant. (Stopping) Or was it one of these parrots. (Loud squawk). Oh no, it's a ...."
Children	"It's an elephant"
Barham	"That's not an elephant ! That's a big grey bird. What is it, a stork or something ?"
Children	(Reading a sign) "It's a Sor.... us. It's a Sorus Crane."
Barham	"Oh it's a crane. (Loud squawks now from two cranes) Well they're having a good laugh aren't they ? Right, okay let's make them laugh a bit more. Who's got another joke ? Right come on then now, nice and loud."
Fourth Boy	(Shouting) "What did the wally call his zebra ?"
Barham	(Shouting) "What did the wally call his zebra ?"
Fourth Boy	(Shouting) "Spot."
Barham	"Spot ! (Laughs, then goes quiet). They're not laughing".
Girls	(Giggle).

Barham	"They've stopped laughing. Got another joke for them ?" Who's got another joke ? (To another boy) Right, come on."
Fifth Boy	(Shouting) "What do you call a sheep with no legs and no head ?"
Barham	"They're looking this way, they heard that. Go on, tell them."
Fifth Boy	"A cloud."
Barham	"….a what ?"
Fifth Boy	"A cloud."
Barham	"A cloud ?"
Fifth Boy	"Hmm".
Barham	"That's beyond me. A quick word with your teacher."
Teacher	"Hello."
Barham	"Shirley isn't it ?"
Teacher	"Yes."
Barham	"Shirley Williams ?"
Teacher	"Yes."
Barham	"Have you got a joke, Shirley ?"
Teacher	"What animal has two humps and is found at the North Pole ?"
Barham	(Shouting to all the animals in that area). "Did you hear that ? What animal has two humps and is found at the North Pole ?"
Teacher (Silence)	"A lost camel."
Barham	"They're still not laughing."
Teacher	(Laughing) "No they're not laughing are they ?"
Barham	"Well I'll tell you what you've achieved, you've stopped the cranes laughing.Who writes your jokes?"
Children	"We all do."
Boy	"On the compu'er."

I really enjoyed that. They were great

kids, and I was so lucky over those years to meet so many good people, young and old, and they so often come back to me in my thoughts now, drifting in at quiet moments like ghosts.

Some of these ghosts are frequent visitors, but I really don't know which memories will last the longest. Will it be the people, or the places ?

Throughout those years, every day I passed through towns and villages that appeared on the road like old friends, and spread across the map there were the gems. Special places unique to my patch. Gems like the jagged rocks of Tryfan's crown, home of Adam and Eve. The perfect pinnacle of Snowdon, seen sometimes fleetingly between the black clouds of night, caked white in gleaming snow. The ruined mansion high on the Denbigh moors where it sometimes took four people to close the door against the wind. The dark and brooding River Dee as it comes slowly to the A5 bridge at Corwen.   Telford's dizzy aqueduct that so incredibly carries a canal high across the sky, and a little to the south and west, busy little dark blue waves splash upon the shore of the ancient mountain sea that is Llyn Tegid – lake Bala, where the monster bides his time. There are the massive grey stone castles of Edward the first, perched proud and arrogant around the coast, and there are those of the Welsh, small but even now stubbornly standing their ground high upon their hills, looking down upon the summer-time English as they pass below, seeing nothing but the view. There are the vast open heather clad vistas of the Berwyn hills, where without a doubt across those hazy purple moors you can see eternity. The deep green bristling pine forests of Coed-y-Brenin, Clocaenog and Gwydir, constantly dark and impenetrable, and those precious border lands of Powis, hardly explored, a peaceful land of knobbly green hills hiding in their folds a treasured maze of nowhere villages, twisting streams and half timbered houses. Then there are those hard and windswept beaches like Anglesey's Benllech, washed and swept clean for cricket every day, while elsewhere less energetic souls drift into sleep upon the silky soft sand dunes of Aberffraw and Harlech. The golden estuary sands of the gleaming Mawddach and the Dyfi so easily capture the heart, as do the tidal races of the Swellies and South Stack, where the lighthouse beam comes scything through the mist along that narrow twisting cliff-top road, and at Penmon point, beyond the ruins of the priory, the light house bell clangs in time with the tide, while across the fields of that magical island of Anglesey, there are the standing stones, those ancient giants that stand as strangers still. To the far west beyond the tip of the Lleyn peninsular, there's another, much smaller island. The secretive island of Bardsey where a thousand pilgrims sleep forever hidden behind Bardsey's great mountain. Here is an island that's often difficult to reach, and always difficult to leave, and wherever you travel in Wales there are the narrow lanes. Little lanes centuries old and filled with tiny flowers and the song of small summer birds hidden among the hedgerows that often drop steeply down to sandy coves like Whistling Sands where the wind stings and the surf thunders, and the sparkling sand whistles and squeaks beneath your feet. And then there are the more daunting roads that climb into the mountains. Many of these are narrow and twisting too. Roads that cling precariously and recklessly to the very edge of oblivion. Roads like those that soar over from Bala to Vyrnwy or Dinas Mawddwy – snow and ice permitting.

I don't see those sights very often now. In the end the last programme I was with folded up and the slot was filled by a phone-in programme. In contrast my phone has fallen silent. No longer are there stories for me to chase. As a reporter I'd met hundreds of people who'd been made redundant and here I was joining the club. I'd always felt sorry for them, but you can't really understand what it's like until you fall in with them.

Quite apart from the redundancies at the BBC, I saw thousands of others made redundant, as I've said, right across the land, from engineering works, steel and iron works, collieries and quarries. In fact, in every town and city, even villages, there were slag heaps of able-bodied men and women absolutely wasted, and among them were often the self-employed, who in their own way had depended on those industries. And of course there were those who'd even been forced to close down by a tidal wave of bureaucracy, much of it coming from Brussels. Men like 'Bob the Milk' of Dolwyddelan come immediately to mind. I felt particularly sorry for him. In the end the ever-deepening layers of restrictions forced him to hang up his cycle clips and leave his bike in the shed.

For forty years he'd quietly got on with milking his cows and selling their good creamy milk from a crate on his handlebars. Before that his aunt had delivered the milk from a hand cart. They'd been an important part of that community and I always gave him a 'thumbs up' as I drove through. One day though he had to pack up. " New regulations." he said quietly.

The best way to reach Bob the milk is to walk down a long path to the broad River Lledr, and then cross it on a footbridge. It was dark that night he told me of his troubles, and it was Christmas eve. Seated with him in the parlour he told me that he couldn't afford the new equipment. It was a shame, and then his elderly aunt came from the kitchen with a Christmas cake, and sitting by that big cosy fire with slices of cake, we drank to the future, for whatever it might hold for us. I will always remember that. Always.

On my walk back I stopped on the bridge and for a while watched the moon dancing on the water, and I felt so very sad. I'm not Welsh, but in Wales there's a way of life that I so admire. It's a very fragile tapestry now, and every now and then another piece is ripped from it. Often by people so far away they've never even been here.

Now though, as my alphabetical ramble stumbles towards its end, I would like to play one last tape for you. It comes under 'Z' because, for me at least, it's a 'zenith' and to put it simply – it's my favourite. It was recorded on a day in 1975, and it was one of those rare occasions when everything just fell perfectly into place. That's what makes it remarkable.

I was never content with a straight interview but I could never have orchestrated anything this well. I knew how I wanted it to go, but in such chaos there was very little chance of it going quite as well as it did. None of the people you will hear were spoken to beforehand. Nothing was arranged with anyone, and to be honest it was quite amazing that anyone was able to say anything in the noise and smoke of all that cannon fire. Visibility was so bad I quite literally kept bumping into people, and they were marvellous. Even the two girls, who I'm sure were twins, drifted out of a pale blue haze as if in a dream, and it shows again how it pays the reporter to get right into the heart of the action.

It was a Sunday, the second day of an ancient battle weekend. Dressed in their 'olde worlde' costumes, the massed ranks of the Sealed Knot Society were at Gwrych Castle near Abergele to fight a bloody Royalists versus Roundheads battle to the death, and it was a great location for it too. Not that this fairytale castle had ever seen a battle, but built into a spectacular backdrop of white cliffs and forest, this former seat of Victorian high society provided a perfect setting, and when the Royalists started their charge and the cannons started to roar, the whole scene sprang to life. The noise was deafening as the troops tore into each other with pikes, swords, and muskets, and wandering around in the midst of all that carnage was a medieval radio reporter.

BWB 6T7
(Huge cannon and musket fire, lots of yelling and screaming).

Commander   (Shouting) "To your left hand face !!"

Barham   (Cheerfully) "Good afternoon and welcome to the Battle of Gwrych Castle. It's going awfully well at the moment but of course its a lovely day for it. The sun is shining overhead, not too hot. You've come in at the second half of the battle. The first half was held yesterday evening when the Roundheads took the castle from the Royalists. So, in the second half, the Royalists are trying to (Huge bang) take it back again. (Huge bang). Sorry about that noise. So at the moment it's one-nil to the Roundheads. And I think the Royalists are massing again at the bottom of the hill for another charge. I'm just moving in now among some of the Roundhead forces. I say, this an awfully dangerous game. Good gracious! There's a lady here. Are you really a (huge bang), are you really a lady ?"

Little Voice   (Brightly) "Yes."

Barham   "Oh dear. Here come the Royalists. They're fighting their way up the hill and they're now at the (drums) foot of the castle, right under the very noses of the guns (huge bang). Oh, oh. I forgot I was standing a little near to that one. Real cannons, real reality. All the dress, talking about dress I'm dressed as a sort of Medieval Knave, a sort of Buttons I'm afraid." (Lots of shouting).

Soldier   (Frantic) "We've lost about (shouting and bangs) … our Musketeer force has almost vanished, and we're at the most exposed (huge bang) I can think we're at – at the moment, but I doubt if this particular amount will come back !"

Barham   "Oh my goodness me". (Huge bang).

Soldier   "I came here realising this would happen. This castle is in an indefensible position as far as I can see, and it'll probably be worth it if in the final result the man of blood finally loses his head ! Apart from that, I'm afraid I've no more to say."

Barham   "Jolly good. Just listen to how these fellows go in with their pikes. (Crash, crash, much shouting). My goodness me, believe me(even more shouting) there's no room in that group for the faint-hearted. The pikes are about 12 or 15 feet long and they charge at each other, absolutely bashing each other as hard as they can go. Ah, oh ! (alarmed) there's a man pointing a gun at me. He's putting it on a tripod. Hey! Excuse me, I'm a War Correspondent. (whack) Oh that's awfully good, a chap here has knocked him over with his pike. Thank you very much. Do you know you've just saved my life ?"

Soldier	"Oh, that's very good."
Barham	"Oh, Hello girls.(Two girls appear out of the smoke) What are you doing ?"
Both Girls	(Speaking as one) "We're fencers."
Barham	"Are you, yes ?"
Both Girls	"Definitely. Oh, here we go, hang on."
Barham	"What does this mean ?"
First Girl	"It's the Brigadier isn't it ?"
Second Girl	"It's the Brigadier, he's the big man."
Barham	"Is he ?"
Both Girls	"Yes in the Sealed Knot. Yes."
Barham	"Have you got to follow him ?"
Both Girls	"Oh no, he's on the other side."
Barham	(Horrified) "He's on the other side !?"
Both Girls	"Yes."
Barham	"Is he ?"
Both Girls	"Yes, they've just taken our castle."
Barham	(Worried) "They've won then have they ?"
First Girl	"It looks like it, yes."
Barham	"Oh my word, oh dear."

Gwyrch Castle hadn't been lived in for many years. As I write it's not much more than a shell now, but in January 1990 we were told that it had been bought by a Mr.Tavaglione, an American. This guy was amazing. I have rarely seen a bunch of reporters look so astounded. Looking as if he'd stepped straight out of a Hollywood gangster movie, he stood proudly at the door, (it was too dangerous to go in) and told us that he'd paid £750,000 for it, and he was going to spend a million turning it into a hotel, and alongside he was going to build an opera house ! He also told us that he had a partner in the venture, a lady by the name of Rukmini Sukarno, the daughter of Indonesia's ex head of state, President Sukarno.

It was ludicrous. Within minutes there were whispers among my colleagues of money laundering and within days there was a little problem with money in Indonesia. It was found that the lady was facing a fourteen year sentence for fraud, and today Gwyrch castle is still a ruin.

Unlike Gwyrch Castle I'm far from being a ruin, and I'm not lying idle. It was disappointing though, but not surprising. Over the years I saw many of my older colleagues in Wales left by the wayside, and when it came to my turn I didn't resist much. By then I was very tired, and not being able to contact head of programmes, I asked the heads of news and features if there might be another programme I could fit into but there wasn't, and as I really didn't want to scratch for crumbs I wrote to the Controller, and guess what ? (Don't laugh) I didn't get a reply.

A letter saying "Goodbye" would have been nice, and a party would have been even better. So to all Heads of Departments, I say this …..if you didn't appreciate my thirty-two years completely loyal and unbroken service it's a pity, and if you didn't enjoy my career as much as I did then never mind, - I enjoyed it, and that's all that matters.

Toodleoo.

P.S. One last thing. 'Z' as I've already stated, also stands for 'Zero' and many years ago, whilst overlooking Llyn Mymbyr on a very wet day, I sat sharing a flask of coffee with a colleague from Cardiff. "Al," he said. "Working up here is worth an awful lot to you."

It wasn't the first time I'd been told of things going sour in Cardiff, but it was a long time before I tasted the poison. It came when someone upstairs issued an order, through my producer, requiring me to involve more Welsh sounding people in my broadcasts. Naturally only Welsh people sound Welsh and like any self respecting journalist I wanted my broadcasts to include anyone with something to say, irrespective of colour, creed, or nationality. The BBC already has an exclusive Welsh language service so I ignored it. A few months later I was living in retirement.

My failure to help BBC Radio Wales sound more Welsh and my early retirement may have been purely coincidental, but two of my English sounding colleagues considered the ending of their employment had nothing to do with coincidence and took their grievances to the Commission for Racial Equality.

One of them had a letter from a BBC programme organiser which was seen as indefensible. He had his case heard and I was brought out of retirement to join those giving witness support. It was an unpleasant experience. For one thing the Commission had prepared a statement for me to read out, but it was so terribly inaccurate that I refused to read the original. In the end the claimant won his case. The BBC and a programme organiser were judged to have discriminated against the applicant on grounds of his national origins, contrary to section 1 of the Race Relations Act of 1976.

In every way – The End.